D0359705

WHY SOCRATES DIED

by the same author

XENOPHON'S RETREAT: Greece, Persia and the End of the
Golden Age

WHY SOCRATES DIED

Dispelling the Myths

ROBIN WATERFIELD

W. W. NORTON & COMPANY

New York • London

Copyright © 2009 by Robin Waterfield
Maps copyright © 2009 by András Bereznay
First American Edition 2009

All rights reserved
Printed in the United States of America

For information about permission to reproduce selections from this book,
write to Permissions, W. W. Norton & Company, Inc.,
500 Fifth Avenue, New York, NY 10110

For information about special discounts for bulk purchases, please contact
W. W. Norton Special Sales at specialsales@wwnorton.com or 800-233-4830

Manufacturing by The Courier Companies, Inc.

Library of Congress Cataloging-in-Publication Data

Waterfield, Robin, 1952–
Why Socrates died : dispelling the myths / Robin Waterfield. — 1st
American ed.
p. cm.
Includes bibliographical references and index.
ISBN 978-0-393-06527-5 (hardcover)
1. Socrates—Trials, litigation, etc. 2. Socrates—Death and burial.
I. Title.
B316.W38 2009
183'.2—dc22
[B]
2009004317

W. W. Norton & Company, Inc.
500 Fifth Avenue, New York, N.Y. 10110
www.wwnorton.com

W. W. Norton & Company Ltd.
Castle House, 75/76 Wells Street, London W1T 3QT

1 2 3 4 5 6 7 8 9 0

For Kathryn

αέρα στα πανιά μας

Contents

Illustrations

Preface

Everyone has heard of Socrates, and even if they know little or nothing else about the man, they usually know that he was put to death by his fellow Athenians in 399 BCE. The events surrounding Socrates' death have become iconic – more discussed, portrayed or merely mentioned – than any except those surrounding the death, some four hundred years later, of a Jewish prophet called Yehoshua. In fact, the two trials and executions often seem to meld in people's minds, so that Socrates too becomes a kind of martyr – a good man unjustly killed for his views, or for being an outstanding individual in a collectivist society, or something like that. Do a web search for 'Socrates and Jesus' and you will see what I mean. But Socrates would have been the last to want to leave a cultural icon unexamined, and that is what I do in this book: examine all the evidence in order to reach a fuller understanding of Socrates' trial and execution than has been achieved before.

Socrates' trial was a critical moment in ancient Athenian history, and so provides a very good lens through which to study a complex and perennially fascinating, somewhat alien society. That is my second intention: to provide a readable account of as much Athenian history as is necessary to fill in the background of the trial. For we will, of course, never understand the trial without being able to enter, as fully as possible, into the mindset of the Athenians who condemned him to death. This is a book about classical Athenian society as much as it is about Socrates, and especially about the social crisis that Athens endured in the decades immediately preceding Socrates' trial.

Socrates was famous: we have more evidence about him, and about Alcibiades, his beloved (who also features prominently in this book), than any other two figures from classical Athens. But even this good fortune may be two-edged. Socrates himself wrote nothing, and almost all the evidence about him comes from two of his followers, Plato and Xenophon, both of whom had their own agendas and reasons for writing. Among these reasons was a desire to exculpate their mentor – to make their fellow Athenians wonder why they ever condemned him to death (in *this* respect, at least, he truly resembles Jesus). So we may have a greater number of words about Socrates than about any comparable ancient Athenian, but every single word needs to be weighed and treated with caution. And the same goes for Alcibiades, a flamboyant, larger-than-life character whose image became exaggerated over the years, until he became an archetypal dandy, profligate and sexual omnivore, whose tyrannical political intentions could be read off from his private life. As if the dubious source material did not make the work difficult enough, at the heart of this book is a trial. The nature of Athenian society, and of the legal system in particular, means that very few trials – and none of those on social charges such as those of which Socrates was accused – were concerned only with the explicit charges. So all the evidence needs a judicious approach.

Socrates himself wrote nothing, as I have said, and there is a temptation to understand this as an eloquent way of asserting his mistrust of the written word. It is true that he preferred the flexibility of living conversation and the spark of pre-verbal knowledge that can occasionally be transmitted in such circumstances, but it is more to the point to remember that disseminating one's ideas by means of the written word was still very rare in his day. But he did have views and opinions, and we need to unearth them from the pages of those who wrote about him, while recognizing that it will never finally be possible to disentangle Socrates' own views from those of his followers.

I have long believed that the historical Socrates is pretty irrecoverable, but also that it would be sheer stupidity to deny that he cast a shadow over the works of Xenophon and Plato. Scholars often cling hopefully or desperately to a distinction between the 'historical' Socrates of Plato's earlier dialogues, and the character 'Socrates' who seems to speak for Plato's own ideas in later dialogues. I no longer believe in this distinction, except that in the light of Plato's genius the shadow of the historical Socrates becomes harder to discern; but in order not to beg the question, I have avoided using Plato's later dialogues for anything except corroborative evidence. I make far more use of Xenophon's testimony than has been normal in the scholarly study of Socrates for the past hundred or so years – but I have already groused enough in print about the neglect of Xenophon, so I will say now only that without his help we are never going to gain a rounded picture of Socrates, or even of just his trial.

Socrates was a philosopher, one of the most influential the world has ever seen. Naturally, then, in this book I make quite a bit of use of philosophical texts. But I do not want to alarm any reader who associates 'philosophy' with 'density and complexity', or even with 'futility'. Neither of these is a fair reaction to the majority of the ancient philosophers, for whom philosophy was, above all, a practical exercise in self-improvement. These early philosophers were dealing with real issues, problems arising from real life, so their work was not futile; many of them were trying in part to reach the ordinary educated man, and when they were making this attempt they did not write with density and complexity. At any rate, the Socratic works of Plato and Xenophon should more properly be classified as intelligent fiction than as tough philosophical textbooks.

In any case, this book is a work of history, and I scarcely scratch the surface of Socrates' philosophy. But in locating political concerns at the heart of Socrates' enterprise, I do present a revisionist picture of his thought. In this book, however, I write not as a philosopher but as a historian, and from a historian's point of view the evidence for a more politically engaged Socrates is as plentiful as that for many reconstructions of the period.

The lofty pedestal that Socrates occupies is due above all to the write-up Plato gave the events surrounding his trial and death. In this version, Socrates became the superbly haughty philosopher, concerned with nothing except his mission to investigate and promote profound moral values. But this picture is a Platonic fiction and has generated the troubling result that, just as Socrates has become apotheosized above the common concerns of humanity, so his philosophy and even philosophy in general (for which Socrates remains the figurehead) is considered to be best studied ahistorically. There is of course some validity in this, since philosophers deal with abstract principles and questions, but there is a danger of distortion if Socrates (or perhaps any philosopher) is read without knowledge of his times.

So Socrates has been through many incarnations, as successive intellectual, spiritual and artistic movements have appropriated him and remade him as the type or antitype of their own ideals. This mythmaking process began a few years after his death and has not yet ended. One way to describe the aim of this book is to say that I have tried to get behind the myths, to uncover the historical person and locate him in his contemporary context. For Plato and Xenophon, Socrates was a moral hero, and it was above all his trial and death that revealed him as such to the world. This veneer, polished and thickened by centuries of acceptance, needs to be chipped away if we are to gain as undistorted a picture of Socrates as we now can. He may indeed turn out to be a moral hero, a great and innovative thinker, and one of the founders of western civilization – but he may also appear at last as a human being, subject to human frailties.

One of the primary tools I have used to tackle the veneer is Socrates' relationship with Alcibiades. There are sound, practical reasons for this: of all Socrates' friends and acquaintances, we know far more about the notorious Alcibiades than anyone else. There is also the fascination of the pairing of these two opposites – a fascination which has long attracted poets (e.g. Hölderlin), sculptors (e.g. Canova) and painters (e.g. Regnault). Socrates frittered away a modest fortune, while Alcibiades flaunted his obscene wealth; Socrates contained his appetites, while Alcibiades indulged them; Alcibiades was a fervent imperialist, wedded to the notion that might is right, while Socrates insisted that it was never right to harm anyone under any circumstances; Socrates focused on inner change as the foundation for moral action in the outer world, while Alcibiades ignored his soul and preferred to conquer the world as he found it. And yet they were a couple, of sorts, and Alcibiades became the vehicle for Socrates' political aspirations. We will not understand Socrates without understanding Alcibiades; hence his prominence in this book.

But they were not only opposites. Both men pushed the envelope in their respective ways (and so came to be accused of impiety, or 'un-Athenian activities'); both men were admired and feared in almost equal measure; neither expected to adjust to the city, but expected the city to adjust to them; both were in a sense scapegoats; both in their interlocking, divergent ways fused two of the greatest and most enduring trends of fifth-century Athenian culture – politics and philosophy.

In both cases, however, the city proved stronger. Perhaps that was inevitable – even inevitable enough to be foreseeable. In Euripides' *Hippolytus* a stubborn, self-absorbed young man quarrels with his father and is driven into exile and killed; in Aristophanes' *Clouds* a teacher, from whom a young man learns how to rationalize and escape the consequences of beating up his father, is attacked in retaliation by the father. But Euripides' play was produced in 428 BCE, thirteen years before Alcibiades' first period of exile and twenty-four years before his assassination, while *Clouds* was first produced in 423, twenty-four years before Socrates was taken to court by a society proclaiming itself 'the constitution of our fathers'.

I have spent a little time here outlining the considerable obstacles presented by the evidence for Socrates and Alcibiades. But despite these obstacles, I believe that the issues underlying and surrounding Socrates' trial are recoverable with a good degree of certainty, even if in order to achieve this recovery we have to take a somewhat roundabout route through relevant aspects of Athenian history. No straightforward route does justice to the complexity of the trial: at stake were impiety and religious innovation, recent developments in education, Socrates' unique personality, various prejudices against him and others associated with him, recent history, politics and political ideologies. If I present the evidence as a jigsaw puzzle that only slowly begins to make sense, this is meant to reflect the mind of an imaginary contemporary of Socrates, asking himself, if he was free of prejudice, why this man was put on trial, and why he had to die. The several answers that would gradually dawn on him are the pathways taken in this book.

Socrates' trial has occasionally brought about something like collective guilt, as if justice had miscarried and an innocent man were condemned to death. In the late 1920s, a Greek lawyer called Paradopoulos applied to the highest court in Athens to have them reverse the verdict of the ancient trial. The court replied, naturally, that this matter was outside its jurisdiction; there is no substantive continuity between ancient Athenian and modern Greek law. In any case, we should not condemn the ancient Athenians for condemning Socrates: as he himself was the first to acknowledge, he was tried and found guilty in accordance with the due processes of law. If in this book I try him all over again, I do not think he would be too dismayed.

Acknowledgements

This is the first book of mine written from start to finish in rural Greece, my home. Trips to libraries from here are time-consuming and costly. I wrote to many academics around the world asking for offprints of their work, and received nothing but generosity and kindness, in the form of the majority of the offprints I had asked for, and some extras too. Too many people were involved to name one by one, so I thank you all collectively. Collective thanks also go to the staff of the Library of the Institute of Classical Studies, London; the British Library; the Library of the British School at Athens; the Blegen Library of the American School of Classical Studies at Athens; and the library of the University of South Florida at Tampa.

As for individuals, I corresponded over details with Philip Buckle, Ed Carawan, Paul Cartledge, Bill Furley, Debra Nails, Robert Parker, Jeffrey Rusten, Stephen Todd and Julian Waterfield, while Michael Pakaluk allowed me to post a query on his 'Dissoi Blogoi' site. My thanks to all of them, and also to my friend Dimitris Peretzis for stimulating conversations, and not least for his play *Saint Alcibiades*, the brevity of whose run in October 2006 at the Athenais theatre in Athens belied a work of rare emotional and intellectual power. As usual, I met with nothing but meticulous care from my copy-editor, Eleanor Rees, and cartographer, András Bereznay. And nothing would have happened without my commissioning editors: Walter Donohue of Faber and Faber in London, Bob Weil of Norton in the States, and Chris Bucci of McClelland and Stewart in Canada.

Several people gave generously of their time and read the penultimate draft of the book in its entirety: Paul Cartledge, Kathryn Dunathan, Andrew Lane, Debra Nails and Bob Wallace. They seem to have enjoyed the experience, and I certainly profited from their comments. The book is also dedicated to Kathryn, because we were married about two-thirds of the way through the writing of it. I have no idea whether the book is better because of this, but I am.

Lakonia, Greece, May 2008

Key Dates

421	Peace of Nicias
420	Quadruple Alliance of Athens, Argos, Elis and Mantineia
418	Sparta defeats Quadruple Alliance in battle of Mantineia
416	Ostracism of Hyperbolus; Alcibiades' Olympics; Melos attacked
415	Desecration of herms
415–413	Athenian invasion of Sicily
414–412	Alcibiades in Sparta
413	Resumption of war between Athens and Sparta; Spartan fortification of Deceleia
412	Revolt of Chios, Naxos, Miletus, etc.
412–411	Alcibiades with Tissaphernes
411	Oligarchic coup of the Four Hundred; Alcibiades recalled by Athenians on Samos
410	Democracy restored; battle of Cyzicus
407	Alcibiades returns to Athens; exiled again after battle of Notium
406	Battle of Arginusae; trial of generals
405	Battle of Aegospotami
404	Defeat of Athens followed by rule of the Thirty; assassination of Alcibiades
403	Civil war; death of Critias; democracy restored
401	Reduction of oligarchic enclave at Eleusis
399	Trial and execution of Socrates

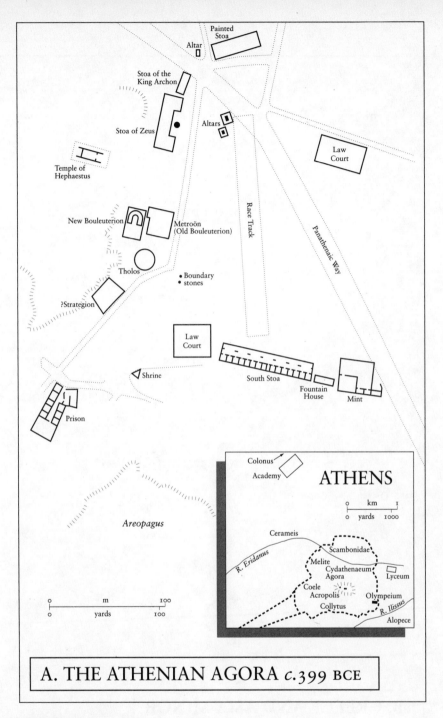

Painted
Stoa

Altar

Stoa of the
King Archon

Stoa of Zeus

Altars

Temple of
Hephaestus

Law
Court

New Bouleuterion

Metroön
(Old Bouleuterion)

Tholos

• Boundary
• stones

?Strategion

Law
Court

Shrine

South Stoa

Fountain
House

Mint

Prison

Race Track

Panathenaic Way

Areopagus

Colonus

Academy

ATHENS

km

yards   1000

Cerameis

Scambonidae

Melite

Cydathenaeum

Agora

Lyceum

Coele

Acropolis

Olympeium

Collytus

R. Eridanus

R. Ilissus

Alopece

m   100

yards   100

A. THE ATHENIAN AGORA *c.*399 BCE

(lightly adapted from Debra Nails, *The People of Plato*, p. 267)

MACEDON

R. Strymon

Amphipolis

CHALCIDICE

Poteidaea

Olympus

Scione

Corcyra

THESSALY

AEGE

ACARNANIA

Euboea

Delphi

IONIAN

Athens

Corinth

Zacynthos

Argos

SEA

Siphnos

MESSENIA

Sparta

Pylos

LACONIA

Melos

Cythera

B. GREECE AND ASIA MINOR

T

BLACK SEA

RACE

ODRYSIANS

Bosporus

Byzantium ● Chrysopolis

Propontis

CHERSONES

Aegospotami
● Lampsacus
Sestus ●
Hellespont
● Abydus

● Cyzicus

P H R Y G I A

Arginusae Islands

Lesbos
● Mytilene

● Cyme

Chios

L Y D I A

● Sardis

km
miles

● Notium
● Ephesus

Samos

Delos

● Miletus

C A R I A

L Y C I A

Rhodes

AEGEAN
SEA

L O C R I S

P H O C I S

Euboea

Delphi

Orchomenus

Thebes

BOEOTIA

Delium

Corinthian

Siphae

Plataea

Parnes

Deceleia

Patrae

Phyle

Marathon

A C H A E A

Eleusis

ATTICA

Megara

Athens

Piraeus

Corinth

Salamis

Phleious

Nemea

PELOPONNESE

LAURIU

Olympia

Mantineia

Argos

Epidaurus

Sunium

R. Alpheius

IONIAN
SEA

Tegea

Hysiae

km 7,5
miles 45

Elis

C. CENTRAL GREECE

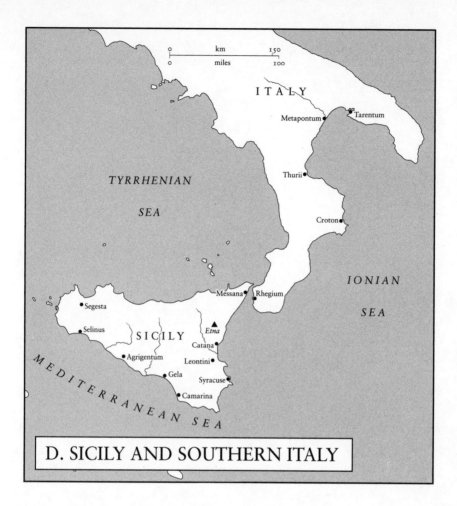

km
miles

ITALY

TYRRHENIAN

SEA

Metapontum

Tarentum

Thurii

Croton

IONIAN

SEA

Messana
Rhegium

Segesta

Etna

Selinus

SICILY

Catana

MEDITERRANEAN SEA

Agrigentum

Leontini

Gela

Syracuse

Camarina

D. SICILY AND SOUTHERN ITALY

THE TRIAL OF SOCRATES

Socrates in Court

In the spring of 399 BCE, the elderly philosopher Socrates, sixty-nine or seventy years old, stood trial in his native Athens. The court was packed. Apart from the hundreds of officials, there was also a shifting crowd of spectators – Socrates' well-wishers and enemies, and those who were simply curious to see what would happen to this man, who had long been a well-known figure in Athenian life.

The case was probably heard in the building known to the excavators of the Athenian Agora as the 'Rectangular Peribolos', a more-or-less square structure in the south-western corner of the Agora. Once the dikasts were seated (the 'jurors', that is, but their functions were so different from those of a modern jury that it is less misleading just to transliterate the ancient Greek term), and the court president, the King Archon, had decided that everything was ready, Socrates and his prosecutors entered through the main entrance in the north wall. The inside of the building was, at this date, still just an open space, about twenty-five metres square, lined on three sides with benches for the dikasts, for witnesses (if there were any to be called), and for onlookers, who were distinguishable from dikasts only by the fact that the dikasts had been issued with voting tokens with which to cast their verdict at the end of the trial. The fourth side of the building held chairs for the presiding archon, the prosecutors and defendant, and their separate podiums.

The walls were lightly decorated and although in its previous incarnation the building had been open to the sky, it had been rebuilt after the Persian sack of Athens in 480 and was now roofed. The klepsydra – literally 'water-stealer', the clock by which the proceedings were timed – was manned by a responsible publicly owned slave, and kept outside, by the north wall, just to the west of the entrance. It was a terracotta jar with an overflow hole close to the rim and a bronze pipe acting as an outlet at the base. The jar was filled with water up to the overflow hole and the water ran out of the pipe into another similar jar, placed below the first one; speeches were timed in multiples of jars, and the original function of the water-clock was not to limit the length of speeches so much as to ensure that both litigants would have the same time to speak. Different kinds of trial were allowed speeches of different lengths, but no trial lasted longer than a day and many lasted considerably less, so that a court could get through a number of cases in a single day. Socrates' trial lasted a full day, but he still complained, with considerable justification, about the time restriction.*

The number of dikasts employed in Athenian trials seems enormous by modern standards: the smallest jury we hear of, for a private case later in the fourth century, was 201; the most critical public cases might be heard by the entire pool of six thousand. The commitment by ordinary people of their time and energy to the pursuit of democratic justice in classical Athens is astonishing. At the beginning of every year, six thousand citizens were enrolled as dikasts, and the courts drew on this pool every time they met; as many of the six thousand as were needed were at the last minute (to curb bribery) divided by lot among the courts. The size of the jury too was partly a hedge against bribery, but more importantly, the law courts were an integral tool of the democracy, and the numbers were meant to ensure that the will of the people was done.

The jury was a fair cross-section of adult male Athenian society, in terms of age groups, wealth distinctions, modes of employment and so on, with something of a bias towards the poor, who needed the state pay for attendance. Since the 420s, dikasts were paid three obols for a day's session – an amount that, on its own, would barely keep a single person alive, but on top of other sources of income was enough to improve the quality of a poor man's life. For Socrates' trial, there were almost certainly five hundred or 501 dikasts, the normal minimum at the time. Following the devastating losses of the long-drawn-out war with Sparta, which had recently ended with the Athenians' defeat, there were probably no more than twenty thousand citizens available for jury duty (for which one had to be male and over thirty years old), so Socrates was tried by a good percentage of his citizen peers.

With the dikasts assembled, the indictment was read out by one of the archon's assistants. The prosecution speech or speeches followed, and then those of the defendant and, if he had them, one or two

---

* References can be found on pp. 209–26. Unattributed facts derive from a variety of sources, which can be tracked down via the bibliography on pp. 227–45.

supporting speakers. The dikasts then voted – immediately, with no further time for deliberation – on the defendant's guilt or innocence. The voting system in use for Socrates' trial in 399 was still relatively new, but vastly improved on its predecessor. Dikasts were given two ballots, which were clearly differentiated, so that one recognizably meant 'I vote for the prosecution' and the other 'I vote for the defence'. The ballot was a small bronze disc pierced through the centre either by a hollow tube ('for the prosecution') or by a solid tube ('for the defence'). Each dikast approached a jar and dropped into it one or the other of his two ballots; he then approached a second jar and dropped into it his unused ballot. When every dikast had voted, votes from the first jar were counted, and could be checked by counting the discarded ballots from the second jar. Secrecy was ensured by the fact that the dikasts could hold the ballots with their fingers covering the spindles, so that no one could see whether they were solid or pierced, but in general the use of ballot-voting in ancient Athens was a way of ensuring accuracy rather than secrecy, since votes could be counted rather than just estimated, by vociferous acclaim or a show of hands.

Socrates' trial fell into a common category, technically known as 'assessed trials' (*agōnes timētoi*), in which further, shorter speeches were allowed. These were cases where the state acknowledged that there could be degrees of guilt, and so after the chief prosecutor had proposed a penalty, the defendant proposed a lesser counter-penalty, and then there was a second round of voting by the dikasts, on which of the two proposed penalties to enforce. For both rounds of voting, a simple majority was all that was required; a tied vote counted in favour of the defendant.

The trial attracted a great deal of attention on the day, and became even more notorious afterwards. This helps to explain the fortunate accident of the preservation, albeit by a biographer writing over six centuries later (drawing on an only somewhat earlier historian, who claimed to have found the document preserved in the Athenian archives), of the exact wording of the charges against him:

> This indictment and affidavit is sworn by Meletus Meletou of
> Pitthus, against Socrates Sophroniscou of Alopece. Socrates is
> guilty of not acknowledging the gods the city acknowledges, and
> of introducing other new divinities. He is also guilty of subverting
> the young men of the city. The penalty demanded is death.

Socrates' trial, then, was one of a number known to us in which the fundamental charge was impiety (*asebeia*), a prosecutable offence under Athenian law. Meletus had demanded the death penalty, and he got his way; I will later outline what we know or can reasonably guess about Meletus and his fellow prosecutors, Anytus of Euonymon and Lycon of Thoricus. Death was a penalty or possible penalty for a surprisingly wide number of serious charges in classical Athens. Having lost the case, Socrates was led by public slaves straight from the court to prison, not far distant in the Athenian Agora. Imprisonment was not, as now, a common punishment; the usual penalties were death, disenfranchisement, exile, confiscation of property or a fine. Prisons were used less as places of long-term internment than as temporary holding-stations, for those awaiting execution, for public debtors, and for some categories of criminals awaiting trial; they fell under the jurisdiction of an annually selected board known, banally rather than sinisterly, as the Eleven, and were staffed by a few lowly workers such as turnkeys, who were probably state-owned slaves.

Execution usually followed a guilty verdict within a day or two, but fate intervened to prolong Socrates' life for a brief span. No executions were permitted while the Delia, the annual festival of Apollo on his island of Delos, was being celebrated, because the sacred island had to remain free of pollution. So Socrates lingered in prison for thirty days, awaiting the return of the official Athenian ship from the festival (it set off for Delos the day before his trial and its return was delayed by adverse winds). Apollo, the god to whom Socrates felt closest, was looking after him to the last.

If Plato is to be trusted, Socrates passed the time conversing with friends and family members, and composing incidental poetry (his only known attempts at writing). Visitors were allowed in the prison at any time of the day or night, and were expected to bring food for the inmates, whose rations were meagre or non-existent. But, until the final day, when he was released as an act of mercy, he was kept in uncomfortable fetters; they were used to reduce the numbers of staff required, and because building materials were such that escape from prison would otherwise have been easy, a matter merely of digging through a relatively soft wall (the ancient Greek for 'burglar' means 'wall-tunneller'). Even so, escaping from prison was not difficult, and some of Socrates' friends made plans to break him out, but Socrates asked them not to. Having earlier turned down the opportunity of

6

exile before the trial (when it was permissible, if not quite legal), he could not now escape illegally. That would be to harm the city, he said; to harm anyone or anything is to commit injustice and to scar one's own soul; and Socrates prided himself on never having wronged anyone throughout his lifetime.

And so at last the ship returned from Delos, and Socrates was executed by drinking hemlock. This form of execution had been introduced only a few years earlier, and had not yet replaced the most common method (a kind of crucifixion), perhaps because it was considered expensive; at any rate, the preparation of the dose was paid for by friends or relatives of the condemned criminal rather than by the state – but what they were really paying for was a more benign death for their friend. The state also approved of the use of hemlock, because it was self-administered and bloodless, and so freed the state from the miasma of guilt.

It used to be thought that death by hemlock was painful and ugly, with spasms, choking and vomiting; but we now know, thanks to classicist and amateur toxicologist Enid Bloch, that the particular species of hemlock used for this purpose in ancient Athens (*Conium maculatum*, available on the slopes of nearby Hymettus) was effective, but not especially violent. Its effects, in fact, are pretty much as Plato described them in the closing pages of his dialogue *Phaedo*, a beautiful and profound work set in prison on the last day of Socrates' life. Plato correctly portrays his beloved mentor dying a gradual death by paralysis, leading finally to asphyxiation. His body was then collected by family and friends and accorded the traditional rites.

BEFORE THE TRIAL

The trial was the culmination of an orderly procedure. First, some weeks or even months earlier, Meletus had had to accost Socrates, and in the presence of two witnesses (perhaps in this case his two fellow prosecutors) read the charges out to him and summon him to appear on a specified date at the office of the King Archon in the stoa named after him in the north-west of the Agora, when Meletus would formally lodge with the King Archon a written copy of the indictment. The King Archon was one of the nine *arkhontes* of Athens, officers annually selected by lot from an elected short-list, who, in the developed Athenian democracy, had little more than formal roles, especially in the religious and judicial spheres. The King Archon's title was an odd residue of the long-gone era of kingship, and he retained some of the prehistoric kings' powers in matters pertaining to religion, so that he was responsible, among other things, for trials for impiety. Socrates' case was slightly complicated by the fact that impiety was only half of the charge, with the other half being subversion of the youth; but since impiety was the more serious charge, it took precedence and the entire procedure was as if for a trial for impiety. Besides, to judge by the phrasing of the charges, the way in which Socrates was supposed to have subverted Athenian young men was by encouraging them to be as impious as himself. That was how Meletus understood the charges.

At the end of this meeting in the Royal Stoa – the dramatic context of Plato's dialogue *Euthyphro*, which has Socrates discussing piety (what else?) with a religious fanatic – the King Archon also set a date for the preliminary hearing, the *anakrisis*. In the intervening days, the King Archon's staff posted a copy of the charges in public, in the heart of the Agora. Then, at the preliminary hearing, it was the King Archon's job to decide whether the case had enough merits to go to court. The indictment was read out, depositions were taken from any relevant witnesses, and Socrates formally denied the charges. If the King Archon was still unsure whether or not there was a case that needed answering, he questioned both Meletus and Socrates until he could reach a decision. After all, the state paid dikasts for their service, and he did not want to waste resources on hopeless or frivolous cases. But these proceedings were more or less a formality, since there were further measures in place to fine prosecutors severely if their cases failed to win twenty per cent of the dikasts' votes in the actual court itself. The people themselves, sitting as dikasts, would decide the merits of the case.

We have no way of knowing what either party said at the *anakrisis*, but Meletus evidently convinced the King Archon that there was a case to be heard, and the archon set a date for the trial. Some weeks passed between the preliminary hearing and the trial. This should have been a time for the defendant to prepare his defence, but on the day Socrates claimed to be speaking off the cuff and even told one of his associates that he had spent his entire life preparing his defence, by consistently doing no wrong. Both Plato and Xenophon were, in some sense, followers of Socrates, and his trial and execution aroused such dismay and anger that they and several others from Socrates' circle devoted at least part of their literary career to defending their mentor's memory. We have all of the Socratic writings of Plato and Xenophon, and too few fragments from a number of others. Above all, in the present context, we have both Plato's and Xenophon's versions of Socrates' defence speeches, each traditionally called in English the *Apology of Socrates*, or just the *Apology* – a transliteration of the Greek word for 'defence speech'.

When such a tiny percentage of ancient Greek literature has survived, and yet *two* versions of a single episode remain, it might seem churlish to complain, but the fact is that we cannot know for certain how much, if anything, of these two versions of Socrates' defence resembles what Socrates actually said on the day. The differences between the two versions are enormous; they cannot both be right. So whom does one trust? It is tempting to rely on Plato's version, because it is brilliant – funny, philosophically profound, essential reading – whereas Xenophon's is far more humdrum, and is in any case an unpolished work. But this is the nub of the whole 'Socratic Problem', as scholars call it: we want to trust Plato, but his very brilliance is precisely what should incline us not to trust him, in the sense that geniuses are more likely than lesser mortals to have their own agendas. And in fact no one doubts that Plato had his own agenda, and came to use Socrates as a spokesman for his own ideas; the only question is when this process started and how developed it is in any given dialogue. The most sensible position is that no dialogue, however early, is sheer biography and no dialogue, however late, is entirely free from the influence of the historical Socrates. Plato, Xenophon and all the other Socratics were writing a kind of fiction – what, in their various views, Socrates might have said had he been in such-and-such a situation, talking with this person and that person on such-and-such a topic. For one thing that is common to all the Socratic writers is that they portray their mentor talking, endlessly talking – either delivering homilies, or engaging others in sharp, dialectical conversation and argument.

What, then, of the two defence speeches? If execution is an attempt by a community to have a trouble-maker disappear, Athens signally failed with Socrates. The trial rapidly became so notorious that a number of *Apologies of Socrates* were written soon afterwards, and at least one prosecution speech purporting to be that of Anytus. If the object had been to report the actual speech or speeches Socrates himself gave in the course of the trial, there would have been no need for more than one or two such publications, and all the rest would have been redundant. The fact that so many versions of Socrates' defence speeches were written strongly suggests that the authors were not reporters of historical truth, but were concerned to write what, in their opinion, Socrates could or should have said – which is what characterizes the whole genre of Socratic writings that sprang up in the decades following Socrates' trial and death. If there is any truth to the stories that Socrates came to court unprepared, a rhetorical innocent, Plato's *Apology* certainly begins to look fictitious: it has long been admired as polished oratory.

Given the unlikelihood of our ever having objective grounds for proving the fictional nature of either or both of these two versions of the defence speeches, it is gratifying, and significant, that we can easily create a plausible case for their fictionality. One of the most famous episodes in Plato's *Apology* is the story that Socrates' friend Chaerephon of Sphettus, famous in comedy for being ascetically emaciated (or at least poor), a con artist and a creature of the night, consulted the oracle at Delphi, the fabulously wealthy shrine of Apollo which was one of only a handful of international cult centres in Greece, and came back with the god's judgement that there was no one wiser or more knowledgeable than Socrates. As Plato tells the story, this oracle was the trigger for Socrates' philosophical mission. He was puzzled by what the god could have meant, and so set about questioning all the experts he could find in Athens, to try to understand what the god meant. And in the end he decided that the god was right, because everyone else suffered from the false conceit that he knew more than he actually knew; none could demonstrate his expertise by responding coherently to Socrates' questions. So Socrates concluded that he alone *did* have a kind of wisdom – the sense to know how little he knew. But by then he was launched on his mission of enquiry, of asking himself and others tough questions to try to uncover the truths underlying our beliefs and opinions.

But why should Chaerephon have approached the oracle with his question in the first place? In order for it to make sense to ask whether there was anyone wiser than Socrates, Socrates must already have had a reputation for wisdom. He had never been famous as anything other than the person in Athens who went around questioning people and finding out if they could define the moral and other concepts they claimed to work with; this enterprise had started around 440 BCE, and had brought him notoriety by the end of the decade. But this is

precisely the kind of questioning that, according to Plato, was supposed to have been triggered by the oracle, rather than going on
beforehand. Another good reason for supposing the oracle a fiction is
that there is no other reference to it by Plato, or by any of the other
Socratics (who would certainly have made hay with it), or anywhere
else in Greek literature, except a mention in Xenophon's *Apology*,
which now begins to look decidedly derivative. It surely would have
been a famous tale.

What Plato was doing with this story is rather subtle. Throughout
his life Plato wanted to establish philosophy, as he understood it, as
the one valid form of higher education, and in order to do so he used
his writings to puncture the claims of rivals – educators, poets, statesmen, orators and other experts. So this is what Plato has his character
'Socrates' do in the early dialogues: question such experts and find
them lacking. This was Plato's mission, and his Socrates was the
mouthpiece for this mission. But this is precisely the mission summarized in Plato's *Apology* in the oracle story. Plato made up the story,
then, as a way of introducing his own mission, the mission he would
give to the character Socrates who was to appear in his works.

Since Xenophon knew Socrates, he knew that Plato's Socrates
was fictional. He was in a position to recognize that Plato's description of Socrates' mission was actually a clever way of outlining and
introducing Plato's own mission. So Xenophon did the same: he used
the same story for the same purpose, and merely tweaked it to suit *his*
mission. The chief difference between the oracle story in Plato and the
version in Xenophon is that in Xenophon the oracle states that there
is no one more free, upright and prudent than Socrates. Xenophon's
mission was to make Socrates out to be a paragon of conventional
virtue (and to explore what inner conditions are required for such
virtue), and so his Socrates is 'free, upright and prudent', rather than
'wise'. Xenophon avoids mentioning wisdom because its corollary
was Socratic ignorance: Plato's Socrates was wiser than anyone else
because he was the only one who was aware of his ignorance. But
ignorance is not one of the traits of Xenophon's Socrates, who spends
most of his time advising others what to do. What we have, then, is an
exquisite case of intertextuality between the two authors. Plato used
the oracle story to establish his mission in writing, and Xenophon,
recognizing that this is what Plato had done, did the same for his own
mission.

'Here before our eyes is the mythmaking process at work,' as Moses Finley once remarked apropos of these two speeches. Perhaps it is the lot of people such as Socrates and Jesus, people who initiate great changes, to be what they become in others' versions. Before long Socrates became such a larger-than-life figure, thanks to the efforts of his followers, that we have to work to uncover the truth about the trial, and the case achieved such fame that, in subsequent centuries, writing defence speeches for Socrates became an exercise for students of rhetoric or concerned philosophers, fuelled by the liveliness of an ongoing debate about the relationship between philosophy and politics. Dozens of Socratic defences were written, and some even 'published', but the only survivor was written by Libanius of Antioch in the fourth century CE, 750 years after the event. The great orator of the late second and early third centuries CE, Maximus of Tyre, alludes to this tradition of writing both prosecution and defence speeches for Socrates' trial, and explains it, at least partly, by reference to the rumour, which started perhaps late in the fourth century, that Socrates himself said nothing at his trial, but just stood there mute and defiant.

SOCRATES' DEFENCE SPEECHES

There may be nuggets of historical truth within either or both of the two works, but we lack the criteria for recognizing them. We will never know for sure what was said on that spring day of 399 BCE. Here, in any case, are summaries of Socrates' main defence speeches, as told by Xenophon and Plato. Plato claims to have been there in person, and Xenophon to have heard about it at second or third hand – but even these claims may be an odd Greek literary convention, a way of creating verisimilitude, rather than a guarantee of truth. Throughout his *Recollections of Socrates*, Xenophon frequently claims to have been present at conversations he could not possibly have witnessed.

Xenophon's version focuses on the current charges. Socrates denies the charge of not acknowledging the gods acknowledged by the state by claiming that he has always performed his religious duties as a citizen. Taking the charge of introducing new gods to be an oblique reference to the supernatural voice that often came to him with advice (more on this later), he argues that listening to this voice is no more irreligious than making use of any other form of divination to receive communications from the gods. The only difference is that this supernatural voice is exclusive to him, to Socrates – but that he is particularly favoured by the gods is also proved by Apollo's response to Chaerephon. This claim to be the special agent of the gods naturally provokes uproar in the court, and Socrates does not help matters by going on to argue that he is such a paragon of virtue that it makes no sense to charge him with corrupting or subverting anyone. Meletus, when questioned by Socrates about the sense of this charge, falls back on the claim that Socrates attracted young men to himself and took them away from the traditional, family-based forms of education. Socrates admits this, and justifies it by saying that he is an education-al expert, so naturally people come to him for education, just as they would go to a doctor on matters of health.

Plato's version is considerably longer and more complex. In this version, Socrates' defence rests crucially on a distinction between his 'old accusers' and his 'new accusers', as he calls them. The 'new accusers' are simply Meletus, Lycon and Anytus, with the specific charges brought at this trial, but the 'old accusers' are largely faceless and nameless: they are the common people, with their prejudices against the new learning that had swept the upper echelons of Athenian society in the last thirty or forty years of the fifth century. They are ill-informed, and incapable of distinguishing between different types of intellectual, and so they project on to Socrates a confused picture in which he becomes simultaneously an archetypal scientist, sophist and orator, along with all their fears about the dangers of such intellectuals – atheism and other forms of moral subversion. Tabloid newspapers used to do the same with the gurus and 'cult leaders' of the 1970s.

Luckily, we are in a position to validate this complaint of Plato's. Socrates often featured in comic plays from the late 430s onwards, and apart from fragments we have an entire work in which he plays an important part. This is Aristophanes' *Clouds*, originally produced in 423, but extensively rewritten some time between then and 414. And in this play we find that Socrates is just such an amalgam: a scientist, a sharp talker, a hair-splitting quibbler, who undermines conventional moral norms and prefers bizarre gods such as Chaos, Clouds and Tongue to the Olympic pantheon. If this was meant to be farce, it became mistaken as satire – and satire of Socrates himself, not of a conglomerate intellectual. And so Socrates was widely taken to be an irreligious corrupter of the young – exactly as in the indictment. It may have been meant to be funny at the time, but things had changed by 399 and people were more inclined to take Aristophanes' charges seriously.

Plato even includes in his *Apology* a specific reference to this play as a source of the old accusers' prejudices against Socrates. Aristophanes chose Socrates as his figurehead intellectual for no better reason than that he was a native Athenian, whereas the vast majority of other current intellectuals were foreigners. Aristophanes returned to the theme in two later plays, where Socrates is tarred as a corrupter of the young, a kind of cult leader or hypnotist necromancer, and other comic poets (especially Eupolis and Ameipsias, whose work unfortunately has scarcely survived) frequently mocked and expressed comic concern about Socrates and his circle.

Socrates' point here, in Plato's *Apology*, is that there is no way for him to combat such confused and deep-rooted prejudices. He denies them, but in the 440s he had taken an interest in current scientific ideas, and that may still have been vaguely remembered. And his distinction of himself from the sophists (which depended, anyway, on grouping a mass of diverse people together as 'sophists') would have been regarded by most of his audience as mere hair-splitting, just as, to non-initiates today, a logical positivist and a Platonist would seem to share more similarities than differences.

It is even likely that the distinction of Socrates from the sophists was an invention of Plato's. The sophists were educators, and Plato tries to make out that Socrates never claimed to be a teacher (in the sense of a transmitter of his own ideas), and simply followed the course of arguments wherever they led, whether the upshot was the refutation of one of his own beliefs, or those of his interlocutors. Xenophon's Socrates, however, is a fully fledged teacher, offering advice to all and sundry, and Plato's portrait is pretty unconvincing anyway, as a piece of history, because it is hard to imagine that Socrates spent his whole time on refutational argument, that this was the beginning and end of his philosophical mission. He must have spent some time teaching too, and this is what Xenophon portrays. One minor difference is that Socrates did not take money from his students, as the sophists did; he preferred not to be obligated to take pupils on just because they had the means to pay him. Where the testimonies of Plato and Xenophon coincide, however, is in their condemnation of the sophists for the superficiality of their arguments. They were not educators in genuine morality, because they taught their students only the eristic art of winning arguments, whether or not that involved searching for the truth. Only Socrates had at heart his students' moral improvement. This shaky foundation is all that allows us to distinguish Socrates from those whom his followers lumped together as 'sophists'.

There was no reason for those who were outside Socrates' exclusive circle not to believe that Socrates was as he was portrayed in *Clouds*: an atheistic scientist-cum-sophist who taught wealthy young men his weird and dangerous notions. In Plato's defence speech, Socrates claims that the source of these prejudices is his mission to interrogate people (so this is where he introduces the story of the Delphic oracle). Not only has this made those whose conceit to knowledge he punctured angry with him (imagine a contemporary critic who day after day demolished the pretensions of our religious, political and artistic leaders, in public debates broadcast on television to millions), but some young men have imitated his method of interrogation, and even misused it as a way to try to score points off their opponents, rather than as a way of trying to get to the truth. And so, in order to divert attention away from their own ignorance, people have gone around slandering Socrates and fuelling prejudice against him.

The next few pages of Plato's *Apology* are taken up with a short dialogue between Socrates and Meletus, in the course of which Socrates sarcastically ties his prosecutor up in knots over the issues of subverting young men and of atheism; for all the guardedness of his responses, Meletus is made painfully aware that he is not Socrates' intellectual equal. Since there was almost certainly no provision for such dialogue in Athenian courtroom procedure, this too is a feature of Plato's *Apology* that we can safely take to be fictional; and, again, it was one that was imitated, though at considerably less length, by Xenophon in his version. Plato used it, presumably, as a way of letting his readers know one or two of the things Meletus had said in his speech; he had stressed that the proper source of education for young men was the family-based perpetuation of what Sir Gilbert Murray called the 'inherited conglomerate' – the moral and religious code passed down, by example and oral teaching as much as by instruction, from generation to generation – and he had accused Socrates of being an outright atheist.

Socrates goes on to affirm his commitment to his philosophical mission. It was given to him by Apollo, and it would be arrogant sacrilege to abandon it, even on pain of death. He compares himself to the Homeric hero Achilles, who had to choose between a short, brilliant life and a long, undistinguished one, and insists that he will not stop philosophizing even if the court makes it a condition of his acquittal that he should do so. He claims that, so far from being a source of corruption, his service to the god is the best thing that has ever happened to Athens. He likens the city to a sluggish, dozing horse, and himself to a horsefly, sent by the god to stir it out of its slumbers, and at risk of being swatted dead by the horse's tail.

But if this is his job, why has he not played a greater part in Athenian public life, as a more direct way to galvanize the city? Because, he says, there is no place for an honest man in the city's politics. His supernatural voice has consistently prevented him from playing a part in the city's public affairs, and the reason must be that had he done so he would have been put to death long ago. As it happens, in the normal course of events he found himself in a position of some responsibility once in 406, when he tried to stop what he saw as an immoral procedure; and once in 404 or 403, during the rule of the Thirty Tyrants, they wanted him to arrest Leon of Salamis, but he refused, again on the grounds of the immorality of the proposed action. Despite his evident survival, he says that both times he was in danger of death, and so he uses these cases to support the point that, had he chosen to act politically, whatever the regime, he would have been killed. And then he winds down his speech with a couple of stock rhetorical points: the prosecution's claim that he corrupts people is undermined by the fact that none of the relatives of those he is supposed to have corrupted have ever taken him to court; and he refuses to demean himself by employing the kind of pity-arousing tactics that others employ in court when threatened by the death sentence.

Socrates was found guilty by a narrow margin: 'If a mere thirty votes had gone the other way, I'd have been acquitted.' In other words, on the assumption that there were five hundred dikasts at the trial, 280 voted for his guilt and 220 for his innocence. Then it was his turn to propose a counter-penalty, in face of his prosecutors' demand for death. Since he believed that he was the best thing ever to have happened to Athens, he semi-seriously proposed, according to Plato, that he be fed at public expense for the rest of his life. This was an extraordinary honour, usually reserved for those who had conspicuously enhanced the honour of the city, perhaps by winning an event at the Olympic games, or for the descendants of those who were taken to have established democracy in Athens. Socrates was just being provocative. In a more serious vein, pleading his well-known poverty, he proposed that he be fined one hundred drachmas (the cost of a small flock of sheep and goats, say), which was promptly increased by the offers of friends, including Plato, to three thousand drachmas.

This was the kind of penalty the court might have accepted, but Plato's Socrates had gone out of his way to alienate wavering dikasts by his arrogance, and a majority still voted for the death penalty. What kind of a majority? A late biographer says that eighty dikasts changed their vote because they were angry at Socrates for his arrogance: that would make it 360 against 140, and this is the figure most scholars accept. But Socrates' own words (in Plato) suggest a different story: *after* the death penalty had been passed he addressed the 220 who voted to acquit him as true dikasts – a strange thing to call them if some of them had subsequently voted to put him to death. In other words, it is possible that *fewer* voted to put him to death, so that the margin was perhaps as little as 260 against 240.

This post-trial address to the dikasts occurs in both Plato and Xenophon, but it again flies in the face of what we know of Athenian courtroom procedure. The core of both versions is that, like the legendary hero Palamedes, the archetypal wronged innocent, he, Socrates, has nothing to worry about, because no harm can come to a just man. It is those who have condemned him to death, and especially his prosecutors, who should worry about the effect on their souls of their wrongdoing, and about the effect on the city of their removal of the one man who could have helped it. Plato's version ends with Socrates voicing some thoughts on death: since his supernatural voice did not prevent him from attending the court today, he is confident that death cannot be a bad thing for him. It is either a blank state, like dreamless sleep, or he can look forward to philosophical conversations in Hades with interesting men of the past. His final words are: 'And so it is time for us to leave. I go to die, and you to live, but which of these two states is better is unclear to all except the god.'

Plato's *Apology* is brilliant; no summary can do it justice. It contains startling, thought-provoking claims, such as that his prosecutors may be able to kill him, but they cannot harm him, because it is a law that a good man cannot be harmed by a worse man; it contains resonant suggestions such as that wherever one has been posted by a superior, man or god, there it is one's duty to remain. Scholars still mine the book not just for details of Socrates' life, but in the attempt to understand some of his core ethical views. Socrates' equanimity, resolution, defiance, wit and clarity greet one on every page – but this Socrates may, in some part, be Plato's creation rather than the historical man.

Apart from those I have already mentioned in passing, there are a few more or less trivial details common to both Xenophon's and Plato's versions; more importantly, both writers create a certain atmosphere for the trial, and in this, at least, they seem to be reflecting the events of that day. The courts in Athens were not as dignified and solemn as we might nowadays expect and, more than once, dikasts and spectators raised a hubbub of indignant protest at what Socrates was saying, or at his outrageous attitude and refusal to kow-tow to them.

The attitude Plato's Socrates displays to the dikasts, the common people of Athens, is consistently one of defiance and arrogance. Socrates argues that any just man, such as himself, who takes part in democratic politics will be killed; he accepts that he is commonly viewed as an enemy of democracy; he denies the educational value of the democratic inherited conglomerate and even suggests that this kind of education is a major cause of corruption; he states his preference for following his own conscience rather than the collective will of the masses; he makes himself out to be morally superior to the jury, because they expect him to resort to the usual methods of invoking pity, which he says are beneath his dignity; he expresses surprise that so many people voted for him in the first instance – which is to express surprise that the Athenian legal system might actually work in favour of an innocent man; he criticizes the legal system for restricting the time allowed for his defence; he charges the dikasts with acquitting only flatterers and yes-men; so far from directly addressing the charge of impiety, he claims that he would be an atheist if he *stopped* doing what he did, and to have a superior sense of piety to that of the dikasts; and, finally, his suggestion that he should be fed at public expense amounts to a refusal to accept the authority of the dikasts to find him guilty.

Socrates undoubtedly did adopt this tactless approach; it is Xenophon's express purpose to explain why this tone of voice was not as ill-considered as it might seem (because, according to Xenophon, the elderly philosopher preferred death to a prolonged old age). And the upshot is that, even if we conclude that Socrates did mount a defence against the charges (as recent scholars have argued, contrary to an earlier tendency to see the speeches as sheer provocation), it was one that would have worked only if the majority of the dikasts had already been confirmed Socratics. Plato was aware of this: on one of the several occasions when he refers in later works, more or less obliquely, to the trial, he has Socrates say: 'My trial will be equivalent to a doctor being prosecuted by a pastry-cook before a jury of children'; and on another occasion he celebrates the unworldliness of philosophers and how useless they are in court. Both Plato and Xenophon wanted to give their readers the impression that a high-minded philosopher was convicted by the stupidity of a mob, but this was also an attempt to distract attention from the real reasons why Socrates was killed.

TWO

How the System Worked

Socrates was tried, condemned and executed; these bare facts alone have spread ripples of puzzlement and indignation down the centuries. But proper understanding of the trial – of any trial – needs context. What kind of society was classical Athens at the time? How did it work? What had it done? What were its hopes and fears? Who were its heroes and villains? We need an outline, at least, of relevant aspects of the classical Athenian political and legal systems. Even such a sketch will show how intertwined the two were. Classical Athens was a radical democracy – the most radical, in certain respects, the world has ever seen – and the courts often acted as another way for the people to wield power. The ancient Greek for 'the people' is *dēmos*, and so, along with the democratic ideal, the Athenians gave us the word 'democracy', 'the rule of the people'.

The author of the fourth-century BCE *The Athenian Constitution* (either Aristotle or, more likely, one of his students) was no fan of democracy, and he ruefully agreed that it is only when the people have control of the courts that they are in full control of the constitution. The people's courts had gained political power above all in the 460s, when they were given the job of assessing the suitability of political officers before they took up their positions, and of judging their performance at the end of their year of office too; by 415 the courts were also hearing cases where the defendant was accused of having introduced an unconstitutional proposal in the Assembly.

But such powers were not the only factors that politicized the law courts; the incredible and enduring competitiveness of upper-class Athenian society also played a part, in that political rivalries often spilled over into the courts. The competitiveness of trials was recognized: the usual word for a court case in ancient Greek was *agōn*, literally a 'contest'. The courts were arenas where what would once have been feuds were played out in more civilized circumstances. Any kind of case could become an arena for political showboating by one or both of the litigants.

This also means that Plato's (rather obscure) attribution of personal motives to each of Socrates' prosecutors is perfectly plausible. Since anyone who wanted to could act on behalf of the city as a whole and initiate a court case on a wide range of charges, including impiety, personal motives were to be expected: 'Extant evidence reveals', concludes Danielle Allen, 'that the Athenians typically prosecuted only in cases where they were victims or personally involved in the matter at trial. The surviving oratorical corpus yields only four cases in which a prosecutor claims to act as a purely disinterested public actor.' And so the prosecutor of a case would typically begin by claiming that, as a good citizen of the community, his personal grievances coincided with harm done to the city. These generalizations will prove to have enormous implications for Socrates' trial.

THE ATHENIAN CONSTITUTION

The population of Athens at the time of Socrates' trial in 399 was around 220,000: 120,000 citizens (men, women and children), thirty thousand 'metics' (resident non-Athenians) and seventy thousand slaves. Of these, only the thirty thousand or so male citizens had full political rights; admirers of the Athenian democracy in the past tended to gloss over the fact that it was a slave-owning society, and that full citizenship was restricted.

As in most societies, there were huge differences between the incomes of ancient Athenians. They themselves generally spoke in broad terms of the 'rich' and the 'poor'; the 'rich' were indeed rich, but the term 'poor' was applied (usually, it has to be said, by the snobbish rich) to anyone who had to work for his living, rather than purchase labour and generate wealth from the surplus value. More precisely, among the thirty thousand full citizens, there were about twelve hundred super-rich, who were liable to 'liturgies' (mandatory and usually *very* expensive benefactions to the state, in lieu of taxation, such as funding a religious festival, or a warship for a year); after this class, there were about three thousand men with sufficiently large estates for them not to have to work or worry much (in peacetime, at any rate), to be able to speculate with their capital, and to occupy a territory close to either side of the liturgical boundary, and another three thousand had enough of an income, from whatever sources, to make them liable to emergency taxation (*eisphora*) by the state, especially in times of war; then there were about fourteen thousand small farmers and businessmen with sufficient income to serve as hoplites, heavy-armed infantry, who were required to provide their own arms and armour when called up for active service; finally, there were about nine thousand 'thetes' – smallholding peasants, casual labourers, menial workers. The Peloponnesian War, which ran intermittently from 431 until Athens's defeat in 404, devastated the last two of these wealth classes, and reduced the numbers of slaves as well – either by death or by giving them the opportunity to run away. The overall population of 220,000 was down from 335,000 at the start of the war.

For all the democracy's claims to egalitarianism and its promise that everyone, however poor, could take part in the city's affairs, it took money to play a major role. There were perks (such as the occasional bribe from abroad, or booty if you were elected general and conducted a successful campaign), but until late in the fifth century there was no remuneration for most political posts, and they were full-time jobs. As well as money, the job was facilitated by recognized standing in society, and above all by a more or less loyal circle of friends and dependants. Aristocratic culture had long been underpinned by such networks, woven partly by a tradition of complex intermarriages between and within clans, and partly by judicious largess. For much of the fifth century BCE, important political offices remained in the hands of wealthy aristocrats, and even when this monopoly became weakened, they were replaced only by nouveaux riches.

Networks thrived on *kharis*, an impossible word to translate because it means simultaneously 'favour' and the feeling of gratitude a favour evokes. It refers to the reciprocity that governed traditional Greek thinking in many areas of life, and it would be only a little too crude to gloss it as 'You scratch my back and I'll scratch yours.' But *kharis* could extend beyond kinship groups and other alliances: a wealthy politician might endow the city with a park, for instance, as a way of winning the favour of the common people; in return, he expected them to support his political career. Favouritism and a marked lack of concern for altruism were two of the consequences of the way Athenian politics were conducted. Politicians did at least pretend to have altruistic motives, but favouritism was openly acknowledged and was not generally thought immoral.

Friends were important, above all, because there were no political parties in ancient Athens; there were programmes initiated by individuals, which withered when the individual died or lost influence. Of course, one person's programme might resemble another's, but even so it makes little sense to speak of political *parties*, with all the machinery, ideology and endurance the word implies. The phenomenon of a politician changing his mind even about fundamental issues such as war and peace, or whether power should be in the hands of the common people or those of an elite, was more familiar in ancient Athens than in any state organized on party political lines. What a politician was promoting, in the first instance, was not so much a platform as himself, as a statesman or trouble-shooter. A proposal was helped on its way by an individual's core network, and by temporary alliances with other politicians (and their networks) who approved or could be persuaded to approve of that particular proposal. The kaleidoscopic ebb and flow of such alliances, and the behind-the-scenes negotiations, may be left to the imagination. Until very late in the fifth century, there was no civil service to speak of, no permanent committees and sub-committees to see that government progressed relatively smoothly. Friendship was the way things got done.

Nothing shows the individualistic nature of Athenian politics more clearly than the extraordinary institution of ostracism. Once a year, since the foundations of democracy had been laid by Cleisthenes in 508, the people had the option of sending a prominent man into exile for a maximum of ten years – not because he had committed any crime (and so his estates and property were not confiscated while he was away), but just because he was felt to be a threat to the stability of the democracy, especially as a result of bitter rivalry with an aristocratic opponent. Once the decision had been made to conduct an ostracism, feuding among the most powerful politicians reached fever pitch, as each tried to turn the spotlight on to anyone rather than himself. Then, on the day, each attending citizen wrote on a broken piece of pottery (*ostrakon* in Greek) the name of the person he wanted to see removed, or got hold of a pre-inscribed shard. If we see ostracism as a vestige of the prehistoric practice of scapegoating (and sometimes literally killing) the king, *ostraka* are virtual curses, spelled out by ordinary people against their leaders. Though the opportunity was there every year, the Assembly had first to vote to conduct an ostracism, and a minimum of six thousand votes had to be cast in total on the day; but then the person who had the most votes against him was banished.

The very existence of the institution of ostracism shows that the people were aware of the tensions created by the fact that they needed the continuity, professionalism and contacts (both at home and abroad) that wealthy and ambitious individuals brought to government, and yet had to curb them. One might expect that the members of the elite who held political power would gradually have imposed their own agenda on the community; remarkably, it was not so. One of the great strengths of the Athenian democracy, as a true democracy, was that the general populace found ways to control the elite, and even to make use of their education, wealth and status for democratic ends. Generally speaking, the system worked well; the Athenian democracy ran more or less smoothly, with brief interruptions in 411 and 404–403, for most of its almost-two-hundred-year history (it was overthrown in 322 BCE, after an unsuccessful rebellion against Macedonian dominion), and found a good middle ground between the chaos of aristocratic feuding and a collectivist, totalitarian consensus.

While recognizing the need for elite leadership, because initiative comes from individuals, the people kept for themselves the right to decide which initiatives to implement. They dictated what was and was not acceptable content for speeches heard in the Assembly and the courts, the ever-present threat of their courts kept officials transparent and accountable, and they taxed the rich in various ways. It was almost impossible for a single individual to gain the kinds of powers that in our lifetimes successive Russian presidents (to take just one prominent example) have awarded themselves. Almost all political positions were changed annually, and certain positions (such as Council member) could not be held consecutively, or more than twice in a lifetime; most positions were not unique, but involved membership of a committee; above all, there was the use of the lottery.

Only the boards of generals and of financial officers were elected (since they were taken to require special expertise), while everyone else was chosen by lot (though in the case of the Council, the lottery was applied to a pre-elected pool). In the fifth century, the best ways to achieve long-lasting prominence were to use generalship as if it were a political position (especially since the post could be held in consecutive years), or to bypass the system altogether by being a notable speaker, capable of swaying the Assembly, even without holding any official position. Pericles, for instance, used successive generalships as the foundation of his power in Athens in the 440s and 430s, while after him it became more common to use rhetorical ability for the same end – so much so that the Greek word for 'public speaker', *rhētōr*, came to mean 'professional politician'. But, strictly speaking, as Harvey Yunis says: 'Athenian *rhētores* had no professional standing and constituted no restricted or recognized class; held no office, legal position, or any formal power greater than the right to advocate a particular policy; enjoyed no special prerogatives and officially were on a par with all other citizens in and outside the Assembly; were not leaders of parties or factions upon whose support they could call; and had to persuade the *dēmos* anew every time they mounted the platform to advocate a policy or move a proposal.' The system encouraged demagoguery.

The most important check on an individual's gaining excessive power was simply the fact that the Assembly was the executive branch of government. The Assembly could be attended by any male citizen over the age of twenty, though in practice, since many citizens lived too far away (especially before the days of good roads) or were otherwise occupied, it was rare for more than four thousand people to attend, at least until the city became packed by refugees during the war years, and until the Pnyx (the meeting-place) was expanded around 400 and pay was introduced for attendance. The Assembly met at least ten times a year, though emergency meetings could be summoned between these mandatory sessions. Some issues came up regularly and recurrently, such as provisions for the supply of grain; others, such as ostracism, came up once a year. Otherwise, the agenda for each Assembly meeting was prepared by the second main administrative body, the Council of five hundred men over the age of thirty, fifty from each of the ten tribes to which all Athenians belonged for administrative purposes.

The Council met every day, and was in effect the daily government of Athens. It controlled the state's finances through its supervision of the relevant committees, it negotiated with foreign states and received their representatives, it heard petitions from Athenian citizens, and it had certain judicial functions. But its most important work related to the Assembly: it debated and prepared the Assembly's agenda, attached its recommendations to every item on the agenda, counted the Assembly votes, and saw that Assembly decisions were carried out (by means of its authority over all the various bureaucratic committees and sub-committees). It posted the business for all ordinary meetings of the Assembly and had the right to call extraordinary meetings if necessary. The Assembly could not debate a matter which was not on the agenda prepared by the Council, but they could insist that an item be included in the agenda for the next Assembly.

To avoid all five hundred Council members being inconveniently occupied all year round (though they were paid a small daily allowance), the Council year was divided into ten prytanies (slightly variable periods of time), one for each tribe. During its prytany, the fifty men from that tribe were on daily duty, and they reported back to the full Council when it next met; they were chaired by one of their number, chosen on a daily basis by lot, who became for that day the head of the Athenian state, symbolized by his custody of the city's seal (whose device we can only guess at: an owl? The goddess Athena?) and the keys to the temples where the state's treasures and archives were stored. Since any adult male citizen could be a member of the Council, and it was the best way to become educated about the city's political systems, this in turn guaranteed a politicized Assembly, because the people who served as councillors also attended the Assembly. If the historians' record of speeches is anything to go by, the farmers and peasants who attended the Assembly were politically sophisticated – capable of absorbing a commentary in the *New York Times*, say, not just the *Daily Mail*.

One of the remarkable features of the classical Athenian democracy is the degree of involvement by people at all levels of society in the running of the state. Six thousand citizens were enrolled every year as the bank from which to draw personnel to man the jury courts; another seven hundred or so sat on committees or held more prestigious jobs; there were five hundred members of the Council; and thousands also attended each Assembly meeting (though, in the nature of things, only a very few of those thousands spoke at any given meeting, while the rest listened, applauded and heckled). If we count religious festivals as political – as the Greeks would, since it was part of one's civic duty to maintain a good relationship between the gods and the city – then we can include the thousands who filled the streets or the theatre during the great festivals, for which Athens was famous. Wealthy individuals supported the state by maintaining its navy and funding its spectacular festivals – and, generally speaking, were proud to do so. Every citizen was also on stand-by, from the age of eighteen until he reached sixty, to serve in the branch of the military appropriate to his social status and wealth: a very rich man in the cavalry, a middle-income man in the hoplite phalanx, and a poor man as an oarsman in the navy. Their future prosperity depended directly on their own efforts, but they could not have devoted so much time to public matters if Athens had not been a slave-owning and wealthy society.

THE ATHENIAN LEGAL SYSTEM

Legal systems are value-laden; they offer a good route towards understanding a society's values. The classical Athenian legal system is bound to seem, to our minds, somewhat strange, but we are now, thankfully, leaving behind the tendency merely to damn it for its 'deficiencies', assessed against some modern standard. It should rather be seen as a system that worked by its own lights, and as a genuine attempt to bring social justice to a community, to safeguard its welfare, to make its leaders accountable, and to put judicial power in the hands of the majority. We should not expect it to be more than it could have been: it was in transition between the kind of primitive justice where settlement is reached by flexible agreement among the interested parties, and the more rigid, developed system where settlement is reached by reference to the terms of a standing legal code. The Athenians retained a higher degree of flexibility or vagueness than we would nowadays feel comfortable with, and relied more or less entirely on concerned citizens rather than legal professionals.

Scholars speak of ancient Athenian law as being 'procedural' rather than 'substantive'. To take the case most relevant to this book, in so far as we can reconstruct the Athenian law about impiety, it read somewhat as follows: 'If a man is guilty of impiety, he is to be tried in the court of the King Archon and made liable to death or confiscation of property. Any citizen who so wishes may bring the prosecution.' Here the emphasis is procedural, because the focus is on the legal action to be taken, and 'impiety' is not substantively defined. But even though many Athenian laws tended to be phrased as threats in this fashion, there were areas of law (such as property law and family law) where clear definitions were more essential, and a substantive element was far more prominent.

Crimes such as impiety, which were taken to affect the community as a whole and to transgress the community's largely unwritten moral code, were left vague precisely because it was up to the community itself to bring the prosecution (by means of one or two concerned citizens), and to interpret and apply its moral code in reaching a verdict

and choosing a penalty. Within broad parameters, then, the understanding of a particular offence could change from case to case,
depending on how the dikasts themselves judged it. Of course, there
could be no doubt in anyone's mind that certain actions, such as de-
facing statues of the gods or stealing sacred property, constituted
impiety, but matters rapidly blurred beyond this core. We can go some
way towards reconstructing the oath taken by dikasts: in addition to
what one would expect about impartiality and so on, there was a provision for voting according to one's sense of justice, in cases where that
sense of justice was not guided by any substantive law. Hence the
dikasts were occasionally addressed even as law-*makers*, rather than
as law-interpreters.

There was no public prosecutor; for most kinds of cases where the
public good was felt to be at stake, any citizen could take any other
citizen to court. The main curiosity here is that even for the most serious crimes, such as murder, the state offered no help; if no individual
chose to prosecute a case, it would not come to court. The main abuse
of the system was that it became an arena for personal vendettas. A
case could be reopened by bringing a charge against one of your opponent's witnesses, but more commonly, to quote Josiah Ober, 'The prosecutor in one action, dissatisfied with a jury's acquittal, might indict the
same person, for the same crime, in front of a different jury by use of a
different class of action. Similarly a convicted defendant could prolong
proceedings by turning prosecutor.' In the fourth century, Demosthenes
and Aeschines spent the best part of ten years trying to destroy each
other's careers in a series of vicious lawsuits, when the real issues
between them were how to perceive the Macedonian threat – and who
was to be the leading statesman of Athens.

There was a protracted attempt at the very end of the fifth century
to tidy things up, but until then laws had arisen piecemeal, without
adequate protection against contradiction and vagueness. Written
laws were idealized as equalizers, but in practice tradition, gossip and
other factors played just as large a part in legal procedure. Precedent
was recognized, if at all, as a weak factor, whose surface appearance
was more important than consideration of why a previous jury had
reached such a decision in the first place. It was easy for speakers to
base arguments on biased versions and interpretations of Athenian
laws while expecting the dikasts not to spot the bias. The laws, especially those that were phrased vaguely, were regarded more as a kind

of evidence, to be wielded as instruments of persuasion, than as the system of regulations on the basis of which a verdict should be reached.

There was little concern in the courts with what we might recognize as valid or relevant evidence. In the first place, there was nothing in Athens remotely resembling a police force; gathering evidence was up to the litigants themselves, and even then they were not always obliged to produce it in court. In the second place, there was no opportunity in court to cross-examine witnesses or one's opponent (whatever Plato and Xenophon may have implied in their versions of Socrates' defence). Evidence was presented chiefly by an exchange of speeches by two sides, and usually consisted of circumstantial evidence, backed up by arguments from plausibility, along the lines of: 'Is it likely that I, an elderly weakling, would have assaulted such a strapping young fellow?'

In many categories of case, one could say the most outrageous or innuendo-laden things about one's opponent and his ancestors and friends – precisely the kind of tactic that Socrates refused to employ in his defence speeches. The most popular accusations included foreign or servile birth, low social status and deviant sexual behaviour. There was hardly any need to prove these slurs, and they were introduced whether or not they were strictly relevant to the case. By contrast, one presented oneself as a true bearer of the most noble and valuable Athenian characteristics. Contrast this with the relative isolation of modern democratic courts, where (ideally) *only* the case at hand is to be judged, whatever the litigants' behaviour in the past; for us, the fact that the defendant needs a shave and a haircut should be entirely irrelevant to the question whether or not he committed the crime for which he finds himself in court, but for ancient Athenian dikasts it was precisely relevant.

There was no judge to instruct the dikasts, and dikasts were untrained men selected at random from the citizen body, who had to decide by themselves matters of law as well as of fact. Precise interpretation of fine legal points would have required a body of experts, and the very existence of such experts would have detracted from the democratic nature of the courts. Dikasts were more likely to be persuaded by the most impressive speaker, or the one they warmed to most for other reasons (such as his political usefulness to them in the near future). Hence speakers tended to skate over complex issues, in speeches that were theatrical (literally: there was influence both ways between forensic and tragic oratory) and combative, and which included a whole host of extralegal matters, deliberately to appeal to the emotions of the jurors, rather than to employ a dispassionate and strictly legal approach. Weak speakers were at a terrible disadvantage; professional speech-writers were available for those who needed them and could afford them.

Juries were large to reduce the possibility of bribery, and because they were supposed to represent the democracy, but their large size could encourage irresponsibility. When a jury consists of twelve, each person is bound to appreciate that his or her vote makes a substantial difference; the same does not apply to a jury numbering well into the hundreds. Moreover, though the dikasts were obliged to reach a verdict, they were not obliged to say why they reached it. However complex the case, it was not allowed to last more than a day. At the end of the day, the dikasts' decision was final. There was no right of appeal, because the dikasts already were an assembly of the sovereign Athenian people: to whom else could an appeal be made?

One quirk of the system was that it made it possible for unscrupulous people to make money by threatening to take someone to court. In many cases the threatened person would make an out-of-court payment to the blackmailer, either to avoid the nuisance of a court case, or in fear of losing more if the case came to court; even innocent men were tempted to pay, because the open nature of the system made it possible for a man to be convicted even of a crime he had not committed, if he was otherwise unpopular or if his opponent impressed the dikasts. These blackmailers were called 'sycophants' – a word that has a curious origin. Ever since the beginning of the sixth century, it had been illegal to export any foodstuffs except olive products out of Athenian territory; there was to be no profiteering when Athenians needed all the land could produce. Occasionally, however, people tried to smuggle figs across a border. If one of your fellow citizens denounced you as a fig-smuggler, he was a *sykophantēs*, a 'tale-teller about figs'; if it was part of his purpose to ingratiate himself with the authorities, he was close to being a sycophant in the modern sense of the word. Sycophancy in ancient Athens was a genuine nuisance, and steps were periodically taken to curb it, but it was an inevitable consequence of the virtual lack of a police force, of the system whereby individual citizens themselves acted as prosecutors, and of the rewards given to successful prosecutors of cases involving crimes where the state's interests were felt to be at stake.

The impulse for all the essential features of Athenian law was that the workings of the courts were expressly considered to be part of the workings of the democracy as a whole; hence the boundary between court matters and the rest of the political life of the community could be thin (and court cases were usually heard, anyway, in more or less public places, where onlookers were welcome). In a modern democracy, the legislative and judicial branches of government are, or are supposed to be, independent, so that they can act as checks against each other; in ancient Athens both were unified in the common people. One important upshot of this was that dikasts tended to rule conservatively: the spirit of the law was as important as the letter (if there was a 'letter' in the first place) and, fundamentally, the law was animated by a desire to preserve the community. This is a true reflection of the capaciousness of the Greek word for law: *nomos* means not only 'law', but also 'custom' or 'convention' – the way a given society traditionally goes about things.

Political scientist John Wallach succinctly summarizes the necessary conclusions:

> The Athenians' criteria of guilt were not wholly legal in nature, or at least not legal in our sense. Because their conception of legality included conformity to everything signified by *nomoi* – legislative enactments, their constitutional heritage, and sanctioned social customs – guilt for violating such laws could be much more loosely defined than it is in contemporary western courtrooms, where the line between political and legal charges is, or at least is supposed to be, firmly drawn.

Every route by which we approach classical Athenian law brings us sooner or later to the same realization: precisely those aspects that we might see as deficiencies are what enabled it to be a powerful tool of the democracy.

THREE

The Charge of Impiety

All Athenian trials on social charges such as the one Socrates faced were potentially or evidently political. Undercurrents and subtexts were usual, and these undercurrents were political, at least in the sense that it was up to the dikasts to decide whether the defendant was a good citizen, and whether condemnation or acquittal would best serve the city, as much as whether he was guilty of the particular crime with which he was charged. 'Impiety' was exactly the kind of amorphous charge that opened up the texture of the Athenian legal system. The vagueness of its definition placed it squarely among those kinds of charges where it was expected, even required, that dikasts would assess the man as much as the crime.

This is what we find in other impiety trials we know of (too few, and usually in far too little detail). Later in the fourth century, at least two other philosophers resident in Athens, Aristotle of Stagira and his right-hand man Theophrastus of Eresus, were threatened with trials for impiety, when everyone knew that the real issue was that they were in favour of Macedonian rule of Athens. Aristotle fled Athens and quipped, with a neat reference to Socrates' trial, that he was leaving to stop the Athenians wronging philosophy for a second time. Theophrastus, whose case came to court, was acquitted.

There were other Athenian impiety trials at more or less the same time as that of Socrates, two of which, those of Andocides and Nicomachus, were similarly high-profile. With possibly as many as six impiety trials in the space of a year or two, some scholars have inferred that there was a conservative backlash at the time, but the haphazard nature of our knowledge of Athenian trials, and the tiny percentage we know of, make this an unsafe inference. It would take us too far afield to examine in any detail the only other two trials about which we know much, but Andocides of Cydathenaeum was a man with an extremely dubious political past, from a democratic point of view, and with many enemies in Athens; we will later explore in more detail the scandal in which he was caught up in 415 BCE, but for our present purposes it is enough to agree with the scholarly consensus that his prosecutors were out to settle old political scores.

As for Nicomachus, the facts of the case are obscure, and the attempt to achieve clarity is not helped by the weakness of the prosecution speech that survives. He was clearly a man of considerable talent, since he rose from being a public slave to membership of the board entrusted in 410 BCE with tidying up Athenian laws – a position of some political power. He was charged, among other things, with innovations that had caused the neglect of certain religious rites, to the detriment of the Athenian people. In the course of the speech, his prosecutor also accused him of various kinds of anti-democratic behaviour. In neither case, then, would it be safe to rule out the kind of political subtext that impiety trials made possible. It even begins to look as though a prosecution for impiety could be a prosecution for 'un-Athenian activity': certainly, as Stephen Todd remarks, 'a surprisingly high proportion of known impiety trials reveal, on examination, a surprisingly strong political agenda.'

The corollary of this is the degree to which the Athenian people had the power to address religious matters, even those that in our day might be the province of a synod of priests, considered to be experts in such things. In classical Athens, however, since religion was largely non-dogmatic, priesthood was not a vocation, but a position which one generally either inherited or gained by lottery. Usually intermittently, and often for no more than a year, a priest looked after the sanctuary, and saw that the rites were properly performed (by him or by someone else). Priests and priestesses scarcely felt responsible for the welfare of their 'flocks': it was the job of the assembled people to ensure that the channel of goodwill from the gods to the citizen body remained open, as it was their job to authorize new sacred buildings or the introduction of a new cult. The gods were so closely involved in Athenian public life (social and political) that ensuring the gods' goodwill was the responsibility of those who held ultimate responsibility for the Athenian public.

Where did Socrates fit into all this? Athens was, by our standards, a relatively small town, and it relied on a number of small-town mechanisms of social control, such as gossip and ridicule. Socrates was visible – ugly, loquacious and pugnacious – and had attracted attention from the comic poets and at street level (or, in Athenian terms, in the Agora). Despite the fact that, on their enrolment, the dikasts swore to bear in mind only the present charges against the defendant, and to ignore anything else they knew or guessed about him, many of them would already have formed opinions about him. We will see how easy it would have been to misunderstand Socrates' religious views.

ATHENIAN RELIGION

Socrates was charged with impiety, not to be confused with 'heresy': in ancient Greece, there was no sacred text to whose provisions one had to adhere, no elaborate body of doctrine in which one had to believe, no professional priestly hierarchy as we understand it, no confessional books in which a writer furthered orthodoxy or heterodoxy by revealing his or her personal beliefs. Religion was largely ritualistic. One had to perform certain actions, and they presumably involved emotional commitment, but there was little dogma in the background. A great deal of religious practice was not personal, but was an obligation one automatically assumed as a member of some community or other – the civic community, the community of peasants, one's family and household, as a craftsman or a soldier.

The chief means of communicating with the gods were offerings and prayer. Most of these rites were based on reciprocity: either you were giving to the gods in expectation of a return from them in the future, or you were repaying them for a perceived token of goodwill. Animal sacrifices ranged from a bull ox down to a pigeon or a goose: blood was shed and fire burnt the offering and sent it as smoke up to the gods. But these were sacrifices for special occasions; daily domestic sacrifices involved tossing a bun, perhaps, or a handful of grain on to the hearth, or pouring a libation of oil, milk or wine.

Libations and sacrifices were usually accompanied by prayers; music might be played and incense burnt, on the understanding that what was pleasing to human beings might well be pleasing to the gods. Prayers could also be offered up at any time. Gods were addressed humbly, and in an elaborate prayer you were expected to rehearse a number of their titles, out of politeness and your natural concern to make sure you got their attention. You would also mention the deity's obligation to you: you have been a loyal devotee, you have a good record of copious sacrifices, and you expect him or her to answer your prayer in return. The gods were not always reasonable – they both were and were not similar to human beings – but in all your dealings with them you acted as though they might be.

34

Apart from daily rituals, and crisis rituals such as sacrificing before battle to test the omens, the Greek city calendar was marked by festivals, some just for men, some just for women, the greatest for the whole community, including children. Whichever group was involved came together for the purpose of the festival, many of which involved a procession, perhaps carrying through the streets the cult statue and objects sacred to the deity, dancing and singing hymns, while slaves herded the animals to be sacrificed. Quite a few festivals included entertainment, where the general public got to watch athletic, musical and dramatic contests. Most of them involved communal eating; in the Greek world, meat was generally eaten only after an animal sacrifice.

Divination was an important feature of ancient Greek religion. If you needed to know the future, a sneeze or a dream or a chance meeting or a stray remark or the pattern of a bird of prey's flight could all be significant. Professional diviners examined the liver of a sacrificial victim before battle and, in order to judge whether the outcome would be favourable, watched to see how the tail curled in the fire, how quickly the flames spread, and so on, and went on sacrificing until they obtained a favourable omen. The biggest form of divination was consulting an oracle. The gods gave signs, but they were ambiguous and hard to interpret. If a particular shrine turned out to be good at interpretation, it could gain international recognition. In the Greek world this happened at various places, but especially at Cumae in what is now Italy, at Dodona in north-west Greece, and at Delphi in central Greece.

A pious person, then, was one who carried out his fair share of all these rituals. But ritual action rested on a bedrock of minimal beliefs, never fully articulated until they came under threat. One had to believe that rituals were effective, and this carried with it further beliefs: that the gods took thought for human beings, and that they knew more and were more powerful than mortals. And so there were some moral features embedded within normal Greek religion, in the sense that certain acts were regarded as pleasing or offending the gods. The gods were usually concerned with justice and would see that, sooner or later, criminals were brought to book. They wanted one to be hospitable to strangers, kind to one's friends, dutiful to one's community and one's parents, fierce with one's enemies; and they believed that – in the long run, at least – arrogance and excess would be humbled.

Most fundamentally, piety also required that one believe in the existence of gods. Rituals can always be performed by people without belief or commitment, but for practical purposes belief and action were taken to be mutually supporting: your performance of ritual indicated that you believed in the gods, and your belief in the gods underpinned your performance of ritual. This is reflected, in fact, in the ambiguity of the charges that Socrates faced in court. As I translated it earlier, the central sentence of the affidavit went as follows: 'Socrates is guilty of not acknowledging the gods the city acknowledges.' But the sentence could also be translated 'Socrates is guilty of failing to perform the customary rites for the gods traditionally recognized by the state.' If Socrates failed to worship them in the prescribed manner, he might as well not have believed in them, and if he did not believe in them, he would hardly be worshipping them in the prescribed manner. Hence both Xenophon and Plato talk as if Socrates was suspected of outright atheism.

Even given the ritual basis of Greek religion, atheism and agnosticism, in senses of the words that we would recognize today, were possible as responses to belief in the existence of the relevant gods, in their involvement in the lives of human beings, and in the efficacy of the means of communicating with them. The acts of communication kept the gods happy with you and your community. This is why impiety was taken to be such a serious crime. The gods looked after Athens as a whole, helped it to prosper in politics, warfare and agriculture, and allowed its citizens to have fair hopes for the future, as long as they performed the traditional sacrifices and rites and avoided pollution. Any major catastrophe affecting the state as a whole was automatically assumed to be due to the anger of the gods. The very fabric of the state depended on the goodwill of the gods, and this in turn depended on everyone's playing a part, not just in the public festivals of the city, but also in domestic rituals. Patriotism and piety were inseparable. Socrates knew the risks when he came to court on these charges. If your politics were suspect, you could be put to death for damaging olive trees attached to a temple, let alone for angering the gods in the way he was accused of doing.

AGNOSTICISM AND ATHEISM

Atheism, or at least disbelief in the traditional gods, spread far more widely in the fourth century, as philosophers developed their own, often bizarrely magnificent views of the divine. But in the fifth century

BCE and even earlier there were thinkers who were forerunners at a time when most Athenians were less inclined to be flexible in religious matters.

Among Socrates' contemporaries, Protagoras of Abdera famously expressed his agnosticism by saying, pompously but precisely: 'Where the gods are concerned, I am not in a position to ascertain that they exist, or that they do not exist. There are many impediments to such knowledge, including the obscurity of the matter and the shortness of human life.' Protagoras's profound scepticism paved the way for the view expressed by Prodicus of Ceos that what men call gods were simply important natural phenomena or people (Dionysus, then, was no more than the inspired human being who invented viticulture). The philosopher Democritus of Abdera denied the immortality of the gods and argued that religion was based on fear. Thrasymachus of Chalcedon seems to have invented the familiar and powerful argument that the patent unfairness of the world (in which, for instance, innocent children die in agony) proves that the gods take no thought for us. Diagoras of Melos, a poet of otherwise little consequence, argued that means of communicating with the gods were ineffective, and fled Athens in order not to face a trial for having revealed some of the secrets of the Eleusinian Mysteries. Diagoras was so famous as an atheist that just to call someone 'the Melian' (as Aristophanes called Socrates in *Clouds*) was to call him an atheist, and his crimes were long remembered.

The frequency with which characters in written works express atheism shows that such ideas were current in Athens towards the end of the fifth century. Above all, Euripides so loved to include such challenging ideas in his plays that Aristophanes mocked him for it: he had a garland-seller complain that Euripides had almost put her out of business, because no one wanted garlands for religious ceremonies any more. In some famous lines, the tragedian first whisks us through the development of civilization, up to the point when open lawlessness had been brought under control by the invention of laws. But what about secret crimes?

> Next, since the laws made it impossible
> For people to commit obvious crimes by force,
> They began to act in secret. This was the point, I think,
> At which some shrewd and clever man first

Invented fear of the gods for mortal men, so that
The wicked might have something to fear, even if
Their deeds or words or thoughts were secret.
So that is why he introduced the divine, saying:
'There is a god, and he teems with life undying.
He shall hear all that is said among mortals
And shall see all that you do.
Your evil schemes, plotted in silence,
Will be noticed by the gods. For intelligence
Is one of their qualities.' With these words
He introduced the crucial doctrine
And covered up the truth with a fiction.

In other words, the idea that the gods exist is a mere human invention, and so is the notion that they take thought for the human race. There is no point at all, then, to any of the rituals by which we attempt to communicate with them. Religion is founded on a deliberate lie; it is just a means of social and political control. Nor do Euripidean characters stop there: others doubt the existence of gods on the grounds that we patently do not live in a world governed by just gods, or on the grounds that the gods, as described in the traditional tales, act immorally and so license immoral behaviour among humans too, or that they are no more than projections of human needs.

Almost all of the most potent arguments against the existence of a divinity or the validity of worship were deployed by Socrates' contemporaries, and this fact exacerbates the puzzle of Socrates' trial. Since the Athenians were clearly prepared to tolerate impiety in some contexts, we will be forced to look deeper than the charge of impiety to see why Socrates was taken to court.

SOCRATIC PIETY

We are never going to be absolutely certain that we can reconstruct the elements of Socrates' conception of piety. A certain amount of avoidance of potential quicksands is bound to have taken place in our sources, since one of their concerns was to make their mentor's execution appear deranged. Nevertheless, the Socratic writers were committed to quasi-factual writing: 'What if Socrates had discussed piety with Euthyphro outside the office of the King Archon? What might he have said?' And so we can confidently use the evidence of Plato and Xenophon, as far as it goes, while suspecting that it might fall short of the full picture.

If Socrates was impious, either he failed to carry out his ritual obligations, or he denied one or all of the three central tenets of Greek worship: the existence of traditional gods, their involvement in the lives of human beings, and the efficacy of ritual for communicating with the gods. Xenophon says that Socrates carried out his ritual obligations: 'Everyone could see that he sacrificed regularly at home and also at the public altars of the state.' We can take Xenophon's word for this, because it is far more likely that Socrates was suspected of impiety because of his beliefs, not his actions – in other words, that even though he might have fulfilled his ritual obligations, they were suspected of being meaningless for him.

Socrates' view of the gods rested fundamentally on the belief that they were always and only good. Xenophon, for instance, has Socrates invent the argument from design: the main manifestation of their goodness is that they have arranged the world in such a way that everything is useful for us human beings. They have given us sunlight so that we can see and rain so that plants can grow and feed us; they have given us fire to warm our bones and light our ways, and to enable us to develop the arts and crafts; they have made our teeth perfect for breaking up food, our hands perfect for life-preserving skills, and so on: Xenophon's Socrates does no more than outline the kind of way he would have us think about everything.

Plato's Socrates showed how the belief in the gods' essential goodness could clash with ordinary Greek thinking about the gods: 'Since the god is good, he cannot be responsible for everything, as is commonly said . . . He and he alone must be held responsible for good things, but responsibility for bad things must be looked for elsewhere and not attributed to the god.' In normal Greek thinking about the gods, Apollo, for instance, was not just the god of light and culture, but also the bringer of plagues; Poseidon made earthquakes. Nevertheless, just as it is inconceivable to us now that anyone could get into trouble for stressing the goodness of the gods, so it was just as inconceivable then. Even Homer, the founder of much Greek thinking about the gods, has Zeus complain at one point that humans attribute their troubles to the gods, when in fact they bring them on themselves. If Socrates was guilty of impiety, this belief of his is not the place to look for it. At the most, he could be considered mildly eccentric in this respect.

One of the consequences of Socrates' belief in the absolute goodness of the gods, however, looks more promising. He must also have held that many of the traditional stories about the gods were wrong, because they portrayed the gods behaving immorally – quarrelling, fighting, castrating their fathers, committing adultery, lying and so on. And Plato has Socrates himself wonder out loud whether his disbelief in such stories could have played a part in his prosecution. But this is a red herring: several of Socrates' contemporaries also had reservations about the propriety of some of the myths, and in general rationalization of myths and legends was a minor industry, involving a number of admired writers. Perhaps the most strident was again Euripides. In a typical passage, he has Heracles say: 'I cannot believe that the gods either acquiesce in illicit affairs or put one another in chains. I have never believed these things . . . Any true god needs nothing. These are just the debased tales of poets.' In criticizing the myths, and trying to purge Greek religion of false views of the gods, Socrates was in distinguished company, with not a trace of a prosecution among them.

In any case, these stories were not gospel to ancient Greeks. Every tragic playwright tampered with the myths and legends for the purposes of the play he was composing. There is a danger of ignoring the metaphorical character of some Greek thinking about the gods. They did not literally believe that the gods lived on the top of Mount Olympus, because they could clamber up there and fail to find them; if they portrayed their gods as young and beautiful, this does not necessarily mean that they thought of them as young and beautiful, but only that they were trying to encapsulate some features of divinity by applying the attributes 'young' and 'beautiful'. It is likely that they took all the stories with generous pinches of salt – which paved the way for the kind of rationalizations that Socrates and some of his contemporaries preferred, and which therefore suggests that Socrates was not thought impious because of disbelief in the literal level of the myths.

There is one more consequence of Socrates' belief in the goodness of the gods to consider. If the gods are good and can only ever be the source of good things, why bother to sacrifice to them? Besides, if the gods are self-sufficient, as Plato has Socrates come close to suggesting, they need nothing from us. Or again, to suggest that the gods are to be won over by sacrifices is to reduce piety to vulgar trading. It is true that Xenophon's Socrates is conventionally pious where sacrificing was concerned, but could this be a whitewash?

Socrates' belief in the goodness of the gods could have led him to reject sacrifice only if sacrifice is seen as a rite of propitiation required by beings who are not always good. But sacrifice and the accompanying prayer need not be restricted to such a purpose. You can use them to ask the gods for something good, if it seems good to them too, and that falls well short of vulgar trading. Socrates' sacrificing seems to have been of this kind:

> Socrates prayed to the gods simply to give him what was good, recognizing that they know best what is good for us . . . He thought that in offering small sacrifices to the gods from small resources he was in no way falling behind those who offered ample ones from ample resources. He said that it was a poor thing for the gods if they took more pleasure in great sacrifices than in small ones, because then they would often be better pleased with the offerings of the wicked than with those of the good.

What Socrates is doing here is attempting to purge tradition of its vulgarity. Close to the start of *Republic* Plato has a minor character argue that one of the benefits of wealth is that one can be sure to fulfil all one's ritual obligations, and in a collection of maxims written probably in the late 370s, the orator Isocrates of Erchia says: 'Revere the gods always, but especially during the city's festivals, because then you will gain the reputation of being the kind of person who performs sacrifices and abides by rules and regulations.' Piety was taken to be measurable, and it was others who took the measure of it. These are the kinds of shallow conceptions of sacrifice that Socrates intended to combat.

Moreover, it was perfectly acceptable, within standard Greek religion, to ask for the gods' help in doing someone harm. A central tenet of Greek popular morality was the injunction to do good to one's friends and harm to one's enemies; and in extreme circumstances one was expected to help one's friends even in dubious or downright immoral activities (such as fixing an election) and harm one's enemies just because they were one's enemies, not because they deserved it for any particular crime. Then again, and on Homer's authority, it was taken to be possible to redeem sin by lavish sacrifices, much as various medieval popes absolved thugs from past crimes if they undertook to join a crusade. Socrates also rejected these muddle-headed beliefs.

Socrates urged moderation and simplicity in one's dealings with the gods, with the point being to petition the gods, not to impress one's fellow men. Socratic gods do not have the same kinds of desires as us; they only want us to be good. He was deeply religious, then, but in a way that was unconventional in his own day, and probably would seem so in any culture. He saw himself as a servant of the gods in try- ing to promote human happiness in the Athens of his time, but he thought that happiness was identical to, or at least a necessary conse- quence of, a virtuous state of the soul, thanks to which one could prac- tise moral virtue. The path to happiness, then, involved painstaking and often painful self-examination, or examination by someone as skilled at it as Socrates. And so he walked the path by questioning himself and others to see if anyone knew what they were talking about when it came to ethical issues, and by giving advice. The promotion of virtue was carrying out the gods' will, since they want human beings to be good and happy. But if this is piety, piety is something we have to think about and work towards: it is not just a matter of unthinking conformity to certain rituals.

These unconventional thoughts do tend to marginalize traditional Greek rituals, in the sense that prayers and sacrifices that asked for anything other than happiness, or were not just expressions of grati- tude for bestowed goods, or were not requests for guidance (since Socrates held that humans can never have the whole picture on any matter), become irrelevant or, at best, peripheral to a true understand- ing of the gods. Plato gives us a perfect example of just such a Socratic prayer:

> Dear Pan and all gods here, grant that I may become beautiful
> within and that my external possessions may be congruent with
> my inner state. May I take wisdom for wealth, and may I have just
> as much gold as a moderate person, and no one else, could bear
> and carry by himself.

The gods are not there to fulfil our petty desires, but to help us in the great work of self-perfection, which is largely undertaken by one's own efforts. But is this impious? It could be if Socrates was saying that the work of improving oneself and others is something one can do *only* by oneself, but this is not what he said: the gods still play a part, and we need to petition them in the usual ways, even if not for the usual things. In working for the perfection of oneself and others, we are instruments of the gods, carrying out their work on earth. So far from Socrates' views reducing the gods to an ancillary role, it is we who have or should have the ancillary role: we should carry out the gods' wishes.

This is not far removed from an insight we find in Homer. In the Homeric poems there is a phenomenon which scholars call 'double causation': whatever I do, I can say either that a god possessed me, or that the deed was mine, or even both at once. Socrates' views are no more obviously impious than it was obviously impious for Antigone in Sophocles' *Antigone* to claim to be doing the gods' work in burying her brother. Socrates was saying that piety is being the gods' servant, and this was perfectly acceptable within Greek religion – how could it not have been? But he was also saying that the special relationship he enjoyed with the god, as his servant, was possible for each and every one of us.

Socrates was skating on thin ice, but was not impious. But it was hardly difficult to make someone out to be impious when Athenians were encouraged to feel that piety consisted in 'not doing away with any of the practices their ancestors had handed down to them, and not adding anything to the traditional ways'. Piety was conformity. The protocol of an ancient Athenian courtroom made it impossible for Socrates to explain his views to the dikasts, within the space of an hour or so. Plato's Socrates seems aware that his views were liable to be thought unconventional, and were too open to misunderstanding to go into on the day in court: he never, in his defence speech, straight-forwardly addresses the charge of failing to acknowledge the gods of the city. He establishes that he believes in gods, but he fails to say they are those of the city, and the reason for his reticence is that his conception of the divine involved too purged and refined a version of Greek religion for the dikasts readily to accept.

In any case, there is something odd about the charge that Socrates failed to acknowledge the gods of the state. There was no specified set of deities that Athenian citizens had to worship or acknowledge, by law or by convention. There were about two thousand cults in Athens and Attica at the time, so it was impossible to worship them all; one was selective, focusing on the major public deities and on those relevant to one's life or to a particular situation. The prosecutors must have used this charge (as Plato suggests by means of the dialogue between Socrates and Meletus) to imply that Socrates did not recognize any proper gods at all – that is, that he was, to all intents and purposes, an atheist. It would have been hard to make this charge stick, but even harder for Socrates to have explained his views to the dikasts. He could have relied on the let-out that the gods were inscrutable (as he undoubtedly believed, along with all other Greeks) and so neither he nor anyone else could be certain about such things, but that would have been tantamount to an admission of guilt under the circumstances of a trial. The prosecutors were happy: innuendo served their purposes just as well as facts.

The prosecutors relished all the popular conceptions and misconceptions about Socrates and his followers. The comic poets had consistently portrayed them as a kind of mystical cabal, with Socrates as their guru. There is such a strong religious dimension to Socrates' work that he can be portrayed as a fully fledged mystic, as one scholar has recently, and mystics have always been the butts of bemused and self-righteous incomprehension. I suspect that the prosecutors presented a weird mish-mash of quasi-Socratic thoughts and practices, confusing him with representatives of various intellectual streams, while reminding the dikasts that he was known to associate with Pythagoreans (a famous mystical sect) and to fall into trances. Even so, the prosecutors must have known that, if push came to shove, it was going to be hard to get Socrates convicted merely on the vague charge of impiety. And so they specified his major impiety: introducing new gods.

INTRODUCING NEW GODS

Socrates was not the last person in Athenian history to be accused of introducing new gods, but he was the first. Again, however, there is something odd about the charge, because many new cults had been introduced into Athens in the fifth century. Some were new deities or heroes, or previously undervalued ones who were raised to sudden prominence, such as Athena Nikē, Zeus Eleutherios, Heracles, Ares and Theseus, all of whom were held to be partly responsible for victory over the Persians. Some were suitable personifications, such as 'Fair Fame' (Eukleia) and 'Rumour' (Phēmē), or Artemis Aristoboulē (Artemis the Good Adviser), personally introduced by Themistocles in gratitude for the intelligence that had helped him to win the battle of Salamis. Some came from elsewhere in Greece, such as Pan, an Arcadian deity who was believed to have induced panic in the Persian troops at Marathon and who subsequently achieved international prominence as a result of Athenian interest in him, or the Epidaurian healing god Asclepius, whose introduction was hastened by the plague of 430–428. Some came from further afield: the need to placate the eastern Thracians, the Odrysians (who both controlled vast reserves of timber and threatened the trade route to the Black Sea), in the late 430s led to the introduction of one of their major deities, Bendis, and the small-scale, elective cults of Sabazius and of Cybele, Mother of the Gods, both from the Near East, were tolerated too, as private, small-scale forms of cult have to be in any cosmopolitan city.

So what was Socrates' crime? Polytheism is necessarily flexible and open-ended; it encourages personal choice, experimentation ('God A seems to answer my prayers more than god B') and change. Around 450, however, the people took for themselves the right to introduce new gods, after proper consultation of the oracles or as a result of an authentic epiphany by the god himself. A wealthy individual could sponsor the introduction of a deity, as one did for Asclepius in the 420s, but the ultimate sanction came from the Assembly. The reason for the decision-making body of democratic Athens to want control over such matters is that introducing new gods could lead to other gods being edged out. But since Athens's prosperity and success depended on the goodwill of the gods, and since at the time (and for two heady decades after 450 as well) Athens was conspicuously successful, it followed that it was important for the traditional gods to keep being worshipped.

But this is still not enough to convict Socrates, because minor sects slipped under the net: the worship of Sabazius, for instance, never received the official sanction of the Assembly, and even when such cults were thought disreputable, no legal action was ever taken against them or their devotees, as far as we know. And whatever people thought of Socrates, no one could have imagined that he wanted to introduce any deity requiring worship on a large scale.

We hear of three other trials for introducing new gods, all from considerably later in the fourth century, when it was far easier for individuals to set up private shrines to obscure deities. The defendants were a famous courtesan called Phryne of Thespiae (and her deity Isodaites), the politician Demades of Paeania (who successfully, if briefly, introduced the worship of the Alexander the Great into Athens), and a priestess of Sabazius called Nino (the names of the new deities she wanted to introduce are unknown). The prosecution of Demades was inspired by anti-Macedonian sentiment, while Phryne and Nino were considered to be disruptive influences. Phryne came to court because the revels she conducted were too wild and licentious, and Nino because she was regarded as a sorceress.

It seems likely, then, that introducing new gods was actionable only if the individual or the religion concerned was suspect on other grounds. This will lead us to look further for the real reasons why Socrates was held to be objectionable, but why was the charge even plausible? What new deity or deities was he supposed to have introduced? There is only one candidate.

Socrates called the little voice that spoke inside his head his *daimonion sēmeion*, 'supernatural alarm' or 'divine sign', and the second half of the impiety charge says that he introduced *kaina daimonia*, 'new-fangled supernatural beings' or 'divinities'. Both Plato and Xenophon understand Socrates' *daimonion* as direct contact with the divine, and they both agree that this part of the charge was an implicit reference to it. This remarkable little voice was unique to him, and he had had it since childhood; it occurred frequently enough for him to describe the phenomenon as familiar. It usually said 'no' to something (whether important or trivial), but since saying 'no' to one course can be a recommendation of another course, it was not merely prohibitive. It was, of course, prophetic: it foresaw some aspect of the future and warned Socrates against it.

Xenophon presents Socrates' listening to this voice as no more or less impious than any other form of divination, and this seems to me to be essentially correct. But there were still problems with having such a friendly, private deity: it seemed to privilege Socrates (and by extension his friends and followers) and to exclude others in a most undemocratic fashion. Likewise, Aristophanes had a character condemn comic versions of the scientists' 'gods' as both 'new-fangled' (the same word as in the charge against Socrates) and private, not available to the people of Athens for worship. One of the main reasons the state maintained a high degree of control over religious matters was because religion helped to weld the community together by means of shared rites.

Socrates' supernatural voice was apparently well known in Athens. With the help of the rumours about his trances and his little voice, the prosecutors could have made him out to be a kind of prophet – but a loose cannon, a prophet without civic bounds, the minister of an unknown god that made sudden appearances and seemed not to require all the usual rituals. For Socrates never specified what god he thought the voice came from; for him it was pure experience. It did not start its communications by saying 'Hello! Apollo here again!' (though if pushed he would probably have identified it with Apollo, whose servant he was and who was the main god of divination). It would not have been difficult for Meletus to claim that Socrates was a believer in new deities. And since he said that Socrates was also trying to introduce these new-fangled deities, he must have argued that Socrates spread the word among his followers.

In short, there was nothing in Socrates' supernatural voice that was clearly criminal or impious, but the prosecutors used it to stir up all the old prejudices about him. Introducing new gods was what the scientists did, after all, with their reliance on natural forces instead of the Olympic pantheon – hence the vague plural of the charge, 'introducing new divinities'. They could portray Socrates as the kind of arrogant person who counted himself superior to the whole religious framework of Athenian society, an acolyte of a god not recognized by the state and therefore no true citizen. Plato has Euthyphro superciliously sympathize with Socrates: 'Such things are easily misrepresented to the masses.'

The flexibility of Athenian legal procedures meant that a defendant was rarely, if ever, on trial just for the particular crime mentioned in the indictment; his whole life as an Athenian citizen or resident was explicitly or implicitly scrutinized. Some scholars, who believe that there was more substance to the impiety charge than I do, argue that it was all the prosecutors needed to get Socrates convicted. But even if the impiety charge was such a powerful threat, a political subtext is not ruled out. In fact, it dovetails with it, because impiety was a matter of *public* concern: the thriving of Athens as a political entity was held to depend, in large part, on the favour of the gods, which was jeopardized by impious individuals. And if we believe, as I do, that there was little substance to the impiety charge, then we are obliged to look elsewhere for the real reasons why Socrates was taken to court.

THE WAR YEARS

FOUR

Alcibiades, Socrates and the
Aristocratic Milieu

'Hello, Socrates. Where have you been? Not that I need to ask: you've been chasing after that gorgeous Alcibiades.' Plato began his dialogue *Protagoras* with these teasing words from an unnamed companion of Socrates. The dialogue is set in 433 BCE. Socrates would have been thirty-six years old, and Alcibiades is described in terms that strongly suggest he is in his late teens: Socrates' friend, wondering why Socrates was breaking the norms of Athenian homosexual life, goes on to say, 'When I saw him recently, he struck me as being a handsome man – but a *man*, Socrates, with a bearded chin now.'

Alcibiades' presence is like a refrain in the Platonic dialogues, as a living person and, later, as a symbol. A dialogue simply called *Alcibiades* and consisting entirely of a conversation between Socrates and his young friend purports to be the first, or the first intimate conversation between the two of them; it too can be dated to 433. In *Gorgias* Plato has Socrates declare his love for Alcibiades and philosophy; the dialogue appears to be set in 427, at the time of Gorgias of Leontini's famous ambassadorial visit to Athens, when his purple oratory made such an impression on the Athenians, but it also contains enough anachronisms to make it plausible to think of it as timeless, or at least not datable with any security.

The best evidence for the extent of the relationship comes from Plato's *Symposium*, where Alcibiades outlines, in a wonderful, drunken speech, at least some of the affair. The implication is that it lasted quite a while, since Alcibiades describes an on-off relationship in which, for all his huge attraction to Socrates, he often ran away from him, back to the world of Athenian politics, and just as often returned, hung over and shamefaced. He describes at length one particular night when, convinced that Socrates was in love with him in the normal way, he gave him every opportunity to consummate the relationship, but 'I might as well have been sleeping with my father or an elder brother.'

This episode too can be dated to around 433, because Alcibiades says that it took place before the two of them were together during the Athenian siege of Poteidaea, when they were messmates. Since they were from different demes (ancestral villages) and different tribes, and since they served in different branches of the armed forces (Alcibiades, because of his wealth, in the cavalry, Socrates as a hoplite), it was unusual for them to mess together, and Alcibiades perhaps pulled some strings to make it happen. It is a sign of continuing attraction between the two men.

The siege of Poteidaea, on the Chalcidice peninsula of what is now northern Greece, lasted from 432 until 429, and it is likely that both of them spent most of these years there. Alcibiades may have arrived a year or so later than Socrates, when he came of age to serve abroad, but then it is all the more significant that he chose to mess together with Socrates, after an interval apart. Alcibiades' account of Socrates' behaviour during the campaign is detailed and affectionate: he protests that the prize for valour which was awarded to him should really have gone to the older man – and not least because of his bravery in saving his, Alcibiades', life, during a severe defeat inflicted on the Athenians when they were on their way home after the siege. He also recalls Socrates' exceptional fortitude in enduring the bitter winters up north, and his self-control when times were good and there were plenty of provisions. He omits to mention what a nasty campaign it was, with the inhabitants of Poteidaea reduced eventually to cannibalism, and over a thousand of the Athenian soldiers succumbing to typhoid fever, the plague that was also decimating Athens itself at the time.

By contrast, when he tells of Socrates' calm bravery during the retreat from Delium in 424, he speaks objectively, rather than as someone who was in love with Socrates at the time. Since he was not there, he does not mention the other Athenian campaign in which Socrates took part, back in the north in 422 (aged forty-seven or forty-eight), in a vain Athenian attempt to recover the town of Amphipolis from the Spartans.

The dramatic date of *Symposium* is 416, and Alcibiades is said to be still attracted to Socrates, but in a way that makes it clear that the affair is long over. His tactic now is to keep his former mentor at a distance by putting him on a pedestal of superhumanity. So how long did the affair last? In an obvious attempt to free Socrates of any responsibility for Alcibiades' scandalous life, Xenophon tried to convince his readers that the young man had associated with Socrates only long enough to learn a few argumentative tricks that would help him in politics, but the extended campaign in Poteidaea alone makes that unlikely. Besides, five of the immediate followers of Socrates wrote dialogues featuring Socrates in close conversation with the young aristocrat (though of the two attributed to Plato, the *Second Alcibiades* is a late imitation, neither genuinely Platonic nor authored by any of the other four Socratics). It became standard to depict the course of the affair as on-again-off-again, with Socrates as the only person who could curb the young man's excesses and point him towards better things, before the lure of the world, with its partying and power politics, finally overcame him. In other words, Alcibiades' lawlessness was not the result of his following Socrates' teaching, but of his ignoring it. Let us say, then, that Socrates and Alcibiades were, even if intermittently, an item up to 428 or 427, with the affair petering out well before Delium. The length of the relationship, as well as the subsequent notoriety of Alcibiades, explains why so many Socratic writers depicted the two together. If the affair had been brief, the Socratics would not have felt it important to defend their mentor against the charge of having corrupted Alcibiades; if they had spent no more than a few months in each other's company, eighteen years before Alcibiades first got into really serious trouble, the charge that Socrates was somehow responsible for Alcibiades' transgressions makes no sense.

Another aspect of the affair that made it so fascinating was its utter implausibility. In 433, when the affair began, the young man was dashing, daring, already the darling of Athenian high society, the leader of the fashionable young bloods and notorious for his arrogant and flamboyant escapades, which were excused as high spirits and a sign of future greatness. He seemed destined for glory, with his high birth into two of the greatest families of Athens – the Salaminioi on his father's side and the Alcmaeonids on his mother's side. Membership of one of these old Athenian families was the equivalent of being a high-ranking peer: he was not plain Alcibiades, but, in British terms, Lord Alcibiades. Nor was he an impoverished aristocrat: he owned estates that were exceptionally large by Athenian standards, and was rich enough to include among his slaves his own personal goldsmith. In addition to noble birth and great wealth, he had been made the ward, after the early death of his father Cleinias in 446, of none other than Pericles, the first cousin of his mother Deinomache and the almost undisputed first man of Athenian politics for over twenty years. Apart from any other advantages such an upbringing may have brought,

Pericles was surrounded by the most gifted artists and intellectuals of the time, and Alcibiades would have met and conversed with them too. Hence Plato portrayed him, in *Protagoras*, as present at a glittering intellectual gathering in 433. He had the best teachers, the best of everything money could buy. He was eloquent as well as elegant, with a good, natural speaking voice enhanced by rhetorical tricks learnt from the new breed of educators.

In short, Alcibiades was so intelligent, so full of promise, so good-looking, self-assured and charming that he got away with almost everything that his mercurial nature led him to. Already courted by some of the wealthiest men in town, he took to trailing the end of his cloak along the ground, wearing soft boots and tilting his head in a foppish manner. Even before his full entry into Athenian public life, he was already being referred to by comic poets in a manner that assumed the audience knew him and his mannerisms. They made fun, in particular, of his lambdacism (he pronounced *r* as *l*); of his love of horses, bathing, gambling, drinking and ostentatious sacrifices; of his many affairs ('In his youth he drew husbands from their wives and as a young man he drew wives from their husbands,' as a later wit put it); of his periodic financial difficulties, brought on by extravagance; and of his proclivity for fisticuffs and general unruliness. Later, his fame was such that not only comic poets, but even tragedians portrayed some of their characters in ways that would remind the audience of Alcibiades.

Socrates, however, was a gift to the comic poets in a quite different way: he even *looked* like a comic actor's mask, and behaved with impeccable eccentricity. He was ugly (with receding hair, bulging eyes, thick lips, a snub nose with wide nostrils, a protruding stomach and a rocking gait) and cared nothing for the fads and fashions of this society or any other. His father had perhaps been a successful statue-maker or stonemason, and his mother helped out as a midwife. But, despite later fabrications for tourists, Socrates seems not to have worked for a living, and to have done nothing with the modest fortune he inherited: he single-mindedly pursued his philosophical goals. So far from being attracted towards the luxury of Alcibiades' lifestyle, he was invariably shoeless (in the Spartan fashion), and wore just a thin, threadbare gown, whatever the weather.

What did Alcibiades see in him? Was Socrates a trophy? By the late 430s he was one of the most famous teachers in town, already the guru of a number of well-bred and intelligent young men, and was increasingly being talked about with a mixture of respect and puzzlement. But in fact it is more plausible to see Alcibiades' attraction to Socrates as genuine. Socrates may have been physically ugly, but he was charismatic, and it was one of his standard ploys to use this to attract young aristocratic men. Alcibiades was determined to be the brightest star in the Athenian firmament, and to make his mark in the wider world too; and to provide him with the kind of education that could help him achieve this goal, he chose Socrates over other available mentors.

Meanwhile, what did Socrates see in Alcibiades? The answer anticipates conclusions that will acquire a firmer foundation later, but Socrates was concerned above all with the moral regeneration of Athens, and attracted into his circle precisely those young men who could be expected to become the leaders of Athens. Alcibiades was the pick of the crop, the one with the brightest future and the greatest potential. What Socrates saw in Alcibiades was *megaloprepeia* – the quality that is, literally, 'suitable for a great man'. But such a quality often goes hand in hand with the arrogant assumption that one is greater than society.

What Alcibiades made of his potential will be the topic of the next chapters, after a little more of the background has been filled in. We will not understand Socrates or his trial without understanding Alcibiades, and we will not understand Alcibiades without seeing him in the context of the Peloponnesian War. War is a time of great stress for a society. Alcibiades was twenty-two when the war began, and he died right at the end of it. It consumed his entire adult life, as he tried to ride to glory on the energies created by the same social crisis that brought his former mentor to court.

ATHENIAN HOMOEROTICISM

Socrates used homosexual flirtatiousness to attract young men into his circle; Alcibiades offered Socrates the use of his body and affected habits – the slant of the head, the trailing cloak – that were recognized signs of passive homosexuality. Some readers might be thinking that this was a pretty kinky arrangement, and that Socrates was the guru of a sect of perverts.

In upper-class Athenian society, however, homoeroticism was not regarded as perverted against a standard of heterosexuality as 'normal'.

It was simply accepted that at a certain time of his youth a young man had a kind of beauty, and that older men – heterosexual older men, as well as the occasional homosexual – would be attracted towards him. If an affair took place, the partners would likely be faithful to each other (there was little homosexual promiscuity in Athens) and the affair would probably last only a few years, at the most. The most common form of homosexuality was, literally, pederasty – love for boys – since boys were found attractive from about the age of fourteen; even affairs between older partners tended to feature an age-group gap between the younger and the older man.

Athenian homoeroticism was largely an upper-class phenomenon. Any society that represses its women as much as ancient Athens did runs the risk of forcing its members to find other outlets for their sexuality. Respectable Athenian women would rarely even be seen on the street; their job was to keep house and bring up the children. This impeded the normal interplay between men and women that underpins a heterosexual society. Homoeroticism was more a feature of upper-class Athens, then, simply because these people lived in larger houses, with more opportunity to segregate their womenfolk. Then again, upper-class marriage was rarely for love, more commonly dynastic.

What the boy got out of the affair – and this too is why it was an upper-class phenomenon – was a form of patronage. In return for 'gratifying' his lover, as the Greeks tended somewhat delicately to put it, he would expect the older man to act as an extra guardian in public life, to introduce him into the best social circles, and later, perhaps years after the sexual side of the affair was over, to help him gain a foothold in the political life of the city, in which most upper-class Athenian men were naturally involved. Moreover, the older man was expected to cultivate the boy's mind, to be an intellectual companion as well – a kind of godfather. The institution of homoerotic affairs filled a gap in the educational system by providing a boy with a better grasp of local culture and worldly wisdom.

Homosexual relationships were not widely approved, outside a limited circle of wealthy Athenians. They were sneered at by the Athenian poor as a class practice reeking of effeminacy, luxury and Spartan culture, and many regarded sexual penetration as something only women and slaves had to endure, and therefore inappropriate for a male citizen. But within certain aristocratic circles, such relationships were more widely tolerated. The fathers (we do not know what the mothers thought) worried about their sons being the objects of sexual advances, but they were also concerned to make sure that, if a boy did enter into such an affair, it was with someone who would do him as much good, in terms of social and political advancement, as could be expected. This might seem calculating, but that is an aspect of Greek views on friendship in general: they frankly acknowledged that a friend was not just someone for whom you felt affection, but someone who could help you out.

By and large, then, people turned a convenient blind eye towards the sexual side of the affair. Most societies do the same where lust is concerned. But Socrates himself was consistently portrayed as barely tolerant of the sexual side of such a relationship: he recognized that, human nature being what it is, it was likely to happen, but he did not approve of giving into the baser, animal parts of one's nature under any circumstances. As far as we can tell from the available evidence, he refused to consummate his affair with Alcibiades, and there is no reason to think that he had sex with any of his other young followers, despite his evident attraction towards them: 'Just then, I caught a glimpse inside Charmides' clothes. I was on fire! I was in ecstasy!' Among his followers, his name was especially linked not just with Alcibiades and Charmides, but also with Euthydemus – all three young men of exceptional promise.

Socrates was a non-ordinary homoerotic lover in another sense, too. In the normal course of Athenian events, the older partner pursued the younger. But Socrates flirted intellectually with young men, allowing them to glimpse what *he* had to offer, in order to make them attracted to him and want to spend time with him. He was trying to make them consummate a lifelong affair with philosophy, not with himself; he strongly emphasized the educational function of such relationships, to the exclusion, more or less, of the physical side. He exploited the homoerotic aspect of upper-class Athenian society for his own educational purposes.

THE ARISTOCRATIC MILIEU

Apart from the fact that they were such an unlikely couple, no one in their circle would have thought that the affair between Socrates and Alcibiades was odd. But how did Socrates, from a relatively humble family (his father *worked* for a living), come to penetrate the circles where he could meet young men like Alcibiades and Charmides? All our sources consistently portray him hobnobbing with the rich and famous, hanging out at the gymnasia, which were canonical aristocratic venues, and even attending elite symposia.

Socrates seems to have married well, and well above his station. Somehow, his father had become connected to the family of Aristeides the Just, a prominent figure before and after the Persian Wars, and a political ally of Alcibiades' grandfather. So Socrates had an entrée into the highest strata of Athenian society. Although we know almost nothing of Socrates' wife Xanthippe, her name, with its – *hippe* ending, indicates high birth: such names, which refer to horses and horse-breeding, tended to be given to elite men and women. A later tradition that Socrates simultaneously had a live-in mistress, a granddaughter of Aristeides called Myrto, must be discarded as typical of the hostile biographical tradition. He also had a younger half-brother called Patrocles, from his mother's second marriage, after his father's death; if this was the Patrocles who was the treasurer of Athena in 405 and suffect King Archon in 403, he was probably a wealthy man. At the time of his death, Socrates had three young sons called Lamprocles, Sophroniscus and Menexenus, 'one a stripling [a *meirakion*, aged between eighteen and twenty], the others still children [under eighteen]'; so Socrates married late, around 420, and Xanthippe was considerably younger than him – a not unusual arrangement in ancient Athens. Marriage to Xanthippe would also have brought Socrates a dowry, to top up his inheritance.

Either through family connections, then, or simply as a result of his unique power as an educator, Socrates was admitted into a usually exclusive circle. The elite of Athens were the ones who were interested in taking their education further than the basics provided for boys. They did not have to spend their lives worrying about where their next meal was coming from, and so they had time for education; the ancient Greek word *skholē*, the origin of our 'school', means 'leisure'. Generally, however, they wanted the education they received to bring practical benefits, in the sense of improving their chances in the competitive world of Athenian politics. If it was becoming increasingly hard for them to maintain that nobility of birth automatically gave them the right to political power, they would have to learn how to gain and hold power in the modern world.

Athenian aristocrats usually possessed both landed wealth and membership of an old family, which may even have pretentiously traced its lineage back to a divine or semi-divine ancestor: Alcibiades' family claimed descent from Zeus himself. They had traditionally kept themselves apart from the common herd by living an exclusive kind of life, which emphasized an enduringly Homeric concern with status, the cultivation of leadership qualities, competition of all kinds with others perceived to be of the same rank at home or abroad, honing a beautiful body by means of exercise, competition in the panhellenic games, *xenia* (ritualized, hereditary friendship with peers from outside the community), marrying outside the polis (until Pericles' citizenship law of 451 BCE granted citizenship only to those both of whose parents were Athenian), conspicuous public spending, glorification of the family (for instance, by constructing large tombs and other monuments to celebrate the family's achievements), control of the most important priesthoods, private luxury spending, symposia, refined and even effete manners and mannerisms (including long hair, 'because it is hard to do menial work with long hair', and rich clothing and seal-rings), a degree of dissoluteness among the young, pederasty and homoeroticism, cock-fighting, horse-breeding, hunting, dancing, music-making and versifying, contempt for physical labour, contempt for anyone not of their class – and, of course, marrying and forming political alliances only from within the same class.

Some of these habits and characteristics could perhaps be imitated by those who were not true aristocrats, but one of them, all by itself, marked a man as truly wealthy. Ownership of a horse or two was an ostentatious way of displaying one's membership of this exclusive group. From early times in Europe, horses have been a symbol of prestige and a marker of high social rank – the rank enjoyed by the *hippeis* in ancient Athens, the *equites* of Rome, the chevaliers of the European Middle Ages. The knights of Athens formed a distinct and easily recognizable group; they could ride about town, but more importantly they could frequently be seen training together in the Agora, cuirasses flashing in the sunlight, and they featured prominently in several of the major annual religious festivals and processions.

Athenian aristocrats called themselves the *eupatridai*, the 'well-fathered', or the *kaloi kagathoi*, the 'beautiful and good', and nowhere was a beautiful body prized more than in Athens, where once a year, among the athletic and artistic contests of the Panathenaic festival, there was a contest in *euandria* – 'cutting a fine figure of a man' – which was a kind of beauty contest, in which contestants were judged for their strength as well as their defined musculature and handsome features.

This was the world into which Alcibiades was born, and on which Socrates was a sort of parasite. But Athenian society was changing, especially as a result of the stresses and complexities of democracy and empire. The closed universe of hereditary aristocratic rulership was increasingly giving way to democracy and meritocracy, so that there were brash nouveaux riches politicians, and social climbers who inevitably de-emphasized the family; the state was demanding that *xenia* be subordinate to patriotism, that the Council, not private individuals, should host foreign dignitaries, and that the people should decide with whom to go to war, regardless of aristocratic ties and interests abroad; under state control, some felt liturgies to be more of a burden and less of a privilege; commoners were beginning to make a mark in the panhellenic games; the common people were gaining the right to choose priests and to put on many of the most important religious ceremonies (while demanding financial assistance from rich individuals); display of wealth was now more the province of the state than of individuals, and it was the state that built public buildings and parks; the state was organizing magnificent public funerals and frowned on the elite habit of overspending on their own family funerals. Plato has Socrates complain that everyone is a hero now: 'Even a poor man nowadays gets a beautiful, magnificent funeral; even a man of no consequence receives a eulogy.'

Aristocrats could still dominate Athenian politics because they had more time than anyone else for it, and because, before the five hundred Councillors for that year were chosen by lot, potential members were first elected at deme level, where the elite could still influence things, but there were an increasing number of disincentives to political power. Above all, the people now assessed a man's fitness for office before he took it up, and at the end of his year judged whether or not he had done a good job. And though the rich might hold more of the political offices, the people held most of the cards and kept the elite on the democratic straight and narrow.

Pericles lay on the cusp of these changes and was responsible for some of them. A couple of his actions illustrate the changing world. At the beginning of the Peloponnesian War, the Spartan army invaded, led by one of the Spartan kings, Archidamus; but Archidamus and Pericles were *xenoi*, so Pericles formally made his estates over to the Athenian people, in case out of *xenia* Archidamus was tempted to bypass his land and leave it unravaged. This gesture neatly symbolized the new separation of the private aristocratic world from the public world of politics. Then, not long after getting his new citizenship law passed in 451, by which both parents had to be Athenians in order for a child to qualify as an Athenian citizen, he put aside his Athenian wife and brought into his home the famous and beguiling Aspasia of Miletus, as if to say that his personal interests would not intrude on his public policies, in the way that they had for old-style aristocrats.

Aristocrats were also having to diversify to make enough money to preserve their lifestyle. The traditional and most stable source of wealth was owning land. The rich tended not to own large estates, but a number of smaller ones both in and around Athens, and further abroad. One of the reasons for the decline of wealthy families after the Peloponnesian War was that the loss of the empire simultaneously meant the loss of almost all these foreign estates. A second form of income, owning non-agricultural slaves, became increasingly important towards the end of the fifth century and on into the fourth; such slaves might be put to work in small workshops (lack of sophisticated technology prevented the development of large factories) or rented out to the state, perhaps to work in the state-owned silver mines of Laurium.

A rich man might also own farms or urban dwellings, which he rented out. In Piraeus, above all, houses and apartments were rented out to metics (foreign residents of Athens), who were forbidden by law to own Athenian property themselves. During the imperial years, as Athens's prosperity attracted large numbers of metics, there was a considerable housing boom, which the rich exploited by developing new properties for rent. Another possible source of income was money-lending or investing, especially in overseas trade, where the risks and the returns were commensurably large. Dealing in grain became another good source of income towards the end of the fifth century. And it was always possible for a man to make a great deal of money from war booty (where a general, the highest in the social as well as the military order, got the lion's share) or, as a politician, from 'gifts' from others, at home or abroad. Most Athenians most of the time felt that it would be invidious to describe this as 'bribery' rather than a perk.

When aristocrats claimed that their noble birth gave them the right to rule, they were not talking about genetics and they were hardly talking about education either, though they expected their sons to be imbued with a sense of their abilities as future rulers. They were talking about the natural order of things: the gods, in their providence for the world, had made certain people gifted at leadership, and had also given them the resources that made leadership possible and effective. This is a common view among elites of any time and place. So when certain thinkers began to ask whether statesmanship was in fact given by birth, or whether it might not be teachable, this seemed like an attack on the gods; and when fully fledged democracy made aristocrats the servants of the state, not its leaders, this seemed like a subversion of the natural order. We will not understand the ferment and the torment of late-fifth-century Athens unless we understand that utterly fundamental issues were at stake.

ARISTOCRATIC RESPONSES

Some aristocrats more or less dropped out, becoming what the Greeks called *idiōtai*. This word, the origin of our 'idiot', referred in a political context to someone who chose not to take part in the public life of the city when he could have done so; perhaps the notions of pointlessness and disengagement offer a bridge between the ancient and modern meanings of the word. Only despair, or a particular temperament, could have driven an Athenian aristocrat to follow such a course, since at least some of his peers would have taken it to be equivalent to choosing to be unmanned or servile. But quite a few well-born Athenians, and particularly the disaffected young, took this route from the 420s onward, in response to having lost their automatic right to leadership.

Others retreated to exclusive clubs (*hetaireiai*). There had always been, in aristocratic circles, loose social groups who met for symposia or religious purposes, but these groups became less based on kinship and thicker on the Athenian ground from the late 430s onwards. Within the clubs disaffected aristocrats could preserve something of their fading world, and even exaggerate certain of its traits. Not only were the clubs venues for letting off steam, for partying and gambling, but they became the seed-beds of anti-democratic thinking, the main lines of which now became tempered in the smouldering fire of discontent.

An average club consisted of about thirty members, even if not all attended every meeting. The core of their activities remained the symposium, though not all symposia took place within the context of a club. The symposium was one of the more arcane aristocratic rituals, a hangover from the glory days of the Athenian aristocracy, when these evening meetings had formed the pulse of the city's social and political life. The word *symposion* literally means 'drinking together', but it is best left transliterated rather than translated, because 'drinks party' has misleading connotations: those present did not stand around sipping sherry and nibbling nuts. Like many aspects of Athenian life, the symposium incorporated elements of ritual and religion.

The guests, typically about a dozen, reclined on couches. Their left arms rested on cushions and supported the upper half of their bodies, so that their right hands were free for eating and drinking from the small table which was set in front of them. After a light meal, the tables were removed, and the room was cleared and swept. The diners wiped their hands on pieces of bread and tossed them to the dogs, then ritually washed their hands and dabbed a bit of perfume, perhaps of rose or orris-root, on their bodies.

A 'king' was appointed, to regulate the evening and decide on the proportions of wine and water to be mixed in the great mixing-bowl. The Greeks usually drank their wine diluted with water, in the ratio of about five parts of water to two of wine, and they thought, or affected to think, that over-indulgence in neat wine induced madness. Symposiast drinking-cups were shallow, better for sipping than gulping, to curb drunkenness and encourage conversation between sips. Nevertheless, drunken symposia were not unknown and could be extended: drunken guests might spill out on the street in a *kōmos*, a ritual revel, in which the boisterous party paraded noisily through the city, still dressed as symposiasts and still singing, in search of another house where they could prolong the evening. This was typically aristocratic behaviour; they could still get away with making a nuisance of themselves.

The symposium began with purificatory rituals, the donning of garlands, and libations and hymns to the gods. The guests settled down to make conversation, sing songs (popular songs from the past or present, or, in competition, verse of their own spontaneous composition), play games (such as *kottabos*, the flicking of drops of liquid from the bottom of a cup at a bowl or some other target) and be entertained. The night might include not only the guests' own singing, to the accompaniment of a girl playing the pipes, but also a show put on by hired dancing-girls, acrobats or mimes. Apart from these slave-girls, who were often obliged to have sex with the guests as well, it was a strictly male affair. Symposia were orchestrated to include nothing from the humdrum world: guests ate and drank from crockery decorated with symbolic or realistic versions of symposia – with ever-receding versions of themselves, as it were; they recited special poems, played special games, and focused exclusively on pleasure and past times. The clubs, and symposia more generally, allowed aristocrats temporarily to suspend time.

But some clubs chose exposure. Just as in eighteenth-century Britain young aristocrats formed clubs such as the Hellfire Club, to mock religion and have sex with prostitutes, so Athenian clubs sometimes took provocative names, based on the names of hostile peoples (compare the 'Mohocks', a street gang in London of the early eighteenth century) or on cocking a more or less serious snook at society in some other way. In Athens there were, among others, 'The Hard-On Club' and 'The Wankers', though these date from the fourth century. In our period there were the 'Acolytes of the Evil God', a mock inversion of a deity known only as the Good God, who was invoked by libations at the end of meals. Hence this dining club met on unpropitious days of the calendar, to tease the superstitious. Usually, however, the clubs were named after the day on which they met, or their most prominent member or members: we hear, for instance, of 'Charicles and Critias and their club'.

There were rumours that a few of the clubs had outrageous initiation ceremonies (reminiscent of some American college fraternities, or army regiments), and more than a few required an oath of allegiance from their members; hence, as well as *hetaireiai* ('groups of comrades'), they were also known as *synōmosiai* ('groups bound by a common oath'). The most famous oath of secrecy in the ancient Athenian world was that required of initiates at the Eleusinian Mysteries, and it was not uncommon for the clubs to make their oaths parodies of the Eleusinian ceremony, a practice that could be overlooked in normal circumstances. No doubt such oaths were often hardly meant to be seriously

64

binding, but occasionally they were, if the subversive goals of a club outweighed its social activities. Even more rarely, but infinitely more sinisterly, members might be required to confirm their oaths by a 'proof of loyalty' (*pistis*). The most extreme of these occurred in 411 when an anti-democratic club arranged the assassination of the Athenian democrat Hyperbolus, as just such a pledge. Members were thus bound together by shared complicity.

Clubs also undertook less sinister political tasks, such as influencing elections, trials and judicial hearings, or distributing pamphlets. They could provide a vociferous block of men at assemblies, to give speeches, heckle, cheer, intimidate, filibuster, or otherwise move things in their preferred direction; or they could canvas support by bribery or in other more legitimate ways. Rival clubs could form temporary alliances, perhaps to try to get a common enemy ostracized; and then when the day came for people to vote, club members could write names down on *ostraka* for those in a hurry or the illiterate, as a heap of 190 *ostraka* archaeologists have recovered with Themistocles' name were written by only fourteen hands. None of these activities was exclusive to the clubs, but they were typical of them.

ALCIBIADES THE ARISTOCRAT

The historian Thucydides, our chief source for the events of the Peloponnesian War, gave Alcibiades two set-piece speeches. In the context of the aristocratic milieu, and as an introduction to Alcibiades' stance in public life, the general tenor of these speeches is highly revealing. The first, delivered during the debate in the Assembly about whether to invade Sicily in 415, starts as a defence of his suitability for high command and political power in Athens. He speaks of himself as a ruler rather than as a general and identifies himself and the city to the extent of claiming that his personal display of wealth abroad (as at the recent Olympics) impresses foreigners with the power of the city as a whole. And then he says that ordinary people should submit to the disdain of the successful man, such as himself, who is favoured by the gods. All this is sheer aristocratic ideology, and the attempt to make political capital out of his fame at home and abroad would have been recognized and admired by aristocrats of an earlier generation.

Alcibiades' second speech, addressed to the Spartans after his defection later that same year, again begins with self-defence, as part of an attempt to persuade his hosts, the enemies of Athens, to give such a prominent Athenian a home. He claims to have supported democracy only as a vehicle for self-aggrandizement and is scathing in his comments about the Athenian constitution, famously calling it at one point 'unequivocal folly'. He hints that he and some others had considered launching a coup in Athens, and held back only because the time was not right. Once again, the kind of political arrangement that he favours is based entirely on the existence of the exceptional aristocrat – himself, in other words. These are bitter words, directed at his native city, but the bitterness too is thoroughly aristocratic: no self-respecting member of the Greek elite would fail to retaliate for perceived insults and wrongs, and Alcibiades saw his banishment from Athens as a personal slight, and as proof that Athens was corrupt.

Alcibiades was different from those of his Athenian peers who were prepared to adapt. He was never going to respond to the changes that were overtaking Athenian society by dropping out. Although he was certainly the leader of a club, and possibly a member of others, they were venues where he could develop political networks, not places of retreat. He was something of a throwback: an old-style, pure aristocrat who exploited his many *xenoi* abroad and relentlessly, publicly and competitively pursued his own and his family's glory. While insisting that his personal fame and successes were good for the city, he also expected to convert them into political capital and clientele.

He seemed to others to be able to adapt himself to circumstances like a chameleon, but in one respect he never changed. And the single-mindedness of his pursuit of glory made politics a game for him, because he felt himself to be outside all constitutions and regimes. This is why the Athenians were conflicted about him: they admired and needed his aristocratic leadership qualities, and loved him for his charm and his successes, but he was also a throwback to a time when aristocrats had been beyond their control, and they feared his ambition. And so they also came to fear those who were held to have fuelled his ambition.

FIVE

Pestilence and War

Alcibiades came of age just as, after a long and uneasy gestation, the Peloponnesian War between Athens and Sparta came to life. Even if his temperament had not predetermined the matter, he had no choice but to make warfare and wartime politics the fields in which he would seek glory. The war lasted intermittently – too intermittently for his taste – for twenty-seven years and ended in defeat for Athens, and the end of the empire it had diplomatically nurtured and ruthlessly maintained for decades. Over the course of these twenty-seven years, many Athenians sought their brief moments of fame in the harsh light of warfare, but by the skin of his teeth Alcibiades lasted longer than most, until in the end there were those, including the historian Thucydides, who were inclined to attribute their defeat above all to him.

Alcibiades is the only person in Thucydides' austere history who is awarded a coherently written character sketch. Other comments Thucydides makes about Alcibiades elsewhere are also strangely revealing of his personality. Some scholars have speculated that Thucydides knew him personally and even that Alcibiades was his main informant for some of the events of the history. Be that as it may, this is what Thucydides says:

> Alcibiades Cleiniou was the one who pushed most forcefully for the expedition [to Sicily]. He wanted to oppose Nicias, not only because of the ongoing political enmity between them, but also because of the disparaging remarks that Nicias had just made in his speech. Above all, however, he wanted command of the expedition, in the hope that he would be the one to whom Sicily and Carthage would fall, and that his success would bring him personal glory and wealth. For in order to maintain his public image, he spent more than he could afford on indulging his desire for extravagances such as horse-breeding. This, in fact, was one of the chief causes of the subsequent defeat of Athens, in the sense that his readiness to overstep the bounds of convention in his private life, and his presumption in every walk of life, alarmed the Athenian people so

much that they assumed he was aiming at tyranny and turned against him. Even though he was a brilliant military commander, his fellow citizens found his private conduct so objectionable that they entrusted their affairs to others, and this led before long to the downfall of the city.

Thucydides' syllogism is transparent, but was he blaming Alcibiades for the defeat any more than he was blaming the Athenians for turning against him? We need to know enough of the history of the Peloponnesian War to see what Athens went through, in terms of military and moral suffering, and what part Alcibiades played in it all.

THE OUTBREAK OF THE PELOPONNESIAN WAR

Athens and Sparta had been rivals almost since the end of the Persian Wars in 479. Though they committed themselves then to the joint defence of Greece against the continuing Persian threat, this was largely a maritime enterprise, and since Athens was the chief naval power in the Aegean, it was Athens that grew in authority and power, while Sparta focused on maintaining its supremacy at land warfare by means of its militaristic regime. Athens became the head of the league that committed itself to the defence of the Aegean, and received tribute from the other members of the league, which was used to keep its substantial navy operational. The Persians were driven from Asia Minor, and the defence of the Aegean culminated in the battle of Eurymedon (the modern river Köprü Irmagi in southern Turkey) in 469 or thereabouts, in which Cimon Miltiadou crushed the Persians on sea and land, and put an end to their last serious military effort against the Greeks. It was as significant a battle as Marathon or Salamis, but it lacked a Herodotus to write it up in detail, and even its date is uncertain.

Before long, the Athenians had a virtual monopoly on naval experience in the Aegean. Realizing the opportunity this gave them, and encouraged by their allies' continuing need for protection, they began to behave from time to time with more arrogance: they used their military muscle to compel some Aegean states, especially those with strategic importance to Athens itself, to join the alliance, and to punish others for wanting to withdraw from it; they dispossessed recalcitrant islanders from their land and installed their own citizens to exploit agricultural resources; they moved the League Bank, with its vast funds, from the sacred island of Delos, the symbolic centre of the league, to Athens; they continued to exact tribute and to treat their allies as their subjects even after they had signed a peace treaty with Persia in 449. Over the years a league of allies became, in all but name, an Athenian empire.

The Spartans and their allies looked on these developments with increasing and increasingly justified suspicion. It was a true Cold War, with many moments of heightened tension, punctuated by occasional and sometimes serious clashes, and by treaties and truces that did little to disguise the fact that each side was actually positioning itself for war. Despite a thirty-year peace treaty between Athens and Sparta, drawn up in 446, the Cold War rapidly heated up in the 430s, with Corinth, Sparta's greatest ally, usually the target of Athenian manoeuvring.

On top of an alliance with the Acarnanians, on the west coast of the mainland, which the Corinthians regarded as their own colonial territory, came Athenian interference in the war between Corinth and Corcyra (modern Corfu); on top of that came the terrible business of Poteidaea, which was a tributary of Athens while retaining strong links with Corinth, its mother city. Athens had recently increased Poteidaea's tribute, and then in 432, worried about Corinthian intrigues in the area, it insisted that Poteidaea break off relations with Corinth and demolish some of its defences. The Athenians trumped the Poteidaeans' attempt to stall and negotiate by sending a sizeable army into the area (which included Socrates and Alcibiades).

Corinth was now consumed by unremitting hostility towards Athens, and threatened to leave the Peloponnesian League if Sparta failed to help. The Spartans promised Poteidaea that they would send armed help, which arrived in the form of a largely Corinthian army. The two armies clashed, the Athenians won, and the Corinthians were trapped inside the city, along with the city's inhabitants. The siege lasted until spring 429 and cost the Athenians an enormous two thousand talents (as well as at least a thousand men); they could give no clearer sign of their commitment to war.

By August 432 the Peloponnesian League had voted for war, claiming speciously that the unenforceable economic embargo Athens had placed upon one of its members, the town of Megara, constituted an act of violence against the treaty of 446. Fighting finally broke out when the Thebans, anticipating an Athenian invasion of Boeotia, attacked Plataea, a Boeotian town that had long been Athens's ally and was a holdout against Theban domination of Boeotia. Thucydides opens his history of the war with a statement of his belief that it would be the greatest war in Greek history, and he was right, at least in the sense that much of the Greek world was convulsed. From Thrace and Macedon to the coast of Asia Minor and the shores of Sicily and southern Italy, Greek cities took the opportunity to settle old scores with their neighbours, protected by an alliance with one or the other of the two superpowers. Moreover, the political rift between Sparta with her support for oligarchy and Athens with her support for democracy was echoed in strife that tore apart many communities. All over the Mediterranean world, Greeks were killing Greeks.

THE ARCHIDAMIAN WAR

At the start of the war, the Spartans could count on allies from all over the Peloponnese (except for Argos and the Achaean towns on the north coast, which were neutral), Megara, most of Boeotia, the Phocians and Locrians on the mainland, and various other mainland states. In the west they had military alliances with Syracuse, the most powerful Greek city in Sicily, and some towns in southern Italy. The Athenians had as allies the two hundred or more states of their empire, and could also call on Thessalian cavalry units, Plataea, Corcyra, Zacynthos and mainland Acarnania. The Spartans were regarded as invincible on land, and the Athenian navy had the same reputation at sea.

The first, ten-year phase of the war is named after King Archidamus of Sparta, though he was opposed to war in 431 and died in 427. Sparta's avowed intention was 'to free Greece' – to put an end to the Athenian empire, which was portrayed as a form of enslavement of fellow Greeks. The best way for Sparta to achieve this goal was to approach the allies directly, and to separate them from Athens by force or diplomacy. But this required a fleet, and Sparta lacked the money and expertise to conduct naval warfare. Even Corinth, with a long-standing navy, was rightly reluctant to challenge Athenian supremacy at sea. At the beginning of the war, Sparta requested some ships from her Sicilian and Italian allies, but the western Greeks preferred to avoid for as long as possible involvement in the problems of the mainland and the Aegean. Sparta was compelled to adopt a second-best course, dictated by its acknowledged superiority on land.

Canonical land warfare invariably involved the devastation of farmland, in order to provoke the enemy to give battle; often, a single, swift battle would decide a whole war. The Spartans invaded Attica in many of the first years of the war; they arrived between the middle and the end of May, when grain crops were ripe enough either to burn or to steal for food, and stayed between sixteen and forty days, depending on provisions and the need of the army to be elsewhere: farmers needed to return to their lands, and the Spartans could not afford to keep their army away from Laconia for too long in force, in case their vast servile population seized the opportunity to revolt.

The destruction of crops and farmhouses was depressing, but inflicted no long-lasting damage, and was not an economic catastrophe. As long as Athens had the Long Walls (completed by 445) connecting the city to the port of Piraeus, food and other necessities could get through. Siege engines capable of destroying the walls would not be invented for several decades. And Athens had the vast financial resources (in terms of both capital and regular income) of the empire. Pericles' strategy was to sit behind the walls and wait, hoping that the Peloponnesians would give up before Athenian money gave out. So the Peloponnesians invaded Athenian territory and the Athenians invaded Megarian territory; no more than skirmishing was involved in either case. Squadrons of the Athenian navy devastated selected areas of the Peloponnesian coastline, and bottled up the Corinthian fleet in the Corinthian Gulf; and the war continued in Chalcidice even after the fall of Poteidaea in 429. But none of these actions resulted in important gains or delivered a decisive advantage.

The strategies of both sides were flawed. The regular Spartan invasions of Attica did not tempt the Athenians to risk a pitched battle on land. On the other hand, Pericles had underestimated the costs of maintaining a navy on a war footing and the stubbornness of the Peloponnesian League. The Spartan tactic did, however, have an unforeseen side effect. Each time they invaded Attica, everyone who had no other place of refuge moved (with as much of his property as was feasible) within the walls of Athens – not just inside the city itself, but along the narrow corridor of walls leading down to the sea. For some part of every year, there was severe overcrowding. In 430 typhoid fever ravaged the city, and over the next four years it wiped out at least a quarter of the Athenian population. There were no hospitals: people died at home or in the streets, and so the plague succeeded where the Spartans were failing. It broke many Athenians' spirits and thinned the ranks of fighting men. From then on, paying mercenaries was something else for which the Athenians had to budget.

Thoroughly dispirited, the Athenian people listened as Pericles' political opponents accused him of cowardice and inactivity, when the real reason was that he had taken them into a war they could present as a failure. They suspended his generalship and charged him with embezzlement; he was found guilty, and fined the enormous sum of fifteen talents. Pericles was reinstated at the beginning of 429, but the elderly statesman died only a few weeks later from the effects of the plague. He had been at the helm of Athenian affairs for many years, and the Athenians would soon learn to miss his experience and statesmanship. None of Pericles' successors had his stature, or at any rate the circumstances impeded their attaining it. Since they were more nearly equals, U-turns became more a feature of Athenian politics, as the Assembly's decisions depended on which politician's views were found persuasive at any given moment.

Nothing illustrates this better than the most important event of 428, which almost provoked one of the worst atrocities of the war. The oligarchic authorities in Mytilene, the largest town on the island of Lesbos, seceded from the empire, taking with them their not insubstantial fleet. The attempt was badly timed: Athenian morale, already lowered by the plague, had plummeted when the Spartans sent a naval patrol for the first time to the Aegean, which the Athenians had come to consider their own waters. The Athenians first blockaded the island, and then besieged the city of Mytilene itself. The Spartans promised help, but delayed and arrived too late. If they had energetically supported the rebellion of one of the Athenian allies, others might have taken heart and followed.

The next year, Mytilenean resistance collapsed. The Athenians took possession of the town, sent the ringleaders to Athens, and waited for the Assembly's decision about the town's future – and the Assembly decided to kill all the male citizens of Mytilene, and to enslave the women and children. They felt they had to stop the rot: if they made an example of Mytilene, perhaps that would prevent further rebellions. After all, their security now depended entirely on their empire.

The Athenian Assembly had voted to execute several thousand people and destroy an entire city. A ship was sent to Mytilene, but the very next day a less harsh mood prevailed in the Assembly. All they could do, however, was send another ship and hope that it would arrive on time. The oarsmen of the second ship put in a special effort, even eating at their oars, and in an archetypal nick-of-time climax arrived just as the original orders were about to be executed. But the revised orders were still brutal: a thousand men were executed, while the city had to tear down its defences, and accept a heavy fine and a garrison of Athenian soldiers.

As he did with other critical points of the war, Thucydides dramatized the issues by having two speakers debate and duel, in this case Cleon of Cydathenaeum and the otherwise unknown Diodotus. Although the people regretted their harsh decision of the previous day, Cleon argued that they should not change their mind. His speech appealed to expediency and attacked any form of moderate imperialism: he wanted to see terror tactics applied to keep the empire's subjects truly in subjection. But Diodotus argued that it was more in Athens's interest to be seen to be lenient. This is what is truly disturbing about the debate: Diodotus did not argue on moral grounds that Cleon's proposals were too harsh and cruel; both parties appealed in different ways only to the criterion of self-interest.

THE END OF THE ARCHIDAMIAN WAR

The following years saw the usual swings and roundabouts of Athenian and Spartan successes and setbacks. Athens signally failed to help Plataea, which finally fell to the Spartans and Thebans in 427; the following year the Athenians defeated a small Boeotian force; on Corcyra democrats and oligarchs massacred one another, with the democrats proving the more successful and the more bloodthirsty; the Athenians achieved some successes in Sicily, in hindering the spread of Syracusan influence and the passage of goods to the Peloponnese from the farms of Sicily; the plague died out; the Spartans carried out their usual invasions of Athenian territory. But there was one critical exception to the generally indecisive state of affairs.

In 425 the enterprising Athenian general Demosthenes of Aphidna successfully fortified the Messenian peninsula of Pylos on the southwest of the Peloponnese. This was a clever idea: it could act as a base for disaffected Messenian helots (Spartan serfs) to stir up rebellion, and it was through the helots that the Spartans were most vulnerable.

It had the potential to be a war-winning scheme. The Spartans clearly thought so, because they lost no time in attacking the peninsula, with its hastily built fortifications, by land and sea. But their assault was unsuccessful.

The Spartans had landed 420 men on the islet of Sphacteria, just off Pylos. With the defeat and withdrawal of the Peloponnesian fleet, these men became cut off. The numbers may seem small, but they represented some ten per cent of the Spartan army, and many of them were proud Spartiates, full-blooded Spartan aristocrats. The Spartan authorities could not endure this loss, and they arranged a truce at Pylos, while they sent delegates to Athens to negotiate an end to the war. They offered to enter into a full alliance with Athens, with each side keeping the territory it currently had. Partly out of fear of the Spartans' inability to rein in their allies, but mainly because their blood was up and they seemed to have the upper hand, the Athenians, led by Cleon, turned down the offer.

Fighting resumed, but the men on Sphacteria held out longer than expected. There was water on the island, and shade, and when the Spartans offered freedom to any helot willing to run the blockade with provisions for their trapped troops, many jumped at the chance. Back in Athens Cleon, whose refusal of the Spartan peace offer was responsible for the continued fighting, offered to take over command, despite the fact that he had not been elected one of the generals for that year. He boasted that he would bring things rapidly to an end – and indeed he and Demosthenes overran the island. The surviving Spartans surrendered – to everyone's surprise, since Spartans were not supposed to surrender but to die in battle. Almost three hundred prisoners, among them 120 Spartiates, were taken to Athens. Captured Spartan shields made a glorious display in the Agora.

The Athenians were now in a very strong position. They were facing a dispirited and weakened enemy, they held hostages, and they undertook a radical upward revision of the allies' tribute in order to secure their precarious finances. Alcibiades' first known appearance in Athenian public life was as a member of the board that revised the tribute. The Athenians renewed their peace treaty with Persia, and simultaneously interrupted Spartan delegations to the Great King's satrap in Sardis. They could probably have negotiated peace on very favourable terms, and there was certainly heated discussion of this possibility in both Athens and Sparta, but nothing was done about it. In the meantime, the Athenians waged a more aggressive war – not the kind of war Pericles had envisaged: they took the island of Cythera, which they could use as a base for interrupting Spartan supplies from Egypt and for raids on the Peloponnese, and nearly risked a hoplite battle with the Spartans near Megara in 424.

Impelled ever onwards by their run of successes, the Athenians devised a bold plan to remove Boeotia from the war, by fomenting democratic rebellion in the towns there, supported by a large invasion. Demosthenes was to occupy the town of Siphae in western Boeotia, while Hippocrates of Cholarges seized Delium in the east. Everything that could go wrong did go wrong: word leaked out and what was supposed to be a surprise attack met stiff resistance from the Boeotians; and the two generals failed to co-ordinate their attacks, but arrived at their destinations a day apart, so that the Boeotians could deal with them separately. Over a thousand Athenian or hired soldiers lost their lives. The Athenian cavalry, with Alcibiades among them, played little part due to the unsuitable terrain, but they were useful in protecting the troops as they straggled back across Mount Parnes to Athenian territory. Socrates was notable during the retreat for his self-control and for keeping his companions calm.

The Spartans followed up this success with an attack on Athenian possessions in the north, under their brilliant general Brasidas, who had made his name over the previous few years. The plan was to threaten the Athenian supply of precious metals and timber from Thrace and Macedon, and the grain route from the Black Sea; lacking an effective fleet, it was the closest the Spartans could get to an assault on the empire. With a combination of diplomacy and the threat of force, Brasidas succeeded in persuading several towns in and around Chalcidice to leave the Athenian alliance, and then laid siege to Amphipolis, the most important Athenian possession in the region. Before an Athenian fleet, commanded by the historian Thucydides, could bring help, Brasidas had offered such favourable terms to the inhabitants of Amphipolis that they surrendered the city to him without a fight. Despite repeated efforts, Athens never recovered this crucial outpost. Thucydides' failure to save Amphipolis led to his prosecution by Cleon (the historian's animosity towards the politician shows in his writing) and lifelong exile. He retired to his family's estate in Thrace, from where he could survey the war and work on his remarkable history.

Having restored the balance somewhat, the Spartans sued once more for peace. Early in 423 the two sides entered into a one-year truce: each side was to keep the possessions they currently had, and fighting was to stop, to buy time with which to negotiate a lasting peace. Unfortunately, on the Spartan side, the Thebans refused to recognize the truce and Brasidas ignored instructions from home and continued his northern campaign, and on the Athenian side, Cleon and other hawks kept stirring things up. Scione, a small but strategically placed town, was judged to have seceded from the Athenian alliance and surrendered to Brasidas *after* the truce had been signed, and therefore not to be covered by it. The Athenian Assembly was furious, and this time there was no Diodotus to oppose Cleon's proposal that all the male citizens of Scione should be put to death.

In 422, once the truce had expired, Cleon took command of northern operations himself. Scione was by now surrounded by a siege wall, so he could ignore it. He retook several other towns, before turning his attention to Amphipolis. The two armies (with Socrates again among the Athenians) met outside the town, and the Athenians were again badly mauled. They lost hundreds of men, while the Spartans lost only seven. One of the seven, however, was Brasidas – and among the Athenian dead was Cleon. The Athenians may not have regained Amphipolis, but the two most belligerent obstacles to peace had fallen.

The peace treaty that was eventually drawn up in 421 recognized, with minor exceptions, the status quo that had existed before the start of the war. In other words, the Spartans were to abandon Amphipolis and the rest of Chalcidice, leaving Scione to suffer Cleon's posthumous legacy of the execution of all its male citizens. Socrates may have witnessed or even been involved in this horrendous act. Athens, for her part, was to abandon important gains such as Cythera and Pylos. The peace was to be binding not just on the protagonists, but on all the allies too, and was to last for fifty years – unless Alcibiades got his way.

ALCIBIADES IN THE WINGS

Alcibiades played very little part in the early years of the war. He served as a soldier at Poteidaea and at Delium, he was on the board that reassessed the tribute in 424, and in 422 he proposed a decree honouring the people of the island of Siphnos for some benefaction to

Athens. The reason for his inactivity during the Archidamian phase of the war is perfectly mundane: in Athens, one had to be thirty to hold significant public office, and he did not reach this critical birthday till 423 or 422, ten years after he first became eligible to serve abroad, at Poteidaea. It was also around this time that he had a bill passed which granted land and money to the children of Aristeides the Just – a diplomatic move, since Aristeides had earned his nickname as the original assessor of the allies' tribute which, with Alcibiades' help, had just been revised sharply upwards.

Alcibiades was still primarily engaged, however, in perfecting his reputation as a man-about-town; like Oscar Wilde, he was putting his genius into his life and only talent into his work. There are plenty of stories about his wild youth. Many may be fantasies, and some derive from the imaginations of the comic poets, but he was certainly a headstrong young man, with a large appetite for life. His first public appearance would have occurred in March of the year when he gained his majority, aged eighteen; as the orphaned son of a father killed fighting for Athens, he would have been presented to the assembled people at the Festival of Dionysus. The young men were required to dress in armour for the occasion, as a sign that they were now entering on manhood and would themselves fight for the city, and we must surely imagine Alcibiades seizing the opportunity to make a fine display. For this was also the occasion when he would have inherited his share of his father's plentiful estate.

He was also busy extending his honour by more dubious means – sexual conquest. This was always a recognized route among the competitive aristocrats of Athens, despite the fact that it required that what we would consider private behaviour (say, seduction of a famous beauty, or of Socrates) become public knowledge. But he also relied on more conventional methods, such as the prosecution of court cases and the delivery of polished speeches designed to win over the general populace. Although his wealth and family prestige meant that he could have gradually ascended to power in the time-honoured way, he preferred the fast route of the new politicians, by endearing himself to the Athenian people. Some time in the 420s, since he securely belonged to the liturgical class, he was obliged to act as sponsor for a dramatic production at one of the choral festivals, which he did in a typically magnificent fashion; also typically, he became involved in a punch-up with a rival impresario.

ALCIBIADES TAKES THE STAGE

The Archidamian War had ended in disappointment and frustration for both sides – hardly the right conditions for a lasting peace – and Alcibiades and his fellow hawks, such as Hyperbolus of Perithoedae, watched for an opportunity to undermine the fragile treaty. Alcibiades was motivated not only by his warlike ambition, but also by his political enmity with Nicias of Cydantidae. Nicias was a 'new man', not a member of one of the aristocratic families; his father had made an enormous fortune renting slaves to the state, and Nicias came to the fore in the 420s as a competent, if somewhat cautious, military commander. By 421 he was already in his early fifties, and became the chief negotiator of the accord with Sparta.

As both an aristocrat and a narcissist, Alcibiades was particularly piqued that the Spartans chose to negotiate with Nicias. Alcibiades' family had traditionally held the *proxenia* of Sparta, allowing them to represent Spartan interests in Athens, but his grandfather had allowed it to lapse; this had not stopped him being ostracized in 460, but at the time he had needed to demonstrate his loyalty towards Athens rather than its rival. Alcibiades was trying to revive the *proxenia*, especially by making sure that the Spartan prisoners from Sphacteria were reasonably well looked after. After all, even his name was Spartan in origin. A foreign state might have more than one *proxenos* in another state, but at any given time one was more 'official' than the others, in the sense that the foreign state turned first to him. With the rivalry between the two states, and especially with Athens holding eminent Spartan prisoners, the official Spartan *proxenos* would have been highly visible, and Alcibiades always wanted to be visible.

He did not have to wait long for a chance to act on his pique. Sparta and Argos were old rivals, with a long history of fighting for supremacy in the eastern and central Peloponnese. The issue had been resolved early in the fifth century, when Sparta wiped out Argos's fighting force in a single battle. Over the next seventy-five years, Argos recovered enough to feel the sting of the old rivalry, but could never challenge Sparta for supremacy. In 450 the Argives entered into a treaty with the Spartans, which had so far kept them out of the current conflict. In 420, however, the treaty was about to expire.

According to Thucydides, this is what happened. Alcibiades invited a delegation from Argos, Mantineia and Elis to Athens to talk about an alliance with the Athenians, instead of renewing their various treaties with Sparta. This provoked the Spartans to send their own delegation, to try to prevent such a Quadruple Alliance, and to demonstrate their commitment to the Peace of Nicias. As foreign delegations did, the Spartans first addressed the Athenian Council, and told them that they had come with full powers of negotiation on these matters. Alcibiades did not want the reminder of peace to sway the Assembly, when the proposal was put to the people there. At a private meeting with the Spartan delegates, he persuaded them not to mention to the Assembly that they had full powers of negotiation and to leave it to him to shore up the Peace of Nicias. So when the Spartans were presented to the Assembly, and were asked whether they had full powers of negotiation, they denied that they had. The blatant contradiction between what they had told the Council and what they were telling the Assembly made the Athenians mistrust them, and Alcibiades made a stirring appeal that they should bring the Argive delegation forward straight away and enter into an alliance with them. Just at that moment, a slight earth tremor interrupted the proceedings as a bad omen, and the next day Nicias persuaded the Assembly to send him and others to Sparta to try to sort the mess out.

This is incomprehensible. Why would the Spartan delegates trust Alcibiades, a fledgling Athenian politician who was not even their *proxenos*? Why would they believe that a hawk would work for peace? Why would they so stupidly discredit themselves and their mission before the Athenians? Why did they not simply discredit Alcibiades instead, by saying that it was he who had persuaded them to say what they said? Could any or all of the puzzles be solved by remembering that one of the Spartan delegates, a man called Endius, was a *xenos* of Alcibiades? It is simplest to think that Thucydides has written a condensed and misleading account. Since, as we shall see, Alcibiades' efforts really achieved very little, Thucydides' reason for highlighting this episode must have been to portray Alcibiades, on his first appearance in his history, as an ambitious and unscrupulous man, driven by personal motivations; and in his desire not to spend more time over this than he had to, the historian obscured the facts.

The key to untangling the story lies, I believe, with the Boeotians. The Boeotians, led by Thebes, were among Sparta's most important allies, and they were opposed to the peace with Athens. Sparta had undertaken to try to win the Boeotians over to the idea of peace with

79

Athens, but instead had just entered into a fresh military alliance with them. The Athenian position was straightforward: either you cancel this alliance with Boeotia, or we enter into an alliance with Argos. This was exactly the deal Nicias offered the Spartans when he went there following the extraordinary Assembly meeting. Now we can perhaps unpack what happened.

When the Spartans said in the first instance that they came with full powers of negotiation, they meant that they had a free hand to try to persuade the Athenians not to enter into an alliance with Argos, by promising to arrange the exchange of Pylos, still in Athenian hands, for territory the Athenians claimed that was still in the hands of Spartan allies. But when asked in the Assembly – perhaps by Alcibiades or one of his stooges – whether this meant that they would cancel their new alliance with the Boeotians, they said that they could not guarantee that. How could they? Such an important issue would be a matter for the authorities in Sparta itself. This is what Alcibiades had discovered in his private talks with the Spartan delegates, or at least from his friend Endius, and this was what he used to discredit the Spartan envoys. He would have argued, without much difficulty, that the Spartan alliance with the Boeotian federation was the key, and that if the Spartan delegates were powerless in this respect, they were in effect powerless altogether.

Alcibiades spent an anxious few days while Nicias was negotiating in Sparta, but the mission came to nothing: it foundered on the Spartans' refusal to give up their alliance with the Boeotians. Nicias came home with egg on his face and with the Athenian doves in disgrace, since they had already returned the Spartan prisoners from Sphacteria (as they were obliged to by the terms of the treaty) and gained nothing in return. The Athenians immediately entered into a hundred-year treaty with Argos, Mantineia and Elis. Sparta was bound to use military means against such a threat on its doorstep. While the Spartans first hastened to reassure and retain their existing friends, Alcibiades, who had parlayed his success into his first generalship, spent much of 419 touring the Peloponnese, strengthening the Quadruple Alliance and persuading others to join it. There was more than a little show-manship even in this military venture, as Arnold Gomme pointed out: 'It was a grandiose scheme for an Athenian general, at the head of a mainly Peloponnesian army, to march through the Peloponnese cocking a snook at Sparta when her reputation was at its lowest.'

When Patrae proved reluctant to join the alliance, on the grounds that the Athenians would swallow them up, Alcibiades quipped, 'That may be so, but they will do so little by little, and feet first, whereas the Spartans will swallow you down head first in a single gulp.' Alcibiades' intention was to secure the western entrance to the Corinthian Gulf for Athens, but a strong Corinthian force prevented him from doing more than strengthening Patrae's defences and enhancing the Athenian presence there. He also persuaded Argos to attack strategically important Epidaurus, perhaps as an attempt to make the Corinthians feel cornered and to frighten them out of the Peloponnesian League. But Spartan sabre-rattling undermined Argive resolve, even when Alcibiades arrived with a thousand Athenian hoplites; in any case, the Athenians too were wary of meeting the formidable Spartan hoplites in a pitched battle.

Having achieved relatively little, Alcibiades was not elected general for 418. The Spartans cowed the Argives into concluding a four-month truce with them, but Alcibiades was despatched to Argos to stiffen the resolve of the allies and to argue that the truce was not valid, since the Athenians had not been involved in the negotiations. The Quadruple Alliance attacked Orchomenus, and set their sights on Tegea next, on the border of the Spartan heartland, but the Spartans met them at Mantineia and defeated them. This was a critical battle for Sparta: if they had lost, the Peloponnesian League would have collapsed and the Athenians would have won the war. But instead Argos, Elis and Mantineia abandoned the Athenian alliance and joined or rejoined the Peloponnesian League. Although Alcibiades' Peloponnesian policy had failed, he was able to boast that he had brought the Spartans to the brink of defeat, and had forced them to risk all on a single battle, without seriously endangering Athens, since the battle had taken place far from the city. It was not a bad start for someone who had set his sights on being the first man of the city. But Nicias was still in the way.

OSTRACISM

The Peace of Nicias should also have been one of the victims of Mantineia, since Spartans and Athenians clashed there in battle, but they tacitly agreed to regard this as an anomaly and carried on as though the peace were intact. Both Nicias's peace policy and Alcibiades' Peloponnesian programme were more or less in tatters, but Alcibiades maintained contact with the pro-Athenian democrats in troubled Argos, who in 417 bloodily deposed the ruling oligarchy and seized power. At Alcibiades' suggestion, they began to build walls connecting their town to the sea (on the model of the Athenian Long Walls), so that they would be less vulnerable to a Spartan attack. The scheme was spectacularly unsuccessful, since the Spartans attacked and demolished the walls just a few weeks after their completion, but the following year Alcibiades, in his second generalship, sailed to Argos to forestall the possibility of an oligarchic counter-coup. He arrived with twenty ships, arrested the remaining Spartan sympathizers, and deported them to islands under Athenian control. By now, Argos was virtually Alcibiades' client state.

With the two rivals, Nicias and Alcibiades, both forced to retrench, Hyperbolus chose this time to attack them both for ineffective leadership and, by default, to put himself forward as a candidate for the position of first man of Athens. Hyperbolus was a popular politician best known for his advocacy of expansion into the western Mediterranean. He now, in 416, initiated an ostracism, on the grounds that the rivalry between Nicias and Alcibiades was destabilizing the state. As far as he could see, he could only win: either Nicias would be exiled, and that would remove the chief opponent of western expansion, or Alcibiades would go, and that would leave the glory and profit of western conquest to Hyperbolus. Of course, an ostracism was not so straightforward: *ostraka* recovered by archaeologists and plausibly dated to this particular ostracism process bear the names of eleven men, including the four picked out by our literary sources as the chief candidates: Alcibiades, Nicias, Hyperbolus and Phaeax of Acharnae. Phaeax too was an expansionist, remembered for a successful diplomatic mission to Sicily and southern Italy in 422, during which he arranged alliances with or at least neutrality in a number of towns, as a prelude to a future Athenian attack on Sicily.

Alcibiades' response is explicable only on the assumption that he was more or less certain that he would be the one to be banished. First, he allied his networks of political friends with those of Phaeax. This left matters about even: it was no longer certain whether he or Nicias would be sent into exile. Nicias accordingly became worried, and was open to Alcibiades' approach. With typical flamboyance, by forming a temporary alliance also with his main rival, Alcibiades not only secured his own safety, but ensured a topsy-turvy ostracism, because when the votes were counted, it was Hyperbolus himself who had the most. Since Hyperbolus had not originally been seen as a threat to the stability of the democracy, which was the alleged purpose of any ostracism, the whole institution came into disrepute. Alcibiades had demonstrated how easy it was for powerful men to manipulate the system to their own advantage. The Athenians never again resorted to ostracism.

MELOS

The year 416 also demonstrated how far down the path of ruthlessness the Athenians were prepared to go. As one of the generals for the year, Alcibiades would certainly have kept in touch with events, but he was not personally involved. He had other fish to fry, as we shall shortly see. The island of Melos had ancestral ties with Sparta, but was neutral (in so far as that was a recognized status in ancient Greece), despite being surrounded by Athenian allies. The Athenians had from time to time attempted to force the island into full membership of the empire, and now their patience had run out. Since the island had briefly and intermittently paid tribute (up until 425 BCE), the Athenians probably consoled themselves, as they prepared to invade, with the argument that it was a rebel state. Before invading, however, they sent envoys to negotiate with the Melians, to see if they could cow them into submission without committing any troops. Thucydides cast the negotiations in the form of a memorably savage dialogue between the Athenian delegates and members of the oligarchic Melian council – savage, but also futile, since if the Melians won the argument they would be invaded, and if they lost the argument they would be 'enslaved', or forced to join the empire.

Right from the start, according to Thucydides, the Athenians dismissed any reference to justice or international law; there is no place for justice between unequal sides, they insisted, only for the domination of the weaker party by the stronger. Expediency is the issue, not justice; the security of the empire demands the island's capitulation. Besides, it is both a natural law, valid among gods as well as men, that the strong should dominate the weak, and a human convention too, throughout human history. If the Melians had the power that the Athenians currently have, the Melians would act no differently. So the Athenians have nothing to fear from the gods. As for the Melian hope of help from Sparta, this is just plain stupid, the Athenian envoys sneered. The Spartans lead the way in acting only in their own interest, and they will not see it here; there is too much risk involved. They might have added (though it does not play a part in Thucydides' dramatic debate) that the Spartans could not seize the moral high ground, since they had just carried out a massacre themselves, at the Argive town of Hysiae.

Negotiation failed to resolve anything, and Athenians turned to military muscle instead. They attacked the island in the late summer of 416 and by the early winter they had conquered it and more or less depopulated it: the men were all killed, the women and children sold into slavery. Thucydides' style rarely permits him to comment explicitly on an event, but he placed the Melian dialogue right before the debate that led to the Athenians sending out the expedition to Sicily, an act of terminal self-destruction, as if to say that one was sin and the other retribution. If so, Alcibiades, the chief instigator of the Sicilian expedition, was the instrument of retribution.

SIX

The Rise and Fall of Alcibiades

Alcibiades avoided involvement in the massacre at Melos only because he was occupied with a different route to personal glory. Originally, the ancient games at Olympia, in the far west of the Peloponnese, consisted of no more than a few footraces for locals. It was only once the festival became a panhellenic meeting of aristocrats that the chariot race became one of the focal events, with its legendary origin depicted on the pedimental sculptures of the great temple of Zeus at Olympia, erected around 456 BCE. But entering a team was possible only for a very exclusive class, even among the rich. The Athenian statistics bear this out: 'The 44 certain known entries by Athenians of four- and two-horse chariots for international contests during the 300 years from 600 to 300 were made by members of only fourteen families, and . . . three of these families (Alkmeonidai, Philaidai/Kimonids, and the Kleinias-Alkibiades family) account for 25 of them.'

The name of Alcibiades is constantly linked with breeding horses for chariot-racing contests. It was his passion, and one of the main ways in which he chose to make a mark on both Athenian and international society. Even before the almost legendary Olympic games of 416 he had achieved notable successes. He had won at the Panathenaea of 418, which was the most splendid international festival in Athens, and in 416 he commissioned two paintings, to be displayed in a wing of the monumental entrance to the Acropolis: one showed him being crowned by figures representing both the Olympic and the Pythian games (held at Delphi); the second had him seated in the lap of the Nemean games. The international Nemean and Pythian games almost rivalled the Olympic games for prestige, and the paintings can only mean that he had also won there. At the same time he also commissioned a bronze statue of himself driving a chariot – not that he or any of his aristocratic peers drove their racing chariots themselves: it was an extremely dangerous event, best left to expert slaves.

But true glory was to be won at the games at Olympia, and for those of 416 he entered no fewer than *seven* teams, more than most states could manage, let alone individuals. As if that were not enough, he erected an enormous pavilion, in the Persian style, in which he lavishly entertained large numbers of guests with golden tableware, and he performed ostentatiously large sacrifices in the sacred precinct. The cost was enormous (eight talents – perhaps £4,000,000 – a later historian records, but how did he arrive at this figure?), and even Alcibiades had to cut some corners. He had bought a team of horses in Argos on behalf of his friend Teisias Teisimachou, but since Teisias was otherwise engaged at the time, leading the invasion of Melos, Alcibiades entered the team as his own. He appears also to have persuaded the Olympic Committee that another Athenian team, which properly belonged to a certain Diomedes, was his; it is typical of Alcibiades not to have been content with the staggering feat of entering five teams. He also 'borrowed' the golden tableware from the official Athenian delegation to the festival. In short, Alcibiades made sure that he was highly visible at this, the most important meeting of aristocrats from all over the Greek world.

His teams came first, second and fourth (or possibly third). When he got home he commissioned no less a poet than Euripides to write a celebratory ode, and the painters and sculptor he used for his victory portraits were also of the first rank. Victory in one or more of the great international athletic festivals was held to be an almost superhuman achievement, and was regularly taken to bestow the victor with talismanic power, of the sort that could strike terror into the hearts of one's enemies on the battlefield; a victorious athlete might well be fêted in popular songs and celebrated on monuments, and after his death his spirit might be worshipped as a beneficent power. Given Alcibiades' rivalry with Nicias, it is certainly worth mentioning that the previous year the older statesman had paid for a particularly extravagant performance of the choral programme of the Delia, the festival in honour of Apollo on the sacred island of Delos. Alcibiades did not enjoy being in the shade; his display at the Olympics was meant to catapult him way beyond his rival.

In the eyes of many Athenians, however, he had gone too far – and they had a very specific way of describing just how much too far he had gone. The rumour began to spread that Alcibiades would not be satisfied even with the Periclean position of first statesman of Athens, but was aiming for tyranny, unconstitutional sole rule. Although in a speech the following year he argued that his Olympic success and spectacle brought glory to the city as a whole, his behaviour smacked of *replacing* the city, not of representing it. The very actions that, according to Alcibiades, glorified the city, led others to claim that people would mock Athens for their subservience to just one man. From then on, rumours of tyranny blighted Alcibiades' career. If anyone had not heard the rumours earlier, in 414, on stage before an audience of thousands, Aristophanes had a thinly disguised Alcibiades found a new model community in the sky (the play was called *Birds*) and set himself up as an eastern-style tyrant there.

There was a specifically Athenian precedent for the attempt to translate Olympic victory into control of the state; it had happened long before, but the story was still fresh in people's minds, because it led to one of the great scandals of Athenian history, the Alcmaeonid Curse. Even as recently as 431, the Spartans had invoked this curse in an attempt to turn the Athenians against Pericles. Around 630 BCE a would-be tyrant called Cylon, a recent Olympic victor, had seized the Acropolis with his supporters – and with the help of troops supplied by his father-in-law, the tyrant of Megara. The coup failed to garner the local support Cylon had hoped for, and he abandoned the Acropolis once he and his supporters had been promised fair treatment. But an Alcmaeonid archon had some of the Cylonians summarily executed. This was the sacrilege that led to the cursing of the Alcmaeonid family – and to the Spartan recollection of the stigma in their negotiations with Alcmaeonid Pericles.

As if Alcibiades' vainglorious use of Olympic victory were not enough, there were other aspects of his life that his enemies could easily use to support the suggestion that limited, constitutional power was not going to satisfy him. There was his habit of using his charm to make the citizens of foreign states more or less his clients: the Ephesians and the islanders of Chios had supported the cost of his Olympic extravaganza, and the loyalty of the Argive army reminded Athenians of how Peisistratus, on his third and most successful attempt to become tyrant in 547 BCE, had seized power with the help of Argive troops. Then there were his strong links with Asia Minor, when the east was the traditional home of tyranny: the Greek word *turannos* was an adaptation of an Anatolian original, and the Persian king was always regarded as the archetypal tyrant. There were also his many *xenoi* among foreign magnates, which suggested simultaneously a network of alliances that could be used to seize power at home, and a tenuous attachment to Athenian democracy.

Even his appetites told against him: it was a firm aspect of the Greek conception of a tyrant that his unbridled lusts manifested not just as violence, and not just as a desire for absolute power, but also as a desire for excessive sex, even with members of his own family (as Persian kings from time to time married sisters). Alcibiades' sexual escapades were so notorious that no one knew where they would end: he was certainly suspected of kinky sex (threesomes with his uncle in Abydus, the ancient Bangkok, and affairs with both a mother and her daughter there), and within a generation, at the latest, there was gossip that he too was not averse to sleeping with his mother and sister 'in the Persian manner'.

Despite the persistence of the rumours that Alcibiades had tyrannical aspirations, it would have been virtually impossible for a single individual, even one as celebrated as Alcibiades, to have seized autocratic, unconstitutional power in late-fifth-century Athens. Even while these rumours were being spread by Alcibiades' enemies, Aristophanes was mocking fear of tyrants as old-fashioned. But it was a real emotion: curses against tyranny were uttered at the start of every Assembly meeting and there were legal weapons (including ostracism) to combat it. The charge reflected Alcibiades' huge appetites, disregard for convention and patently undemocratic nature; tyranny seemed to be the logical end of the way in which he sought distinction and flaunted his power. And his very popularity threatened a society whose integrity depended on a high degree of notional equality among its citizens. Hero worship had the potential to undo Athenian democracy; this was what Alcibiades' enemies sensed and it gave credibility to their accusations.

SICILY

After the Olympics of 416, Alcibiades and his war policy rode high on a wave of popular adoration; he seemed to be the embodiment of Athenian adventurousness, which had already profited the city immensely and promised to restore its fortunes once again. Many Athenians profited from the war, especially the poorer members of society, who received a stipend for serving in the navy, which had been largely dry-docked for five years. Meanwhile, the war chest had been swelled by a few years of relative inactivity, and a new generation of young soldiers had come of age and restored Athens's military capability. Nationalism was as vigorous as it had ever been.

Athenian imperialists had long looked westward to Sicily. Pericles himself had glanced in that direction in the 430s, but in the face of the reality of war had favoured conservation over aggression. But a few years later, with Pericles dead, Cleon, Hyperbolus and others came out in favour of attacking Sicily: it was always popular for a politician to promise western conquests, to remind the people of western opulence and especially of Sicily's grain and ship-quality timber, two vital commodities of which Athens was always short and sometimes starved. The main and immediate obstacle was Syracuse, a Greek city – an ally of Sparta – as populous and as committed to a course of self-interested ruthlessness as Athens. The next hurdle was Carthage, the wealthy Phoenician trading city on the north African coast, which already had outposts in the western triangle of Sicily. According to Thucydides, Athenian imperialists with an expansionist turn of mind made no secret of the fact that once Sicily had been secured, they had their sights on Carthage – and then Spain, rich in minerals and grain. With the western Mediterranean under their control, the resistance of the Peloponnese would start to seem futile.

Cleon got his way to the extent that the Athenians maintained a largely ineffective military presence in southern Italy from 426 to 424, until with the Treaty of Gela the Sicilian communities, including Athens's allies, united and persuaded Syracuse to shelve its ambition to rule the entire island. Athens no longer had a plausible reason for military intervention in Sicily, but dreams of western conquest lingered; some saw Athens's destiny in a pan-Mediterranean empire, three centuries before the Romans achieved it.

Despite the Treaty of Gela, tension remained just below the surface of Sicilian affairs, occasionally bubbling up into the open. And when Selinus and Segesta were involved, not for the first or last time, in a bitter border war, the Segestans, after exhausting local possibilities, turned for help to Athens. The embassy arrived in Athens late in 416, and was joined by a delegation of exiles from Leontini, who had been expelled in a Syracuse-backed oligarchic coup a few years earlier; even the Segestans complained as much about Syracuse as about Selinus. After some weeks, while Athenian agents in Sicily assessed the situation, the Assembly voted to send a limited force to Sicily; this was not, or not yet, to be a full invasion, and in any case they expected support from their allies in Sicily and southern Italy (more support than they actually received). The mission was 'to help the Segestans against the people of Selinus; to re-establish Leontini, if things were going well in the war; and in general to make the kind of provisions for Sicily that might seem to them most to further Athenian interests'. To judge by the generals' actions in Sicily, this last clause was meant to give them a *carte blanche* where Syracuse was concerned. Three generals were appointed, with Nicias and Alcibiades joined by the elderly firebrand Lamachus of Oa.

But this, the legacy of the failed ostracism, was an inauspicious leadership: Nicias was by now chronically ill with kidney disease, and the bitter enmity between himself and Alcibiades was hardly appropriate for the high command of such a critical expedition; united only by their contempt for Lamachus, the two rivals devoted their energies to a futile attempt to outdo each other in the magnificence of their flagships. All they had going for them, apart from belligerence and the size of the expedition, were Nicias's contacts with the democrats in oligarchic Syracuse (for which he was *proxenos*) and Alcibiades' skill at negotiating; neither Lamachus nor Alcibiades had good track records as successful field commanders. Even when they arrived in southern Italy, they were incapable of agreeing: Lamachus wanted to attack Syracuse straight away; Alcibiades wanted to gather a coalition of Sicilian and southern Italian towns whose troops could be used against Syracuse and whose crops and livestock could supply the army; Nicias wanted to settle Segestan affairs and then either leave, having made a display of force that the Syracusans would remember, or stay if the Segestans could supply the fleet. But this unfortunate beginning merely reflected the palpable aura of doom that had hung over the expedition in the weeks immediately prior to its departure.

HERMS AND MYSTERIES

This is not the place to tell the story of the Sicilian expedition, which has in any case already been done brilliantly and with the thoroughness it deserves, first by Thucydides. Suffice it to say here that the Athenians lost, largely as a result of incompetence. The whole sordid, tragic business took two years, and in the course of these two years the Athenians had voted twice to send reinforcements; the upshot was that the losses may have amounted to almost fifty thousand Athenian soldiers and oarsmen (including allies and mercenaries), among whom were Nicias and Lamachus, and both the generals (one of whom was

Demosthenes) who had been sent out with the second wave of reinforcements. By the end of the catastrophic expedition, the Athenians
probably had fewer than a hundred serviceable ships, had more or less
exhausted their capital reserves, and were just as badly off as before
for grain and timber. Even more importantly, the catastrophe altered
the balance of the war in the Aegean, since the Persians, scenting the
possibility of recovering their long-lost Aegean possessions, decided to
come in on the side of the Spartans.

The pre-expedition omens indicated either success or disaster, but all
paled into insignificance beside the mutilation of the herms. Three or
four weeks before the expedition was due to set sail in all its glory, on a
single night most of the herms in the city were vandalized. Herms were,
as the name implies, figures of the god Hermes, each consisting of a
square-cut, slightly tapering block of stone, with only two sculpted
features: a bearded bust of the god set on top, and an erect phallus in the
appropriate anatomical position. They warded evil from, and so guaranteed prosperity for, the building or street or square at the entrances of
which they were placed, and hence also acted as boundary markers.
Originally, herms were perhaps just logs of olive wood with projecting
branch-stubs (which are still today called 'pricks' in the coarse world of
Greek olive-farming), and in classical Athens some private homes still
had wooden rather than stone herms.

Thucydides says that the faces of the herms were disfigured, and one
defaced herm that has been recovered by archaeologists in the Agora
may date from this episode. Many have succumbed to the temptation
to think that, in some cases at least, the phalluses were broken off. The
temptation is increased by a couple of lines from Aristophanes' play
Lysistrata, produced in 411, in which some Athenians, who are
displaying prominent erections, are warned to keep their clothes on,
'in case a herm-basher catches sight of you'. But the joke may be no
more than: get dressed, or the herm-bashers will mistake you for
herms and smash your faces in.

This was an act of profound and outrageous sacrilege, and it met
with a swift response. The Council convened the Assembly several
times within a few days; a special commission of inquiry was set up;
substantial rewards were offered for information; immunity was guaranteed for anyone who might incriminate himself in informing; and
the promise of freedom tempted slaves to inform on their masters. But
the first information that was received (from a slave of Alcibiades

called Andromachus) only confused matters further. The board heard not about *this* act of desecration, but two others, both of which had taken place in the recent past: first, sacred images had been damaged during a *kōmos* (a lawless, drunken, noisy parade through the streets in the wee hours of the morning, after a symposium); second, the Eleusinian Mysteries had been mocked by being celebrated in private houses. Alcibiades was denounced for both of these crimes.

The most likely reason for putting on a display of the rites of the Mysteries is that it was a form of initiation into a club. The Eleusinian rite lent itself to such parody because initiation was at its heart, as it was of all the Greek mystery cults. Only the Mysteries offered ancient Greeks features that, even in the waning Christian era, we moderns might expect from a religion: personal salvation, and a glimpse of transcendence. Since the Mysteries were the best chance for ancient Greeks to experience these powerful emotions, the whole cult was held in awe. Initiates were charged with secrecy, and over the thousand-year history of the cult, hundreds of thousands of them kept the secret. We know too little about the Mysteries, then, to be sure what the profaners might have done, but the very fact of performing the rites out of their sacred context and before non-initiates was probably enough. The cult was sacred to the goddesses Demeter and her daughter Korē or Persephone, and was open to all Greek-speakers, but was jealously protected by Athens, in whose territory the town of Eleusis fell. Very many Athenian citizens and their wives were initiates.

The mocking of the Mysteries became critically important, but we hear no more about the earlier act of damaging sacred images. Perhaps it had already served its purpose, as a red herring. The idea that sacred images could be damaged during a *kōmos* may have been floated in order to downplay the importance of the mutilation of the herms by making it out to be a drunken prank perpetrated by young aristocrats; indeed, the conspirators may well have disguised their noise by pretending to be drunken revellers. There is a very striking, if somewhat crudely painted, Athenian vase that shows a toppled herm being struck in the face by an axe-wielding satyr. Given the exact coincidence between the picture on the vase (substituting a satyr, symbolizing unruliness, for a drunken human being) and the actions of the herm-mutilators, it is astonishing to learn that this vase pre-dates 415 by some decades. Another vase from the same period shows satyrs, who commonly represent extreme human behaviour on vases, vandalizing a tomb. It looks as though the desecration of sacred objects was familiar, even if rare, drunken behaviour (satyrs were commonly associated with Dionysus, god of wine), and certainly there were those at the time who persuaded themselves that this was no more than youthful high spirits, taken too far – an exaggeration of the kind of dissolute prank aristocratic youths of earlier generations had commonly indulged in, in the days when society had been structured in such a way that they could get away with it.

If this view had prevailed, the fuss over the mutilation of the herms might have died down, but the sheer scale and timing of the affair made that impossible. Athens was famous for its hundreds of herms, and apparently most of them were damaged. To do this amount of noisy damage in a single night, without being detected (even granted that Athenian houses rarely had windows on to the street), took considerable planning and manpower. One of the informants said that he saw about three hundred men, one of the defendants that only twenty-two were involved. Both figures were presumably considered plausible, but since the informant had reasons to exaggerate and the defendant to downplay the affair, the truth probably lies in between. But even if a hundred people were involved, why would so many – a good proportion of the Athenian rich – have taken such a pledge if not for politically subversive reasons?

It seemed like a conspiracy – but to what end? There was much fear at the time of the oligarchic machinations of Sparta; it was thought that the Spartans, in this time of nominal peace between the two states, would try to defeat Athens by encouraging internal dissent, even civil war. And so the dominant theory about the mutilation of the herms was that it was precisely 'part of a conspiracy to bring about a revolution and to subvert the democracy'.

This is why it became a true witch-hunt, marked by the kind of hysterical over-reaction that inevitably mars attempts to get to the truth: 'They did not assess the informants, but in their paranoia accepted everything anyone said, so that perfectly decent people were arrested and imprisoned on the evidence of bad men.' Andocides of Cydathenaeum, a member of one of the city's wealthiest families and a notorious oligarch, was prosecuted for a different act of impiety in 399 BCE, and one of the reasons we know so much about this whole business is because, in his defence speech, he gave the court his version of the events of sixteen years earlier as background information, and his speech has survived. In the course of this speech, no doubt impelled to a little exaggeration by self-righteous indignation over his own summary arrest, he asked his dikasts to imagine the Agora, the thriving, bustling heart of the city, being avoided by terrified people, the innocent and the guilty alike.

Perhaps the conspirators intended to spoil the Sicilian expedition; after all, mysterious Hermes was the god of travel, because the end of a journey is always unknown. But no one stood to gain from the cancellation of the expedition. There were those who wanted peace, but the Sicilian expedition was, strictly, not a breach of the current peace with Sparta, so stopping it would have made no difference. The sacrilege would cast a pall over the expedition, and for that reason alone it was incumbent upon the authorities to do their best to redress the situation, but it is at least as likely that the prevalent view at the time was correct – that the conspirators' misguided intention was just to create enough instability to improve their chances of fomenting revolution while large numbers of poor Athenians were away in Sicily, serving as oarsmen.

If we are inclined to look for symbolism in the act, then, it may be more productive to remember that another of Hermes' provinces was the lottery (always a journey with an uncertain end), the essential tool of Athenian democracy; but in all probability the conspirators chose the herms not for symbolic reasons, but just because their desecration was the easiest way for them to commit an outrage. One of those accused later claimed that the whole affair was a *pistis*, a pledge or proof of loyalty to some over-large club.

The committee appointed to investigate the disfigurement of the herms allayed public fear somewhat just because it seemed to be doing something, but all the evidence they received seemed to confirm the fear of oligarchic conspiracies, just because the accused were the *kinds* of men who met in clubs after dark, and the clubs were the seed-beds of oligarchic disaffection and bluster. Suddenly, the issue was loyalty to the democracy, and when the imitation of the Mysteries also came to light, this affair too became tarred with the same oligarchic, or at least un-Athenian, brush. These sorts of initiation ceremonies had probably been going on in the clubs for a while, and may even have been relatively common knowledge; but now they seemed threatening, to be the work of those who demanded from fellow club-members greater loyalty to the club than to Athens. When the younger Alcibiades, our Alcibiades' son, came to defend his father's memory, he linked in a single sentence the charges that his father's club had met for revolutionary purposes, and that they had put on a performance of the Mysteries.

So once the authorities had heard of the further acts of impiety, in both of which Alcibiades was allegedly implicated, fears spiralled out of control. Further informants came forward to give evidence about the profanation of the Mysteries. A metic called Teucrus denounced twelve people, including himself, for a separate incident in which the Mysteries had been illegally celebrated, and said he also knew of eighteen herm-mutilators; the next, a woman called Agariste, named a few people for illegally celebrating the Mysteries; the next, a slave called Lydus, told the board about yet another occasion on which the Mysteries had been illegally celebrated. In all, we know of five or six occasions on which the Mysteries were illegally performed, a heady brew of impiety and oligarchy. And the Athenians may well have felt that this was the tip of an iceberg. Many of those denounced fled, while a few were hastily put to death; those who were taken to court were tried before juries composed only of fellow initiates from the pool of six thousand enrolled dikasts, to preserve the secrets of the Mysteries.

So far the informers had been two slaves, a metic and a woman – none of them full citizens. As if that were not curious enough, the woman, Agariste, was an Alcmaeonid, a member of one of the oldest and noblest families of Athens, and one of those she named was her kinsman Alcibiades, perhaps in an attempt to keep her family's reputation untainted by the scandals: it must have been 'one of the most sensational events in an uncommonly sensational year', as historian Robert Wallace has said. The next informant was a certain Diocleides, an Athenian citizen. He declared that he had been out late on the night of the mutilation of the herms, and in the light of the full moon (probably 25 May, then) had seen approximately three hundred men up to no good: they must be the mutilators, and he could name over forty of them. One was Andocides.

The two affairs seemed to dovetail; there was even some overlap in the people allegedly involved in one or the other of the crimes. Both smacked of a widespread oligarchic conspiracy in the highest stratum of Athenian society. The Assembly declared a state of emergency, all forty-two people on Diocleides' list were thrown into prison, if they did not flee into exile, and armed citizens patrolled the streets and defensive walls of both Athens and Piraeus. Andocides decided to turn state's evidence, in order to save himself and the nine other members of his family who had been imprisoned – and in order to demonstrate that Diocleides had fabricated his whole story as a way to settle some scores. Andocides did his best to make it sound as though it was all a prank, evolving out of the culture of drunken symposia attended by aristocratic young men, and he played safe by denouncing largely men who had already been denounced by earlier informants. Diocleides confessed to his lies, claiming that he had been put up to it by a couple of Alcibiades' friends, and was duly put to death. Andocides' enemies found a way around the promise of immunity and saw to his exile. Andromachus and Teucrus were the only two who were given the promised rewards; Agariste may have felt it beneath her dignity to accept one.

Alcibiades was deeply implicated: two of the five informers had named him for profaning the Mysteries, and many of the other conspirators had familial or other close links to him; quite a few of them were also associates of Socrates. But by then Alcibiades was no longer in the city. After being denounced by the very first informer, his slave Andromachus, he had tried to insist on an immediate trial, to clear his name before the expedition set sail, but the people did not want to be bulldozed. The expedition sailed on schedule a couple of weeks later, in the middle of June. Then, after the sailing, Teucrus and the other informants came forward, and the atmosphere in the city worsened.

Widespread paranoia was not helped by the appearance early in July of Peloponnesian and Boeotian forces on the borders of Attica. But this was a time of supposed peace, with an alliance in place between Athens and Sparta; it was clearly not going to last much longer, but it had not yet been broken. So what were the troops doing there? Taking part in a threatening military exercise on Athens's borders? Hardly: such training exercises were not an aspect of this Cold War. They were there for a hostile purpose, and most likely because they were hoping to get called in by dissident Athenians; in fact, they had probably expected to be summoned earlier. Their appearance in peacetime confirms that there *was* an oligarchic conspiracy afoot. Where we can be certain of the status of those accused, they were well born and well off (including Oeonias Oeonocharous, the wealthiest man in Athens, a billionaire by today's standards). Where we can be certain of their politics, they were oligarchs; a significant number of the names recur again among the oligarchs involved in the coups of either 411 or 404 or both. When the militia patrolled the walls of Athens, it was not to ward off external enemies, but to prevent some of their fellow citizens opening the gates to the enemy.

A CONSPIRACY THEORY

Everything points, then, to an oligarchic conspiracy – but what went wrong? Why was no coup attempted after all? The simplest answer is to say that the conspirators were unmasked, and were exiled or killed, but this can be no more than part of the picture. The most peculiar aspect of the whole mess is that, although a number of oligarchically inclined Athenians died or fled, some very important oligarchs remained. They may even have been pulling the strings.

The most ardent members of the board that investigated the two scandals and saw that democratic justice was done were Peisander of Acharnae and Charicles Apollodorou. Peisander is one of the many shadowy figures in Athenian political life about whom it would be instructive to know more; he was important enough to feature in a number of literary works (usually portrayed as a coward) and even to have a whole play devoted to him. He was in his early forties, intelligent, wealthy, slightly overweight and a *bon vivant*; he was also a friend of Alcibiades, and so had nothing to do with the accusations against him, but otherwise did an admirable job in purging the city of opponents of democracy. And this is exactly what is odd, because within a very few years he would emerge as the chief architect of an oligarchic coup in Athens. In fact, he pursued his mission to replace the democracy with a narrow oligarchy with considerable ruthlessness: he organized or triggered the first political assassinations in Athens for about forty years. We are asked to believe, then, that some time between 415 and 411, he changed from fervent democrat to fervent oligarch.

This is not impossible. Athenian politicians were openly self-interested and changed allegiances even over major issues. But the distance Peisander is supposed to have travelled, from one *extreme* to the other, is what makes this interpretation implausible in his case, and the plot further thickens when we consider that we are also asked to believe the same about Charicles. He too came to the fore in 411 as an oligarch, and was even more famous as one of the members of the brutal oligarchic regime that briefly ruled Athens after the end of the war. Would either of these men have been acceptable as leaders of the oligarchs in 411 if just a few years earlier they had been instrumental in persecuting oligarchs, if not destroying a potential oligarchic coup? When Andocides first mentions them in his defence speech he describes them as 'supposedly loyal democrats at the time', as if he thought their loyalty to the democracy had been a sham.

Instead of assuming that both these men coincidentally underwent a conversion, we can reconstruct another possible scenario. Suppose that Peisander and Charicles were hardcore oligarchs, and that they and their networks were genuinely committed to revolution. Suppose they were sober men, who knew that such a coup stood a chance of success only if the majority of the populace could be persuaded that it was in their interests. Certainly, then, the eve of the Sicilian expedition was not the appropriate time: the general populace was almost irrationally in favour of the expedition, and by implication of the renewal of war. Political coups require either popular leaders, or dis-content and disunity – or both – but in 415 the Athenian people were fired up and united by a common purpose. The hot-heads who smashed the herms were acting prematurely.

The first result of the mutilation of the herms was the denunciation of Alcibiades for mocking the Mysteries. Alcibiades' enemies leapt at the chance to suggest that Alcibiades was the ringleader of an attempted coup, and I believe that this may be a half truth: he was an ally not of the hot-heads, but of Peisander and the sober men, who were planning a coup in the future – a coup of which Alcibiades intended to be the leader. Obviously, it could not take place while he was away in Sicily; probably the intention was to cruise to power on the strength of his likely successes there. At any rate, in a speech to the Spartans delivered later in 415 (as reported by Thucydides), he admit-ted that he and his friends had been held back from launching a coup only by the consideration that war is not a good time to do so.

So Alcibiades set sail, leaving matters in the hands of his friends Peisander and Charicles. They acted with extreme boldness: it was they, specifically, who turned the investigation into a witch-hunt, by insisting, where the affair of the herms was concerned, that the eighteen men denounced by Teucrus could not have been the only ones involved – 'that what had happened was not the work of an insignificant number of men, but part of an attempt to overthrow the democracy, and that therefore the investigation should continue'.

This was a clever ploy, serving a number of purposes simultaneously. Above all, it was an attempt to divert attention from Alcibiades (though, as it happened, it was too late for that). Alcibiades was not accused of mutilating the herms, but only of mocking the Mysteries, so the more the investigation focused on the herms, the more they hoped to defuse hostility against Alcibiades. It was after the Assembly had received a sequence of denunciations about the Mysteries that Alcibiades' cousin and close friend, Alcibiades of Phegous, got Diocleides to tell the Assembly that three hundred men were involved in the desecration of the herms: with such numbers involved, they would have to focus on it.

Second, the ploy successfully disguised the fact that Peisander and Charicles (and their associates) were *not* loyal democrats, since they seemed to be acting for the democracy. Third, it created a cache of men who were either oligarchs or, by now, angry with the democracy; they would scatter to sympathetic states or friends abroad and forge networks; they could be recalled when the appropriate time came for revolution. This might seem far-fetched, but one of the strangest aspects of the whole business was that most of the forty-two men named by Diocleides fled, even though Diocleides' deposition was false and he was soon executed for it; witch-hunts promote fear of unfair trials, of course, but if Diocleides was lying and these men were innocent, many of them must have had an alibi for the night in question. Why did none of them produce it? So, on my conspiracy theory, no oligarchic coup followed the mutilation of the herms because the surviving hot-heads were in exile, and the hardcore oligarchs were biding their time.

ALCIBIADES' DEFECTION

The profanation of the Mysteries was presumably not supposed to become known outside the closed circle of the clubs, but the mutilation of the herms was a public, shocking act, with sinister political nuances. Alcibiades' enemies, led by a certain Androcles, did a good job of persuading the Athenians that illegally performing the Mysteries – the only crime for which Alcibiades had been denounced – was as politically subversive as mutilating the herms. The two acts became so confused in people's minds that not much more than fifty years later, in the course of summarizing Alcibiades' chequered career, Demosthenes mistakenly said that he had mutilated the herms.

No doubt as a result of Androcles' efforts, the two scandals together were taken, according to Thucydides, to be part of 'an oligarchic and tyrannical conspiracy', wording that can refer only to Alcibiades. Androcles must have reminded the Athenians of the rumours that Alcibiades aspired to tyranny, and spiced the tale with the suggestion that all these pseudo-Eleusinian rites served a common purpose, to unite powerful men behind the banner of Alcibiades. In August an official ship was sent to find him in southern Italy and bring him home to stand trial. Alcibiades knew straight away that he would never return to Athens and, in a gesture that combined bitterness towards Athens with an olive branch towards Sparta, he immediately began to undermine Athenian interests in Sicily. On the way home, while the ship was docked in Thurii, Alcibiades and his closest friends disappeared.

Alcibiades was tried *in absentia* and condemned to death; on hearing of the sentence, he is reported to have said: 'I'll show them I'm alive.' His property was confiscated and auctioned off (as was that of all the other condemned exiles), and the details inscribed as a permanent warning on marble stelae and set up in the shrine of the Eleusinian goddesses in Athens. The sale of the confiscated property of the dead or exiled men took about eighteen months, but it was worth it: the state raised the equivalent of a year's imperial tribute; Oeonias's property alone fetched over eighty-one talents. In the world's first celebrity clothing auction, twenty-two of Alcibiades' gowns were sold.

He and the others implicated in mocking the Mysteries were subjected to an awesome, public curse, pronounced by priests and priestesses as they 'stood facing west [the direction of the infernal gods] and shook out their purple garments'. There was no place for Alcibiades now in Athens, not even a house for him to shelter in, and the curse specifically barred him from the Agora and Athenian cult shrines, as well as threatening any Athenian who came in contact with him with lethal pollution. And so he resurfaced in Elis, in the north-western Peloponnese, but soon made his way to Sparta, once he had extracted a guarantee of safe conduct from the Spartan authorities: he had, after all, done his best in the recent past to bring them to their knees.

His choice of Sparta was, surprisingly, not unambiguous treachery, above all because the two states were supposed to be at peace at the time. Alcibiades' family had traditionally held the *proxenia* of Sparta in Athens, the perks of which were not just prestige at home, but also a place of protection in the foreign state. In any case, he had *xenoi* there, and it was relatively normal for aristocrats to prefer the demands of guest-friendship to those of patriotism. But in the course of the speech in which he persuaded the Spartan authorities to make him welcome, Alcibiades said – and there is no reason to think that his sadness was not sincere – that democracy had corrupted Athens until it was no longer a place to which he owed allegiance. The argument may seem sophistic, but it was one which would have struck a chord with many Athenian aristocrats at the time; and aristocrats all over the Greek world were prepared to betray their city into the hands of a foreign, occupying power, if that was the price of their holding political power. Nor was Alcibiades the only one to defect to Sparta. He was accompanied there by some of his closest political allies (including Alcibiades of Phegous), and other Athenian oligarchs spent their years of exile either there or in Spartan-held Deceleia.

Alcibiades sweetened his not entirely welcome arrival in Sparta with some advice. First, he helped them decide to send help to Syracuse; second, though the matter had long been discussed in the councils of the Peloponnesian League, he added his weight as a high-profile defector to the idea that the Spartans should occupy somewhere in Athenian territory, to match the Athenians' continuing occupation of Pylos; rather than invade for only a few weeks at a time, as they had done in the first phase of the war, they could have a permanent base. At Alcibiades' suggestion, Deceleia was the site chosen for this fortress, though it was not fortified till 413 because by then war between Athens and Sparta had resumed. Deceleia was only about twenty-two kilometres from Athens and, once the Spartans had fortified and garrisoned it, they could threaten Athenian farmland on a permanent basis, and could interrupt the straightforward route from fertile Euboea, so that supplies instead had to be transported by boat around Sunium. The Spartan presence there also made it possible for thousands of Athenian slaves to run away from farms, but especially from the silver mines of Laurium, where appalling conditions gave the slaves working in the galleries and tunnels little to hope for. The restriction of income from the mines was a bad blow for Athens.

There is evidence, though not of an especially convincing kind, that Alcibiades spent some time in Thebes (a Spartan ally) and Thessaly.

These visits could only be fitted into this period of his life, so perhaps he went there on some kind of mission on behalf of the Spartans: his skills at negotiation were recognized. Otherwise, he was relatively idle between 415 and 413, the two years he spent in Sparta, and for a man of his restless energy it must have been a frustrating period. But he had plenty of time to make enemies, specifically of one of the two Spartan kings, Agis II. The only reason given in our sources for the rift sounds suspiciously like gossip:

> While King Agis was out of the country on campaign, Alcibiades set about seducing his wife Timaea, and he was so successful that not only did she get pregnant with his child, but she did not even deny it. The boy she gave birth to was called Leotychidas in public, but in private the child's name, as whispered by the mother to her friends and serving-women, was Alcibiades. That is how infatuated the woman was. As for Alcibiades, he used to say, in his wilful fashion, that it was not defiance or lust that had led him to do it, but rather because he wanted his descendants to rule over the Spartans.

There may be some truth to the story: the combination of sexual conquest, high ambition and arrogance sounds like Alcibiades. And it is true that Leotychidas was later refused the kingship on the grounds that he was not his father's child (though that does not necessarily make him Alcibiades' bastard); and that Spartan culture permitted what Paul Cartledge has described as 'the (to an Athenian) surprising availability of Spartan wives for extra-marital sex'; and that Alcibiades was just the man to take advantage of this. So who knows?

SEVEN

The End of the War

The uncomfortable truth was that, after the Sicilian catastrophe, the Athenians were on the ropes. They were in no position to prevent the Spartans, with Persian help, from turning the Aegean and the Hellespont, which up until then had been safe waters for Athenian patrols, into the main theatres for the final phase of the war (413–404). The Persians saw an opportunity to recover their Greek subjects on the Asia Minor coast, which had been lost to the Athenian alliance since 479. Dissatisfied Athenian allies began to secede with increasing regularity and Spartan encouragement. Most Athenian manoeuvres in the Aegean had the defensive purposes of recovering dissident allies and keeping open the trade route through the Hellespont.

The Spartans finally made use of Alcibiades in 412, following the arrival in Sparta of delegations from several of Athens's most important subject states, with a view to secession. Foremost among the would-be rebels was the island of Chios, with its own fleet of sixty warships, and the oligarchic Chians' plea was supported by representatives of Tissaphernes, the satrap of what the Persians called Sparda (roughly, Lydia, Lycia and Caria), with its capital at Sardis. At the same time, agents of the other Persian satrap in Asia Minor, Pharnabazus II of Phrygia, arrived to suggest an alternative strategy: that the Spartans develop a Hellespontine fleet, to threaten the trade route from the Black Sea. Both satraps were prepared to offer the Spartans cash to develop and maintain a fleet, with which they could contest the Aegean or the Hellespont; both wanted to please their king by being responsible for bringing down the Athenian empire.

The Spartans chose to focus first on central Asia Minor. Alcibiades was sent out to Chios to encourage the oligarchs there, and to stir up rebellion against Athens in the Asiatic Greek towns. Endius and his other friends in Sparta were happy to see him removed from the immediate reach of King Agis's growing hostility. Within a few weeks, several Athenian allies had rebelled, including the important port cities of Miletus and Ephesus and the island of Lesbos. Tissaphernes was impressed by Alcibiades' diplomatic skills, and renewed his promise of money.

A measure of the Athenians' anxiety and bankruptcy was that they chose this moment to break into a special fund of one thousand talents which had been set aside at the beginning of the war for use only in the direst emergency. In 413 they had also replaced the annual payment of tribute by their allies with a five per cent tax on all maritime trade within the empire. The strategically placed island of Samos, with its excellent harbours and bays, had long been the Athenians' main base in the Aegean, but now they had greater plans for it. Once they had got the local democrats to overthrow the long-standing oligarchy, they sent a fleet of about seventy-five ships there, with the fifteen thousand oarsmen, marines and other crewmen required to keep such a fleet operational. Samos became a second Athens.

The Athenians soon succeeded in recovering Lesbos and some of the Asiatic Greek towns (though not Miletus), and even blockaded Chios. This was hardly the widespread rebellion in the Aegean that the Spartans had hoped to see, and that Alcibiades had promised. Late in 412 Agis ordered Astyochus, the Spartan commander at Miletus, to have the Athenian put to death, making him the only person to be condemned to death by both sides in the war. Alcibiades got wind of the threat and took refuge in Sardis with his new friend Tissaphernes, who had also recently fallen out with the Spartans over the precise wording of the prospective treaty between them. They got on so well together that the satrap named his favourite *paradeisos* (an estate combining parkland, orchards, woodland and hunting-grounds) after the Athenian.

ALCIBIADES' INTRIGUES

Alcibiades now embarked upon perhaps the most risky and devious scheme of his entire life. First, he had to persuade Tissaphernes to moderate his support for the Spartans. Under the circumstances, Tissaphernes was inclined to listen as Alcibiades revealed that the Spartans were already considering the possibility of simply replacing the Athenian empire with one of their own. Athens had shown all Greeks the enormous rewards that empire could bring, and even ascetic, militaristic Sparta was prepared to be corrupted. Alcibiades' suggestion, then, which met with a willing response from the satrap, was that Tissaphernes should do his best to play the two Greek powers off against each other, so that even the eventual winner of the war would be so exhausted that it would be in no position to retain the Asiatic Greek cities coveted by the Persians.

So much for phase one. Phase two involved negotiating with the Athenian generals on Samos. Presenting his advice to Tissaphernes as proof of his loyalty to Athens (since the Spartans would not be receiving so much help from the Persian), Alcibiades gave them the impression that Tissaphernes was his to command and told them that he could bring him over to the Athenian side – but only if the democracy was replaced by an oligarchy. Persian policy here coincided with Alcibiades' personal concerns: he was rapidly running out of places to stay, but he could be more certain of a safe haven in Athens without the democracy that had cursed and banished him. He found enough receptive ears among the leading Athenians on Samos for an oligarchic conspiracy to be formed on the island. So far, so good for Alcibiades: the prospect of defeat had made the Athenians desperate, and even the democrats on Samos, fronted by Thrasybulus of Steiria (a friend of Alcibiades), were prepared to sacrifice at least some of the institutions of democracy if the result was the survival of Athens.

The leader of the Athenian oligarchs on Samos was Alcibiades' friend Peisander. He had come to the island not as a general, but as a trierarch, responsible for financing and taking charge of a warship for a year. But Phrynichus of Deiradiotae resisted the plan; despite being a committed oligarch, he was an enemy of Alcibiades and did not want to see him restored to Athens. Alcibiades accordingly fabricated a tale (which found its way into Thucydides' narrative as fact) that Phrynichus was planning to betray the Athenians on Samos to Astyochus, the Spartan commander, and Phrynichus was sent back to Athens.

So the conspiracy on Samos prospered within the Athenian high command, and even Athens was going to be an easier nut to crack than it might have been before the Sicilian expedition. In 413, in the immediate wake of the Sicilian disaster, crypto-oligarchs in Athens had successfully pushed for the appointment of a permanent board of ten elders (including the eighty-four-year-old playwright Sophocles), independent of either the lottery or annual election. The board had uncertain emergency powers (they were called *probouloi*, 'preliminary advisers', so perhaps they took over some of the work of the Council), and the oligarchs hoped that this would pave the way for further limitations of democracy. At the same time, the slogan became current that what was needed was a return to the *patrios politeia*, the 'ancestral constitution', or 'constitution of our fathers'. Although this vague phrase was flexible enough to suit a wide spectrum of political persuasions, it sounded like a return to the good old days – at least to the Cleisthenic model of a blend of aristocracy and democracy.

Under these circumstances, the oligarchs might have thought that things were moving of their own accord in their preferred direction, so that they had no need of violence, but at the same time they could not overlook the fact that they had a good opportunity. The war in the Aegean was finely balanced, especially since early in 411 the Spartans persuaded the main states of the wealthy island of Rhodes to defect from the Athenians, and the prospect of gaining the upper hand with the help of Tissaphernes' cash would be a persuasive argument in the Assembly. At the same time, resentment was fast building up among the Athenian rich, who were of course potential recruits for the oligarchic cause, since they were the ones who would emerge with full political rights and access to resources. The renewed war effort was milking them of their cash and capital, just when they were incapable of profiting from their land thanks to the Spartan fortification of Deceleia; the desertion of slaves also hit both landowners and businessmen, and they still had liturgies to fulfil and war tax to pay. The knights (roughly, the second wealthiest class in Athens) were also likely supporters of an oligarchic coup: many knights had been politicized in the 420s as a result of a prolonged and bitter rivalry with Cleon.

So it was with cautious hope that Peisander led a delegation of Athenian oligarchs from Samos to Athens at the end of February 411. No doubt they found the city awash with rumours and in a state of high tension: news of events on Samos would have reached the city from Phrynichus, if from no other source. There was no point in dissembling, so they addressed the Assembly relatively frankly: recall Alcibiades, and Persian funds will support our war effort and we can quickly win the war; in order to achieve this, 'a different form of democracy', as they delicately put it, will be required. Also, public pay should be restricted to troops on active service, and not made available for service on committees and juries at home – a fiscal measure Peisander presented as wartime belt-tightening, but pay for public service was an essential plank of the democracy, since it enabled the poorer members of society to take part. At first, the Assembly hesitated, with Alcibiades' enemies and the officials of the Eleusinian cult particularly vociferous, but Peisander won them over: the possibility of Persian cash trumped every protest in bankrupt Athens. The Assembly voted to send Peisander with nine others to negotiate with Alcibiades and Tissaphernes in Sardis.

All this might seem pusillanimous on the part of the Assembly, the heart of Athenian democracy, but they were a less strident, more weary and more bewildered majority than they had been a few years earlier, disinclined to privilege ideology over either ending the war or getting paid for their military service. They knew they were voting for an oligarchy, but even the loss of some rights was preferable to the hazards of a lingering war. Besides, Peisander and the others were talking about a broad oligarchy of five thousand full citizens, selected on the criterion of their wealth, and also hinted that this was just an emergency measure – that once the war was won democracy would be restored. The Athenian people, or those who remained in the city and were not stationed on Samos, chose to believe them.

At the same time, however, Peisander was working more surreptitiously: he made the rounds of the clubs, encouraging them to unite and to support the oligarchic cause. He also linked up with the hardcore oligarchs who emerged as the chief architects of the coming coup – the orator Antiphon of Rhamnous, Theramenes of Steiria and the otherwise unknown Aristarchus of Deceleia. Shortly afterwards, the clubs began a campaign of terror, intimidation and the occasional assassination of prominent democrats and opponents of Alcibiades, including Androcles, the man who had worked hardest for his downfall after the mocking of the Eleusinian Mysteries. Fear pervaded meetings of the Assembly and Council, since no one knew who the murderers were and everyone knew what might happen to those who spoke out against Alcibiades or against Peisander's proposals.

Leaving Athens in safe hands, then, Peisander headed the delegation to Sardis, to report on progress on Samos and in Athens, and to bring back details of Tissaphernes' promised support. However straightforward this mission might have seemed, things did not go at all well. Having decided to let both Sparta and Athens exhaust each other, without favouring either side, Tissaphernes was not pleased at being asked to change his mind and support just one side. With Alcibiades as his mouthpiece, Tissaphernes made outrageous demands that the Athenians could never agree to – the return of not just the Asiatic Greek cities, but also some of the islands, and a free hand to patrol the coastline with Persian warships, which had been banned this far west for fifty years. The conference achieved nothing, except to cause a momentous breach between Alcibiades and Peisander, especially dangerous since Tissaphernes was still flirting with the Spartans. On his way back to Athens, Peisander stopped at Samos, where his failure in Sardis alienated Thrasybulus, who still favoured Alcibiades' return (and the promise of Persian cash and an end to the war), but no longer as part of an oligarchic package.

Most of the oligarchic conspirators had a dream: oligarchy in Athens was just the first step towards establishing sympathetic oligarchies elsewhere, as a way of patching up the tattered empire. And so, while Peisander went to Athens to foment oligarchy there, others travelled around the Aegean on equivalent missions. In this way the revolution of 411 contributed directly towards the loss of the Athenian empire and of the war. After the failure of the oligarchy in Athens, most of the new oligarchic governments elsewhere in the empire remained in place, and inevitably turned to Sparta for support.

OLIGARCHY IN ATHENS

Peisander was back in Athens by the end of May. In delivering their report to the Assembly, he and his colleagues suppressed the failure of the Sardis conference and continued to insist that they and they alone could bring the war to a swift and successful conclusion. The Assembly was amenable to a proposal that a board of thirty – the ten *probouloi* and twenty others – should be created to think over the options. But when this new committee came to make its recommendations to the Assembly a few weeks later, the oligarchs arranged for the Assembly to meet not on the Pnyx as usual, but outside the city walls. With King Agis and his army based near by at Deceleia, this arrangement was designed to intimidate those who could not protect themselves in open countryside and who did not have the backing of the Spartans. Moreover, the site chosen for the Assembly, the precinct at Colonus of Poseidon of the Horses, had distinctly upper-class associations: the message of the Assembly was that government was changing in favour of the rich. The only recommendation the new committee put to this pseudo-Assembly was that any Athenian citizen could make any proposal he wanted, with impunity, even if – what had been expressly forbidden by Athenian law for a number of years – such a proposal were unconstitutional.

The proposal immediately made by Peisander, and passed, was oligarchic in nature: a new Council of Four Hundred was to be set up with full powers of government. The method of selection of the Four Hundred was also undemocratic: a committee of five, chosen by lot (but from among those present at Colonus), would select one hundred men, who would each co-opt three more. Official positions were to be limited to five thousand citizens of hoplite rank and above, so that pay for public service could be suspended, since the Five Thousand could afford to do without; and the Council of Four Hundred could convene the general Assembly of all citizens as and when it saw fit. In other words, the Four Hundred were to be the effective rulers of Athens, with the Five Thousand a sop to more moderate oligarchs and fence-sitters among the rich, while the Assembly, being entirely a tool of the Four Hundred, was a parody of the democratic Assembly. Moreover, it would be up to a special committee to conduct the census which would lead to the list of the Five Thousand – a process which could be prolonged indefinitely to keep the Four Hundred in power. For, to the Four Hundred, five thousand seemed little better than 'downright democracy'.

A few days later the oligarchs completed their coup. Supported by armed mercenaries, they took over the offices of the democratic Council, paid off the Councillors for the remainder of the year, and instituted the new Council of Four Hundred in their place. The oligarchs appeared to be well in control. They must have wanted to recall the post-415 exiles, but they had to find a way to do so without recalling Alcibiades, because they were no longer sure where Alcibiades stood.

Matters had not stood still on Samos. An attempted oligarchic coup on the island – part of the Athenian oligarchs' programme of establishing oligarchies all over the empire – had been defeated, and both the Samians and the Athenian troops set their faces firmly against oligarchy. When news reached Samos of the takeover in Athens of the Four Hundred, along with an exaggerated account of their terror tactics (which had been brought starkly home to those on Samos by the assassination there of Hyperbolus, who had retreated to the island after his ostracism), the leading Athenian democrats on the island made the troops swear to maintain democracy, to continue the war against Sparta, to be unremittingly hostile towards the oligarchy in Athens, and not to enter into any negotiations with them. The Athenian poor serving on Samos thus took the initiative which their comrades at home had been too cowed to take, and thereby made themselves into a kind of Athenian democratic government-in-exile.

Alcibiades had been the instigator of the oligarchic coup in Athens, and had expected to be one of them, but after his breach with Peisander the oligarchs went ahead without him. But personal safety was still uppermost in his mind; he still needed to get back to Athens. He now performed a volte-face as perfect as his earlier abandonment of Athens for Sparta – precisely the sort of behaviour that led to his enduring reputation as a chameleon. Knowing that Thrasybulus was sympathetic, he used him to deflect any further opposition. Thrasybulus won the main body of the army over to his side by convincing them that in Alcibiades lay their best hope of a speedy and profitable end to the war, and travelled to Sardis personally to bring Alcibiades back into the Athenian fold. Having taken upon themselves the right, as the only Athenian democratic government, to elect their own generals, they appointed Alcibiades to join the others they had chosen. Alcibiades the would-be oligarch thus re-emerged as a general of the democracy.

Shortly after his return, in the summer of 411, envoys arrived from the oligarchs in Athens. Despite their conciliatory message, the troops wanted to lynch them and sail straight for Athens to topple the oligarchs. Alcibiades must have been tempted, since victory over the oligarchs would have elevated him to undisputed leadership of Athens, but he recognized that it would mean abandoning the Aegean to the Spartans, and the last thing Alcibiades wanted right then was for Sparta to gain such a decisive advantage in the war; after all, one of the Spartan kings had tried to have him assassinated already. Thucydides calls Alcibiades' restraining of the troops an act of patriotism, and the noblest thing Alcibiades ever did, but it is not hard to discern his usual self-interest.

Instead, still acting as the official democratic government, the Athenians on Samos sent a message to Athens, demanding that the Four Hundred stand down immediately in favour of the Five Thousand. The combination of the threat from Samos and Spartan successes in the Hellespont and Propontis (they had gained the strategic towns of Abydus and Byzantium) threw the Athenian oligarchs into disarray. Theramenes saw the writing on the wall and put his not inconsiderable weight behind the moderates and realists among the Four Hundred, who were urging that the list of the Five Thousand should be published sooner rather than later.

The extremists' reaction, however, was extreme: Peisander, Antiphon, Phrynichus and others chose to call in the enemy rather than lose control. They sent a secret delegation to arrange this, but it was too late: always a fragile alliance of different factions, the Four Hundred rapidly lost their grip on the city. Phrynichus was publicly stabbed to death in the Agora. A Spartan fleet sailed close to Athens, expecting to find Piraeus opened by their friends, or the city torn apart by civil strife and easy prey. But the moderates and democrats rose up in the defence of Piraeus, and then marched on Athens, not to fight, but to force the Four Hundred to keep their promise of drawing up the list of the favoured Five Thousand.

The Spartan fleet turned its attention to its secondary target, the island of Euboea, which had been poised to rebel since the Sicilian catastrophe; they defeated a scratch Athenian fleet, and made it possible for the entire island to secede. The Athenians were dismayed not just by the loss of this island, right on their doorstep, but by their danger. The main Athenian fleet was on Samos: the Spartans could have blockaded Piraeus and either forced the city to submit, or tempted the Samian fleet to defend Athens at the cost of leaving the Aegean undefended. But the Spartans failed to seize the opportunity; Thucydides sarcastically described them as the most helpful enemies Athens could have had. But in the longer term, the worst thing was that Euboea had been one of the main sources of grain for the city, and now the Athenians were increasingly dependent on grain from the Black Sea – and the shipping route through the Hellespont was a fragile basket in which to have all one's eggs.

The last remaining support in Athens for the Four Hundred was eroded by the knowledge that the extremists had intended to betray the city to save their skins, and by the fact that they had failed to protect the city's supply of grain. People wanted a rapid victory, not an end to the war at any cost. The Assembly met to transfer power to the Five Thousand, defined now not by means of the still unpublished list, but as all those who could afford their own hoplite equipment (in reality, closer to nine thousand). By taking this decision, the Assembly re-established itself as the proper government of Athens. The old Council was brought back, and the rule of the Four Hundred was over after only four months. Peisander and other oligarchs fled to the Spartans at Deceleia or to the Boeotians; those who remained, such as Antiphon, were taken to court at the instigation of their erstwhile friend Theramenes and executed for treason. Phrynichus was posthumously cursed, his corpse was thrown out of the city, and those of his assassins who had been caught were released. 'The elite', comments

Josiah Ober, 'had proven unable to establish a stable, nondemocratic form of government in the face of their own tendency to intra-class competition, strong Athenian patriotism, and the developed political consciousness of the lower classes of Athenian political society.'

The rule of the hoplites lasted about eight months longer before succumbing to pressure from the oarsmen on Samos. Athens had endured its worst constitutional turmoil since the foundation of democracy almost a century earlier. On the restoration of democracy in 410, every male citizen was required to take a solemn oath that legitimized the killing of anyone who was opposed to democracy. The chief differences from the pre-coup democracy were that state pay for anything but armed service remained suspended, and a new Law Review Board was created, tasked with overhauling the Athenian laws and constitution, an initiative (one of only a handful that we know of) that had been started by the Five Thousand.

ALCIBIADES' RETURN

Even after he had been pardoned, Alcibiades chose not to return to Athens straight away. Along with some of the other exiles, he probably considered the situation in Athens still too volatile. After all, court cases were continuing against the remnants of the Four Hundred and their sympathizers, and it was Alcibiades who had originally pushed for the regime change. Even as late as 405 Aristophanes included in *Frogs*, in serious mode, a plea to forgive and forget, or at least to get on with the backlog of court cases: 'And suppose someone mistakenly fell for Phrynichus's tricks: in my opinion, those who slipped up then should be allowed to free themselves of the charges against them and be pardoned for their past errors.'

By not returning, however, Alcibiades remained on the margins of Athenian political life. Although he continued to fight for the Athenian cause, he did so as a maverick – as a kind of privateer who accepted orders from Athens, as Sir Walter Ralegh did from Elizabethan England. Nevertheless, the three or four years from 411 to 408 were the culmination of his military career, and his successes in battle were supported by his skill at raising money, which endeared him both to his troops and to the power-possessors back in Athens. The consequent increase in morale spiralled his successes in both spheres ever onward and upward.

Spartan gains in the Propontis shifted the theatre of war northwards, to Pharnabazus's domain. Athens's grain route through the Hellespont became the target of the attentions of the Spartans' Hellespontine fleet, based at Abydus. The Athenians responded by moving their own fleet to Sestus, and Alcibiades' help was critical in enabling the Athenian generals to inflict a defeat on the Spartans. This gave Theramenes the opportunity to get the Assembly to pardon Alcibiades and those who fled with him in 415; desperate for a saviour, the Athenian people forgave him his crimes. A little later, the Spartans broke out of Abydus in full force; they had decided to move the fleet to a more favourable location at Cyzicus, closer to Pharnabazus and supplies. Cyzicus was a critical Athenian possession in the Propontis, with strategic harbours facing both east and west, and the Athenian response was swift and effective. Within a couple of weeks, and again with Alcibiades' help, Cyzicus was safely in Athenian hands, and other former or current Athenian allies hastened to affirm their loyalty. Athens had survived another crisis, and it seemed that Alcibiades could not set a foot wrong.

With Byzantium still in Spartan hands, the Athenians fortified Chrysopolis and imposed a whopping ten per cent tax on all shipping through the Bosporus, while Alcibiades freely raided and plundered Pharnabazus's territory. The Spartans approached Athens for peace, but urged on by the popular leader Cleophon, the Athenians rejected the olive branch, thinking they could win the war outright. The celebration of the four-yearly Great Panathenaea that summer was especially joyous and magnificent, and the Athenians used the opportunity to announce that allied tribute was to be reimposed (while the trade tax and the Bosporus tax remained in place). For the remainder of the year, Alcibiades continued to keep things under tight control in the Hellespont, so that the Aegean could once again become a field of operations for official Athenian commanders, in their continuing efforts to undo the losses of the mass rebellions of 412. But the Spartans achieved a notable success close to home in finally recovering Pylos.

Alcibiades was also trying to cap his military successes with a bold diplomatic coup – a Persian alliance with Athens, with Athens keeping her maritime empire, and turning a blind eye to Persian repossession of the Asiatic Greek cities (whereas Sparta would want them for itself). Athens and Persia were to carve up the world between them with the callousness of Roosevelt, Churchill and Stalin at the Yalta conference. This vision of Alcibiades' won over not just Tissaphernes, but eventually (under the pressure of Athenian military successes in the Hellespont) Pharnabazus, who in 408 sponsored a Greek delegation to the Persian king, Darius II, to talk over the possibility of making the vision real. Since the delegation included not just Persians and Athenians, but also Argives and renegade Spartans and Syracusans, the intention was plainly to follow the 'Peace of Alcibiades' with treaties with Athens's main enemies, once these renegades had seized power in their states. As part of the process, the Athenians tactfully welcomed into Athens the eastern deity, the Mother of the Gods, and the old Council House was rededicated as her shrine (the Metroön) and used as the office of the Law Review Board, and as the storehouse of the state archives, which now for the first time had a permanent home.

In 408 Alcibiades and Theramenes succeeded in regaining Byzantium. Throughout the Hellespont and Propontis, the Spartans now held only Abydus, and the Athenians were able to keep them bottled up there. Back in Athens Critias Callaeschrou formally proposed the recall of Alcibiades. Pausing only to sell prisoners of war in Caria, to raise funds to bring back home, Alcibiades returned early in 407 with the aura of a conquering hero who had turned around years of defeat. He gave conciliatory speeches to both Council and Assembly, but popular enthusiasm for his return could hardly have been higher. All the charges against him were dropped, the curses revoked, and he was given property to replace what had been confiscated in 415 and auctioned off. He was even awarded a golden crown by the grateful citizenry – a remarkable and very rare honour. He was elected general with full powers to make field decisions on his own without referring back to the Assembly.

Before setting out again for the front, Alcibiades brought off a typically ostentatious propaganda coup. The Eleusinian cult was extremely important to Athens's self-image and to its relationship with the gods, but, since the Spartan fortification and occupation of Deceleia, an essential aspect had been curtailed, as initiates skulked by boat along the coast to Eleusis, rather than enjoying the full roster of ceremonies involved in the proper land procession. But as a symbol of acceptance of his role as an official Athenian general, and in repentance for his earlier transgressions, Alcibiades provided an armed guard for the procession and it went ahead without interference from the Spartans.

At the same time, however, Alcibiades' enemies were hard at work. His popularity was so great that it was easy for them to claim that he still desired tyranny. And so his friends saw to it that he was bundled off again to the Aegean, burdened by the heavy weight of Athenian expectations, with a substantial force of fifteen hundred hoplites, 150 horsemen and a hundred ships under his command – about the same size as the first wave to Sicily, which Alcibiades was to have commanded. It was as if the Athenians were apologizing for depriving him of his earlier moment of glory.

But there was little for him to do. The Spartan fleet, such as it was (though there was a major rebuilding programme going on), was pinned in Abydus and Chios, and Alcibiades had to keep his troops off Persian territory in order not to jeopardize the embassy to Darius, which had still not returned from its distant destination. But the embassy came to nothing: even as it was on its way to Susa, it met a Spartan delegation on its way back, who no doubt took great delight in informing the Athenians that it was they who had secured Persian support for their side. The king was sending his younger son, Cyrus (still only sixteen years old at the time), to Asia Minor to make sure that the Spartans won the war. The new Spartan commander in the region, Lysander, as good a diplomat as a field commander, ingratiated himself with Cyrus, to make sure that he kept his promise to supply the Spartans with pay better than either Tissaphernes or Pharnabazus had done.

As rapidly as Alcibiades' star had risen, so it fell once again. His enemies in Athens loudly denounced his failure and began to reverse the swing of the pendulum of popular opinion: not only had he achieved no military successes that year, but the emptiness of his promises as regards the Persians had finally been exposed. The Athenian people were uncertain. In their hearts, they knew they were losing the war, and this made them desperate. The problem was that it looked as though their saviour would use his charisma and popularity for tyrannical purposes.

Early in 406 Alcibiades left the fleet at Notium in the hands of his lieutenant, who was tempted into a battle with Lysander, and was soundly beaten, with the loss of fifteen ships. Along with a minor setback on land at Cyme, this was enough to shatter the fragile myth of Alcibiades' invincibility, on which his prestige at Athens depended. His enemies said he spent his time whoring instead of fighting; they said he wanted Pharnabazus to install him as tyrant of Athens. Cleophon called for Alcibiades' deposition and impeachment and, just a few months after his triumphant return, Alcibiades prudently withdrew to his mini-kingdom on the Thracian Chersonese (the Gallipoli peninsula). The Athenians banished him once again. Those who deal with spin rather than reality are eventually unmasked; Alcibiades wanted to be the meteoric hero Achilles, but turned out to be wily Odysseus.

Alcibiades' connections with Thrace are obscure, but they may date back at least to 416, when in his play *Baptae*, one of the targets of which was Alcibiades, the comic poet Eupolis referred scathingly to Athenian *baptae* ('dippers'), or practitioners of the ecstatic rites of the Thracian goddess Kotys or Kotyto. At some point an Odrysian warlord had given him estates and castles on the Chersonese, where he now went. If he could not be top dog in Athens, he could at least rule his own domain as a kind of piratical princeling. He never saw Athens again.

THE END OF THE WAR

Having got rid of the man who, for all his waywardness, was one of their chief military assets, the Athenians continued on the same self-destructive course. A few months later, two of the Athenian generals for 406, including the capable Conon, found themselves blockaded, with almost the entire Aegean fleet of seventy ships, in Mytilene on Lesbos. The Spartan commander Callicratidas was fulfilling his promise to 'stop Conon having his way with my sea'. A ship broke through the blockade to take an urgent message to Athens for reinforcements, and it was a sign of Athenian desperation that for all their consciousness of status they offered full citizenship to any slave or metic who would help defend the city by manning ships; even men of the cavalry class put aside their harnesses and took to the oars, and all the remaining eight generals accompanied the fleet. And it is a measure of their resourcefulness that they managed within a month to put together a fleet of 110 ships.

When this fleet, further reinforced by forty allied ships, was spotted by Callicratidas, he left fifty ships to continue the blockade at Mytilene and sailed out with the rest, still some 120 ships, to do battle off the Arginusae islands (a group of small islands between Lesbos and the Asia Minor coast). It was, in the opinion of at least one ancient historian, 'the greatest sea battle ever fought by Greeks against Greeks'. The Athenians crushed the Spartans and then divided their own forces: while the generals sailed to the relief of Mytilene, Theramenes and Thrasybulus, as trierarchs, were detailed to pick up survivors from the twenty-five or so Athenian ships that had been lost. A storm prevented

Bust of Socrates. A Roman copy of a lost Greek bronze original, and fairly typical of the genre. Socrates became instantly identifiable by his looks and somewhat pugnacious demeanour, though this bust slightly downplays his ugliness. Known to scholars as 'Type B' Socrates busts, they may stem from an original by Lysippus, one of the most famous sculptors of the fourth century BCE.

Good busts of Alcibiades are surprisingly rare, given his ubiquity in our literary sources. This one, a Roman copy of a Greek original, preserves something of his virile good looks, but makes him look far more Roman than Athenian.

This wonderful sculpture has been attributed to Antonio Canova (1757–1822) and Bertel Thorvaldsen (1770–1844), but is perhaps the work of Lorenzo Bartolini (1777–1850). Drawing on the Platonic tradition, that Socrates was the only one who could save Alcibiades from the snares of the world, here a very stern Socrates summons, by force of personality alone, a reluctant Alcibiades from the arms of two young women.

A well-preserved herm from about 550 BCE. Herms were placed at change-over points such as crossroads and doorways. The erect phallus was apotropaic: the herm warded off bad luck and so ensured prosperity for the street or building. They were especially common in Athens, and their mutilation in May 415 BCE was an act of outrageous sacrilege, probably carried out as part of a failed oligarchic coup.

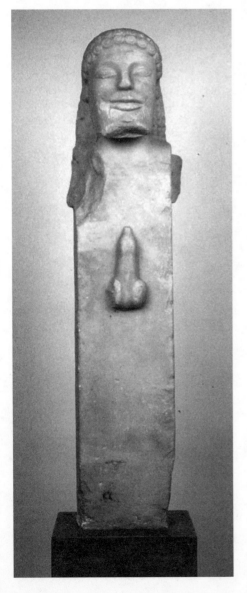

These unassuming ostraka are of fascinating historical value. They are the only ones that have been found with the name of our Alcibiades, dating from the 416 ostracism. Ostraka are broken pieces of pottery, and the names of the candidates for ostracism were written on them. Provided at least 6,000 such votes were cast, the man with the most votes was sent into exile for 10 years. Alcibiades was a candidate, but avoided being sent into exile.

Giambettino Cignaroli, *Death of Socrates*. Cignaroli (1718–1770), from Verona, painted this work in the Neoclassical style in the early 1760s for Count Karl Firmian, then the Austrian governor of Lombardy (Upper Italy), who was a keen ancient historian and patron of the arts. It was originally paired with a *Death of Cato*.

their doing so, but it was nothing compared with the storm that broke over their heads back in Athens.

Disheartened by the loss of as many as five thousand men, the Athenian people stripped the eight generals of their positions and summoned them home to give an account of their actions. This was relatively normal procedure in democratic Athens, but two of the generals chose self-imposed exile over what might greet them back home. The remaining six (who included the same-named son of Pericles) gave their report to the Council and, whatever else they said, they tried to save themselves by pinning responsibility for the failure to pick up the survivors on the two trierarchs. Theramenes and Thrasybulus launched a furious counter-attack: they simply read out the official report sent back to Athens immediately after the battle by the generals themselves, which showed that the storm was the only reason for the failure to recover the floundering sailors. The generals responded that in all fairness, then, they could not be blamed either, since the storm was responsible.

The next day a festival caused a lull in these tense proceedings, and Theramenes resorted to sly tactics. He had the relatives of the dead mingle among the crowds at the festival in their mourning clothes, and whip up anger against the generals. When the Assembly reconvened after the festival, he had one of his stooges introduce the proposal that the assembled people should immediately proceed to a verdict on the generals, since they had heard all the evidence and the speeches at the previous Assembly. Others argued that this was unconstitutional and they had a good case: the speeches the generals had previously been allowed fell well short of the length allowed at a proper trial; they should be tried, one by one, in a court, not by the Assembly. Even by the generous standards of the Athenian legal system, Theramenes' proposal should have been tolerable only if the generals' guilt was so evident that normal rules could be set aside. But his tactics had worked well, and the mass of the people, presumably prompted by more of his stooges, cried out that 'it was intolerable not to let the people do what they wish'. They also silenced the generals' supporters by threatening to include them along with the generals in the mass guilty-or-innocent verdict.

This was the culmination of decades of popular sovereignty: the people should be allowed to do whatever they wanted to do, even if it was unconstitutional bullying. As it turned out, it was the last gasp of such radical democracy, but that was no consolation to the victims then. The final stage of the frenzy saw the proposal – for an immediate verdict on all the generals – put to the vote. It was always the job of the chairman of the prytany to do this, and on this particular day Socrates was the chairman. He of all people was bound to resist: as one who believed that it took both time and calm reasoning to reach the truth, he could not tolerate this hasty procedure. He refused to put the motion to the vote, and had to put up with the abuse of the crowd. But prytany chairmanship lasted only a single day, and it was already late afternoon. The next day a last-ditch attempt to apply common justice was overridden, and the Arginusae Six were found guilty and executed. Before long, however, remorse over these hasty actions led to retaliation against some of those who had instigated them.

After Alcibiades' retirement to Thrace, Athenian naval hopes were pinned on Conon, but Lysander refused to be drawn into another set battle, and preferred to strike in safety against Athens-bound merchant ships and the occasional pro-Athenian town in Asia Minor. Morale was very low among the Athenians both at home and on Samos. When the brilliant Spartan general crowned a series of military and diplomatic victories by taking Lampsacus in 405 and making it his base, the Athenians set up camp at Aegospotami, on the opposite coastline. In the meantime, they gathered supplies from Sestus, twenty-five or so kilometres west down the coast.

Alcibiades' domain was nearby, and there is a story that he spoke to the Athenian generals at Aegospotami, offering help in the form of Thracian troops, and advice to the effect that their position was risky: the men had to roam far to find supplies, and the anchorage there was not suitable; Sestus would be a better location in these respects, and they could still keep an eye on Lysander from there. In return for the help and the advice, he wanted joint command of the Athenian troops – to be the same kind of freelance commander he had been between 411 and 408, the period of his greatest successes. Naturally, he received a curt brush-off: 'We are in command now, not you.'

A few days later, as Alcibiades (in this story) had predicted, Lysander attacked when the men were dispersed. Almost the entire Athenian fleet was captured or destroyed, and the Spartans took three thousand prisoners, though many others fled overland, while Conon and a few ships escaped by sea. It was the end of the war, and in short order Lysander dismantled what was left of the Athenian empire; only the Samians held out for a few months, fired perhaps by the recent gesture of the Athenians in granting them citizenship equivalence, in recognition of their loyalty and role in restoring the democracy in 410. Elsewhere, Lysander ordered all Athenian citizens home (to increase pressure on the soon-to-be-starving city), blocked the grain route (partly by threatening any ship's captain who took grain to Athens with summary execution), and early in 404 appeared with 150 ships off Piraeus itself. No food could get through, and before long Athens was in the grip of a terrible famine. In the besieged city they remembered how they had slaughtered the men of Scione and Melos, and expected the same treatment themselves.

Both Spartan kings took to the field, and Peloponnesian forces camped just outside Athens, within easy view of the walls. Starved of both grain and allies, the Athenians had no choice but to negotiate. There was a division of opinion among their enemies, but in the end Lysander got his way over the ephors (the senior Spartan officials) and Spartan allies: Athens was to lose not all its fortifications – the city walls were to survive – but only the Long Walls that joined the city to the harbour, and the Piraeus defences. Without its lifeline to Piraeus, Athens would never be in a position to recover its empire. Its fleet of warships was limited to a mere twelve; the empire was formally dissolved; the pro-Spartan oligarchs exiled after the coup of 411 were to be allowed back; and the Athenians were, in the time-honoured phraseology, to have the same friends and enemies as the Spartans and to follow their lead by land and sea wherever they might go. The Athenians bowed to the inevitable and accepted these terms. The walls were demolished amid scenes of celebration and the music of pipe-girls: 'People thought that this day marked the beginning of freedom for Greece,' remarked Xenophon, betraying his pro-Spartan and oligarchic proclivities.

ALCIBIADES' MURDER

One person who did not live long enough to see whether or not this promise of freedom was fulfilled was Alcibiades. He was assassinated later in the year in Phrygia, on his way to the new Persian king, Artaxerxes II, partly to find a haven away from the long reach of the Spartans (by betraying to the king details of the intrigues of his brother Cyrus, who would soon launch an attempt, made famous by Xenophon, to seize the Persian throne for himself), and partly, perhaps, to start to build a new power-base from which to continue his mission of seeking international glory. At any rate, that was what his enemies were afraid of: although we will never know who killed him and why – and it may even have had less to do with politics than with a sordid tale of adultery – suspicion falls most readily on the new rulers of Athens, who needed to make sure that Alcibiades could do them no harm, remembering perhaps that he and their rival, Thrasybulus, had long been expedient allies.

Thucydides distributed blame for the downfall of Athens between Alcibiades and the Athenian people. But was Alcibiades responsible for Athens's defeat? Yes, if we think that Nicias and the Athenian doves in 421 had a chance to make the peace stick for any meaningful length of time; yes, but indirectly, if we think Alcibiades could have conquered Sicily and that this would have won the war for Athens; yes, if we think that his advice to Sparta while resident there was at all significant; yes, given that the oligarchic coups around the empire in 411, which he indirectly triggered, weakened the empire.

But perhaps we should not be focusing on Alcibiades' *actions* during the war. After all, Athenian stupidity, over-reaching and incompetence, Persian cash, the brilliance of one or two of the enemy commanders, the plague and the universal hazards and expenses of war were far more potent factors. But this is less important than the fact that, not long before his death, it was widely believed 'that he alone was responsible for their past troubles, and that anything terrible that happened to the city in the future would likely be initiated by him alone'. And this judgement was due not to anything Alcibiades had done or had failed to do, but to something less tangible. The Athenians were aware that their defeat had in large part been due to internal conflict, and Alcibiades seemed to epitomize and even be responsible for such conflict. His private life and his personal ambitions were so extreme and manipulative that they inevitably provoked reaction, at just the time when Athens could least afford it and needed to focus its energies on winning the war. The 'Alcibiades syndrome', as it has been called, is that he preferred personal advantage to public interest, and encouraged others to do so as well.

So Alcibiades – the brilliant, flamboyant, chameleonic, greedy, narcissistic Alcibiades – was dead, but he lived on as an archetype of wasted talent in the minds of Socrates and his associates. The image that remained in the minds of the Athenian people was also of waste, but perhaps it was theirs. Could they have made more use of him? But Alcibiades' good points came in the same package as his bad points, and so they were always ambivalent: 'They miss him, they hate him, they want him by their side,' as Aristophanes said, and summed up the problem in a famous metaphor: 'It's best not to rear a lion cub in the city, but if you do, pander to his moods.' The problem was that pandering to Alcibiades' moods would have spelled the end of the democracy. Centuries after his death he got the reward he always wanted in his lifetime, when the Roman emperor Hadrian instituted a sacrificial ritual at the site of his murder in Phrygia.

EIGHT

Critias and Civil War

The negotiations that led to the terms of Athens's surrender were oddly prolonged. Theramenes arranged to be sent to negotiate with Lysander, and let it be known that he was holding a major trump card, which he could not reveal in advance for fear of devaluing it. Whatever it was, it had to be powerful enough to keep Lysander from destroying the city and enslaving the population, which is what the most important Spartan allies were pushing for. It is a measure of Theramenes' authority in the city in these troubled times that, perhaps somewhat gullibly, the Athenians appointed him their ambassador with full powers to make peace, and he set out for Samos, where Lysander was supervising the blockade of the town and port. Theramenes went alone, but Lysander already had notable Athenian exiles in his camp, including Charicles, Aristotle of Thorae and Critias, all previous allies of Theramenes as oligarchs and friends of Alcibiades.

Theramenes did not return for three months, and then came empty-handed, saying that Athens's fate had to be decided by the proper authorities in Sparta, not by their brilliant but maverick commander. In order to explain his long absence and his failure, he claimed that Lysander had detained him. But it does not seem likely that the 'detention' was anything but amicable, and it is distinctly possible that senior Athenian oligarchs had spent the time assembling on the island from their various places of exile, to discuss the immediate future. Since this conference took place under Lysander's aegis, they must have looked to Lysander to help them to power. And no doubt their discussions were leisurely, because it was in all of their interests to wait until starvation put pressure on the Athenians to come to terms. Theramenes' trump card was the offer of oligarchic rule in Athens by men who would be loyal to Lysander if he managed to use his influence in the Peloponnesian League to get better terms for them.

So Theramenes and others went to Sparta, and returned with the terms outlined towards the end of the previous chapter. Meanwhile, on Lysander's orders, Cleophon, still resisting peace, was arrested on a trumped-up charge and put to death, and the clubs kept the population cowed by the fear of a resumption of their terror tactics of 411. This cleared the way for the Spartan insistence, as relayed to the Council and the Assembly by the oligarchs, that Athens should be governed from now on in accordance with the 'ancestral constitution' – the multivalent phrase that had become a slogan a few years previously. It seemed as though Athens was to be allowed the right of self-government, but as it turned out, the 'ancestral constitution' that was in store for the Athenians was hardly less oligarchic than, and certainly as brutal as, any of the puppet regimes Lysander was imposing on the Asiatic Greeks.

THE THIRTY

Athens was close to anarchy for a while. There was feuding in the courts, and no government to speak of, while the skeletal poor still slumped in the streets, and the rich reeled from the loss of all their foreign properties and argued that the democracy had been responsible for the war, and so now for all their suffering.

A committee was set up in April 404 to try to determine which version of the 'ancestral constitution' Athens would have. This committee proved so ineffective in the face of lobbying by the various factions that the oligarchs, with their confidence restored by the return of their exiled friends, appealed to Lysander. The democratically elected generals were deposed in August, and a temporary board was formed of five ephors ('overseers'), one of whom was Critias, to act as an interim government. The blatant borrowing of Spartan terminology for the members of this board was a sign of things to come. Lysander arrived in Athens in person from Samos in September and used the pretext of Athenian tardiness in carrying out the terms of the surrender to impose on the Athenians an oligarchy of thirty men.

The same whiff of a set-up surrounds the fact that in the Assembly that instituted the Thirty, Theramenes got to choose ten of the Thirty, Critias and his fellow ephors got to choose themselves and another five, and the final ten were chosen from among sympathizers present at the Assembly. Most of the Thirty were politically experienced men, and quite a few had played some part in either or both of the scandals of 415 and the oligarchy of 411; they were also mostly extreme oligarchs, since they had no intention of allowing dissension to split their ranks as it had those of the Four Hundred. A Council of the normal number of five hundred was appointed, but its members came from a select list of only one thousand men (rather than from the entire citizen body), and its job was only to ratify the measures proposed by the Thirty. The same goes for other appointments, such as the Board of Ten, headed by Charicles, that was put in charge of Piraeus. Positions on the Board of Eleven, responsible for executions and Athens's prisons, were also filled by supporters of the Thirty, and the city was policed by three hundred whip-bearing mercenaries (the same number of men as a Spartan king's bodyguard). Once Athens was in the safe hands of fifty-one committed oligarchs, the Spartans withdrew their troops from Athenian soil.

Left to their own devices, one of the first things the Thirty did was put an end to the political powers of the popular courts, by giving them back to the old Council of the Areopagus, to which all archons gained automatic entry at the end of their year of office. The removal of these powers from the Areopagus Council in the 460s had played an important part in extending the powers of the democracy in Athens. The Thirty also undermined the popular courts by trying the most notorious sycophants and putting them to death; although sycophants were an acknowledged menace (even if only to the rich), the elimination of sycophancy was another step towards taking the whole judicial system under central control. They also continued the work of tidying up the laws that had been initiated by the Five Thousand in 410, though the changes they wanted to see were those that suited an oligarchic constitution. These measures were portrayed as the first stages of the moral rearmament of Athens.

One of the few laws they passed was aimed at the perceived menace of rhetorical teaching: no one was to teach the 'art of words'. A similar desire for control can also be read off from the Thirty's reconstruction of the Pnyx, the meeting-place of the Assembly. Under the democracy, the speakers' platform had symbolically faced the sea, the source of political power for the poorest members of Athenian society, who manned the navy; as part of their overhaul of the Pnyx, the Thirty turned the platform so that it faced inland. Their rebuilding of the Pnyx prevented mass meetings from sprawling over the hillside: although no more than a few thousand regularly attended Assembly meetings, there was at least space for more, but the Thirty both limited the space available (to about six thousand in a crush) and made entrance into the meeting-place controllable. They also oversaw ballots in the Council, whereas previously they had been secret: every Council member's vote had to be placed on a table where members of the Thirty sat, rather than deposited secretly in an urn. But then the Council consisted largely of their stooges, so this measure made little difference.

For a radical group, the Thirty's reforms in the first few weeks of their regime were modest. The reason for this relative lack of activity is surely that they were plotting something far more extreme: they wanted to restore to Athens the kind of constitution where less needed to be written down, because the good men and true were in power, who instinctively knew about such things and could confer among themselves. It was democracy, with all its moral complexities and ambiguities, that needed written law. In fact, it seems distinctly possible that the Thirty were intending to establish a Spartan-style constitution in Athens. Sparta too had five ephors, a ruling committee (called the *gerousia*, or Council of Elders) of thirty members, and a general Assembly of a limited number of privileged citizens, with limited powers. The coincidences are too great to ignore. The Thirty were men with a vision, and with the ruthlessness to do whatever it took to see that vision become reality.

Such thorough social engineering was bound to meet with opposition. As a precaution, the Thirty asked the Spartans to send a garrison, and offered to pay for it themselves. Seven hundred Peloponnesian hoplites arrived, to quell disturbance or to see that none arose, and were housed on the Munichia hill in Piraeus, which was, not coincidentally, where the Assembly was meeting while work was in progress on the Pnyx. But the Thirty now had an extra problem: they not only had to make reparations to those of the returned exiles who were clamouring for the restoration of their confiscated property, but they had to pay the Peloponnesian garrison too. They were strapped for cash.

And so they raised money by killing or banishing men of property, focusing especially on wealthy metics and anyone they judged to be a potential opponent of their political programme. This reign of terror earned them their familiar title: the Thirty Tyrants. They go down in European history as the first to make fellow citizens live in fear of the dawn raid. Inevitably, the violence escalated, as many, even among their supporters, withdrew either in disgust or because they would not tolerate a Spartan-style limitation of their rights and privileges, and so became targets themselves. Anytus, later one of Socrates' prosecutors, was one of the lucky ones: he had been an ally of Theramenes, but the Thirty banished him and stole his tannery business with all its valuable slaves.

We hear that in all fifteen hundred people were illegally killed in just a few weeks. Others chose voluntary exile rather than death. Once there was no longer much chance of opposition, the Thirty published the definitive list of the three thousand wealthy Athenians who were to count as full citizens and members of the Assembly (the equivalent of the Spartan 'Peers', the full-blooded Spartiates, who were about the same number at the time). Only they were subject to the laws, while anyone else could be put to death at the whim of the Thirty; only they could bear arms, while the rest were disarmed by the Spartan garrison; only they could live and own property in Athens, while the rest were to be resettled, chiefly in Piraeus, presumably in houses formerly rented by metics who had either fled or been put to death.

Many of those who had the means to do so chose exile over resettlement; a few chose to form the backbone of the resistance movement. Those who stayed in the Piraeus were to be the businessmen of Athens, while the Three Thousand were to be supported by their slave-run farms. Meanwhile, the Thirty fortified and occupied Eleusis, some thirty-five kilometres north-west of the city, perhaps to prevent its becoming a centre of resistance, but also as a future bolt-hole: it had a good harbour, and control of the cult of Demeter and Korē had more than just symbolic value, since the temples were filled with treasure and the storehouses with the grain that was Demeter's province. The takeover of Eleusis involved the arrest and subsequent killing of many of the inhabitants; they also removed potential dissidents from the Athenian-owned island of Salamis. This was Athens's darkest hour.

CRITIAS

Were the Thirty motivated in all this by nothing more than greed for money and power, as hostile sources (and only hostile sources remain) soon began to assert? Though we know little enough about Critias, it is more than we know about the others, and it adds substantially to our picture of the Thirty. Born around 460 BCE, Critias was a member of an old Athenian family, and a highly cultured man, whose written work was admired and edited by no less a critic than Herodes Atticus, the controversial professor and benefactor of Athens in the second century CE; in the Platonic tradition, however, he was known, more disparagingly, as 'an amateur among philosophers, and a philosopher among amateurs'. His close association with Socrates is proved not only by his presence in two of Plato's dialogues (though not the *Critias*, which is named after his grandfather), but by Xenophon's efforts to deny that there was any politics involved in their friendship.

We first hear of Critias when he was named by Diocleides as involved in the desecration of the herms in 415; he was released after Diocleides admitted that he had lied. He does not seem to have been involved in the oligarchy of 411, but he was later banished by the democracy, at Cleophon's instigation, for something, and most likely for his pro-Spartan views, of which he made no secret. At this stage of his career he was chiefly known as a polymath and multi-talented writer, who wrote lectures, verse reflections on political matters, incidental poetry in several metres, tragedy, and a literary symposium, the prototype of Plato's and Xenophon's versions.

None of these works survives in more than meaningless fragments. They included two on Sparta, one in prose and one in verse, which displayed an admiration for all things Spartan. In these encomia he certainly perpetuated, and possibly originated, the 'Spartan mirage' – the state's reputation for incredible toughness, structure and discipline. In fact he spent at least some of his time in exile working for the Spartans in Thessaly, where he tried to replace the relatively lawless state of affairs, loosely led by various hereditary aristocracies and princelings, with a broad oligarchy, a hoplite franchise. This would have given the Spartans a single body of people with whom they could negotiate; they wanted a buffer state there, between the Macedonians and southern Greece.

Critias was present at the Samos conference, returned to Athens at the end of the war, along with all the other oligarchic and pro-Spartan exiles, became one of the ephors, and was then co-opted into the Thirty. Why did his fellow oligarchs rate him so highly? Paradoxically, it is a hostile source, the democrat Lysias, who gives us a clue, when he acknowledges that the original intention of Critias and the Thirty was 'to purge the city of unjust men and turn the rest of the citizens to goodness and justice'. This moral goal is confirmed by whoever wrote the seventh Platonic Epistle (and it just may have been Plato himself), when he says that he (i.e. Plato) was at first tempted to support the Thirty, because he believed that they would turn the city into a place of justice and morality. And he says that it was his relatives who dangled this bait before him: his uncle Charmides was one of the Piraeus Ten, and Critias was another uncle, Charmides' cousin.

This moral aim dovetails perfectly with Critias's professed admiration of Sparta, and with the Spartan-style constitutional changes that the Thirty instituted. Admirers of Sparta found in the Spartan constitution a healthy emphasis on a simple way of life based on physical exercise, the avoidance of commerce, and respect for one's elders; more substantially, they liked to think that all Spartan citizens worked together in concord for the common good and were obedient to the laws. They were sure that the Spartan constitution developed moral excellence in its citizens – and that, no doubt, is why Critias described it as 'the best possible state'.

All this makes plausible the suggestion that Critias was the brains behind the Thirty, and that the moral regeneration of Athens was their purpose. The Thirty were not mindlessly savage tyrants, but were motivated by a genuine concern to do good as they saw it; but then dictators always begin by thinking that they know better than others what is good for all. Critias's aim was perfectly summarized over two thousand years later by another dictator, General Francisco Franco of Spain, who said: 'The Fatherland must be renewed, all evil uprooted, all bad seed extirpated. This is not a time for scruples.' Athens had been corrupted by years of democracy, with its artificial egalitarianism, its lack of structure, and its resolute defiance of the aristocrats' god-given right to rule. To cap it all, the democracy had taken the city into a crippling war and then lost it. It was time to put things right.

CIVIL WAR

The resistance movement began in earnest early in 403, when Thrasybulus, earlier banished by the Thirty, reappeared from abroad with a small band and occupied a steep, defensible hill near the village of Phyle on the rugged border between Boeotia and Attica. The rebels had the support of democrats in Piraeus, such as Lysias, who sent them arms and armour made in his own factory (the only Athenian workshop large enough to deserve the name) – and made himself the target of a hit squad, which he only just evaded. The Thirty tried to persuade Thrasybulus that he could work with them, but that would have been putting his head in the noose, and he remained where he was, with a small but steadily growing band of followers, many of whom had been exiled by or had fled from the oligarchs.

The oligarchs' first attempt to dislodge Thrasybulus and his men, by besieging the hill until the democrats ran out of provisions, was foiled by a wild snowstorm. The city was thrown into crisis, and Theramenes, suspecting that the days of the Thirty were numbered, began to distance himself from his fellow oligarchs – just as he had in 411, and again probably as an attempt to save his skin. (Thanks to his eleventh-hour opposition to the Thirty, a rich streak of heroization of Theramenes has contaminated the historical record about him, but in all probability he was always a hardcore oligarch who pretended otherwise only when it was expedient to do so. At any rate, he seems to have been thought by his contemporaries to be a trimmer: he was nicknamed *kothornos*, after the actors' boot that fitted either foot.) The rift had begun to open when the Thirty decided to restrict Athenian citizenship to only their chosen Three Thousand – 'as though this number necessarily encompasses all the good people,' Theramenes said, with impeccable logic and sarcasm.

The Thirty disarmed everyone who remained in the city apart from the Three Thousand, and this left them free to accelerate their programme of fund-raising by murder. Feeling increasingly cornered and in need of a desperate *pistis*, a pledge of loyalty, to cement their ranks, the Thirty made it a condition of membership that each of them should personally undertake at least one of these assassinations. Theramenes refused, and the Thirty decided to eliminate him. Critias publicly denigrated him in the Council and, with armed knights standing by in case of resistance, removed him from the list of the Three Thousand. Since the Thirty had the power of life or death over anyone not on the list, in the same breath Critias condemned Theramenes to death. Theramenes took refuge at an altar, from where he was dragged away to execution. Diodorus of Sicily's account of Theramenes' death contains the delightful suggestion that Socrates made an attempt to save Theramenes' life at the last minute, but this is rubbish – a mis-transcription at some point of an already dubious story that the orator Isocrates of Erchia made such an attempt.

Meanwhile, Thrasybulus's men had grown in number from seventy to a thousand, consisting of a mixture of Athenians, metics and mercenaries; their morale had also been boosted by the successful repulse of a second assault on Phyle, in the course of which about 120 of the new Peloponnesian garrison were killed. Anytus had joined Thrasybulus, and so changed status from moderate oligarch to hero of the democratic uprising.

Thrasybulus felt confident enough to move his main base of operations to Piraeus, where the Munichia hill offered the same kind of protection as Phyle. The clearance of Athens had made Piraeus the heartland of opposition to the oligarchs; Thrasybulus was making himself available to a pool of new recruits. The Thirty, with the knights and the remains of the Peloponnesian garrison, immediately marched against Piraeus, but they were defeated in a gruesome battle by the outnumbered democrats, who made skilful use of their advantage on the hill, and of their poorer supporters as light-armed skirmishers. Critias and one other member of the Thirty were killed, as was Charmides, one of the ten responsible for Piraeus. Others fled to Eleusis. Critias's tomb was said to have portrayed a personification of Oligarchy setting fire to Democracy and to have been inscribed: 'This is a memorial to good men who for a short while restrained the arrogance of the accursed Athenian populace.'

Piraeus was now a democratic stronghold, and effectively a separate municipality from Athens itself. In Athens, the Thirty were replaced by a board of ten archons, one from each tribe. The King Archon was Patrocles, possibly Socrates' half-brother. The democrats in Piraeus promised equal rights in the future to anyone who joined them, and many metics seized the opportunity to risk improving their lot. The increasing boldness and confidence of the democrats, who began to treat the countryside around Athens as their own, aggravated the fears of those who remained in Athens and prompted one of the nastiest atrocities of the civil war. A band of knights, patrolling the countryside to prevent democratic foragers, came across some peasants, who were doing no more than picking up supplies from their farms, and slaughtered them. In retaliation, the democrats executed one of their prisoners.

The ten archons proved themselves to be no more than Spartan puppets, by asking for aid from Sparta on the grounds that the democrats were, in effect, in revolt against Sparta. The Spartans gave the Ten, who were financially as well as morally bankrupt, a loan to hire mercenaries who, under the command of Lysander and his brother, were to blockade

Piraeus by land and sea. This half-hearted response was a sign of a sea-change in Sparta. The Spartan authorities had long been concerned about Lysander's ambitions: he had proved himself a ruthless and brilliant commander in the last decade of the war, but had also shown that he was not averse to hero-worship from the people he conquered, and to installing governments that were loyal to him personally. When he began to achieve some success against the rebel democrats in Athens, his enemies in Sparta got busy: he was known to be close to the Athenian oligarchs, and they made out that he was planning to make Athens his personal domain.

One of the two Spartan kings, Pausanias, led an army against Piraeus and took over command from Lysander. But faced with stiff resistance from the democrats (though at one point he nearly defeated them just outside the north-western city walls), and with the growing reluctance of important Spartan allies to interfere in Athens, Pausanias chose a course of reconciliation. He persuaded Thrasybulus and the democrats that the archons wanted an end to hostilities, and after some prevarication the archons agreed.

The peace was negotiated under the auspices of the Spartans on the spot. In the short term, the two sides agreed to lay down their arms, and the Spartans withdrew, leaving the Athenians to sort out their own affairs. The chief provisions of the agreement that was hammered out were that all confiscated property was to be returned, while anyone who wished could go and join the oligarchs who had already fled to Eleusis, which was to be a semi-independent enclave. They had ten days to register, and another twenty to get out of town; they would henceforth be banned from holding office in Athens.

As for reparations, the survivors among the fifty-one oligarchic governors of Athens and Piraeus, if they stayed in the city, would face an investigation of their conduct while in office, and the normal penalties if they were found to have transgressed, but only the most egregious crimes, such as murder, would be punished; there was no war crimes tribunal. As a sop to the oligarchs, their conduct would be investigated only by juries of the better-off members of society, to prevent vindictive action from the lower classes. The face of democracy would only be improved by a display of mercy. Athenian understanding of democratic citizenship was closely related to equality: for a while, no one could occupy the moral high ground, because that was exactly what the Thirty had tried to do with their programme of purging the city of what *they* saw as immoral elements. So the restored democracy would be lenient.

In late September 403, the democrats processed from Piraeus back to Athens to sacrifice in gratitude to Athena on the Acropolis. It was a magnificent occasion, with deliberate echoes of the Panathenaea, the most democratic festival of the ritual calendar. An interim board oversaw the transition back to full democracy, and ensured the continuation of the overhaul of the laws. There was friction, but the Spartans never took it upon themselves to interfere – even when in 401, just a couple of years before Socrates' trial, the restored democrats decided to suppress the last remaining oligarchs and reunite Eleusis with Athens. On the pretext that at least some of the oligarchs were beginning to hire mercenaries with a view to retaking Athens, the democrats attacked Eleusis and bloodily put an end to its status as an oligarchic enclave.

AMNESTY?

Against all the odds the peace worked. Apart from the reduction of Eleusis in 401, blood was not shed in recrimination, and Athenian democracy continued and flourished for another eighty years. The Athenians were naturally inclined to brush the civil war under the carpet as much as they could: after all, large numbers of them had been involved in or had connived at the rule of the Thirty, and they needed to forget their collective guilt. Dozens of years understandably passed before ordinary citizens in Germany began to face up to their or their parents' complicit roles in the Holocaust.

Despite this attempt at collective amnesia, the early years of the restored democracy were tense. Thrasybulus was remembered not just as the heroic leader of the resistance movement, but also as the one who kept trying to persuade the Athenians to persevere with the conciliatory mood of the times. His repeated efforts would not have been required if there had been no friction, and he was not always successful: one of the first actions of the restored democracy was to reduce the level of support the knights received from the state towards the expensive upkeep of their horses, and within a couple of years three hundred knights were sent to fight for the Spartans against Tissaphernes in Asia Minor on the grounds that (as Xenophon tendentiously put it) 'democracy would only benefit if these Athenian horsemen went abroad and died there'. They had served the Thirty too well. The clubs were curtailed, and it was more or less impossible for those who had supported the Thirty in any way to gain election to important political positions in the subsequent decades.

The conciliatory veneer did little to stop people referring in court to their own or their opponents' actions during the reign of the Thirty, as a way of embellishing their own characters and slurring those of their opponents. And this went on for many years: nothing casts so long a shadow in the collective memory of a people as civil war. When a court was sitting to assess someone's fitness for office, this was a particularly good opportunity for someone to bring up the past, since a man's character was expressly on trial. Other trials too almost explicitly offered the jury the chance to avenge themselves on the Thirty in the person of the defendant. Lysias's *Against Eratosthenes* is an attack on a member of the Thirty, not for any recent crime, but precisely for having been a member of the Thirty and for having in that capacity ordered the murder of his brother; his *Defence of Mantitheus* shows that Mantitheus had been accused of having served the Thirty as a knight, and his *Defence against the Charge of Subverting the Democracy* does the same for an unnamed defendant. As Andrew Wolpert has said: 'Peace was never final; rather, it was reinvented and renegotiated every time a conflict erupted between members of the former factions and every time a citizen recalled the period of unrest.'

Nevertheless, scholars have invariably spoken of a general amnesty after the civil war, imposed by the restored democracy as a way of rapidly healing wounds, and in order to prevent the system becoming clogged with an avalanche of recriminatory lawsuits. The amnesty was supposed to apply to everyone, except the original sixty-one oligarchs (the Thirty, the Piraeus Ten, the Eleven, and the ten archons who took over after the fall of the Thirty), and even to them if they stayed and survived an assessment of their actions while in power. It was supposed to stop anyone proceeding against anyone else for crimes committed before the agreement.

Though some of the details are unclear, the reconciliation agreement of 403 between the men of Piraeus and the men of the city was, first, a property deal: everyone (or his heirs, if the Thirty had killed him) was to regain his original property, or comparable property if the original had already passed to a third party, except for the Thirty and their henchmen, who were free to go to Eleusis if they wanted. Second, if any of the Thirty and their henchmen chose to stay in Athens and submit to trial, the verdict of that trial was to be taken to be final. There was to be no reprise on either issue. It is this 'no reprise' provision that has been taken to be a general amnesty, a pardon for all past crimes, but it clearly falls short of such a blanket amnesty, since it refers only to the two provisions of the agreement. The term used is common in ancient Athenian contract law and it always refers to the specific terms of a specific agreement. So the fact that there was to be no reprise on either the property deals or the verdicts handed down against those of the oligarchs who stayed in Athens does not amount to a blanket amnesty on all crimes committed before 403. This will prove important for understanding Socrates' trial. Even those scholars who believe that there was a political subtext to the trial tend to think that it had to be conducted at the level of innuendo, since open reference to Socrates' pre-403 associates and their undemocratic politics was banned. But without the amnesty in the background, the picture of the trial looks very different.

A CONSERVATIVE ERA

The 'no reprise' condition was one of several reconciliatory moves. Not the least important was the radical overhaul of the legislative system. Scrutiny of the laws had started in 410 and had continued, despite regime changes, with the board responsible for the work merely receiving, like the British Civil Service, somewhat different instructions from the different regimes. The board had originally been tasked with reinscribing the 'laws of Solon', the earliest of which dated from the beginning of the sixth century, but since these were scattered, the job took longer than the four months initially assigned to it. In any case, it turned out that what was required was not just fresh, legible inscriptions, centrally available in Athens itself; the board successfully argued that they had to do something to iron out inconsistencies and obscurities as well. So the work turned into a major and fundamentally important exercise, requiring a number of years. It was still not quite finished in 404, when the civil war interrupted it.

In 403, a new Legislative Board of fifteen hundred was appointed, to complete this process of rationalizing the laws; the overhauled code was written up on papyrus and stored in the Metroön, with the most important laws inscribed on stone for public viewing. From then on, no law passed before 403 was to be valid, unless it formed part of the new inscriptions and transcriptions: 403 was the start of a new era for Athens, as 1792 was designated 'Year One' in revolutionary France. Moreover, no uninscribed law could validly be referred to in court or enforced, and no decree could override a law; a law was understood to be applicable to all Athenians, while decrees applied only to a segment of the population, or even to a single individual. Further regular reviews of the laws were to be undertaken as seemed desirable, but the passage of a proposal into law now involved several hurdles, as Peter Rhodes explains: 'It was deliberately made difficult to have a law enacted: it could be done only at a certain time of the year; the proposer had to examine the existing code and if necessary propose the repeal of any law with which his new law would conflict; the proposal had to be displayed in public and read out at three meetings of the assembly; and the nomothetae [the Legislative Board] who finally pronounced on it were not any citizens but men who had taken the oath and registered as jurors (*inter alia*, men of thirty and over).'

But the ongoing work assigned to the Legislative Board was even more important. From then on, no laws could be passed solely by the people's Assembly. They gave their approval to a proposed new law, but the Legislative Board had the final say, once they had considered the implications of the proposal, and in particular whether it conflicted with any other existing laws. The Assembly was allowed the final vote only on decrees. This appeased the oligarchs, because no longer could the people, led by some demagogue, insist that whatever they decided on any given day was right (as at the trial of the Arginusae Six); and the democrats were content with being back in power, and with an end to civil strife, so that they could get on with restoring Athens's status and economic conditions, and with healing wounds. Concord, then, was the new watchword, and in theory the only standard by which major issues were to be judged was whether or not it enhanced the collective good.

The ordering of the laws was important not just for stability, but also for deciding the overriding issue of the day: who was to count as Athenian? The Thirty had severely limited the number, and others had other proposals, but the new government reaffirmed Pericles' law of 451: things had lapsed somewhat during the war, but once again, from 403 onwards, citizenship was to depend on both one's parents having been citizens. This reaffirmation of the past responded to a need that was powerful enough for them initially to refuse citizenship to those foreigners who had helped Thrasybulus during the civil war, even though he had offered it to them. The organization and archiving of the laws was important for the restored democracy in part because it made it possible for anyone to refer to laws in order to confirm what it was to be Athenian – that is, what laws he was subject to, what his obligations and privileges were.

To the victor, the spoils. The restored democracy gained the right to settle the debate over which faction got to claim that it was restoring the 'constitution of our fathers'. The mood of the times was as conservative as the slogan implies; whim was to be banished, whether it was the whim of oligarchs or of the assembled people. Published and at least semi-transparent laws were the new guides, supported by better bureaucracy and a more uniform language in official documents. The prohibition on appeal to unwritten laws reminded aristocrats that their instinctive claim to leadership was, in a sense, no longer legal. Written laws seemed objective, impersonal, infinitely repeatable, not arbitrary. The very act of writing a law down gave it apparent permanence and stability. Post-Thirty Athenians wanted freedom from the destabilizing influence of mavericks; Critias and Alcibiades were gone, and they were not to be resurrected.

CRISIS AND CONFLICT

NINE

Symptoms of Change

Social crisis manifests in different ways in different societies, but war-torn Athens, the Athens of the last third of the fifth century BCE, was affected by a striking list of stress factors. Old certainties were being undermined by prolonged warfare, morally subversive ideas, population displacement, relative poverty following a period of relative prosperity, the polarization of rich and poor, turbulence with occasional outbursts of violence, even civil war (especially disturbing since Athens had been so free of civil strife, compared with many Greek states), the reorganization of the law code, changes of fashion, and changes in the economic structure. If these do not add up to a social crisis, it is hard to see what might.

Athenian society was not in meltdown, but it was far from tranquil. Perhaps a useful parallel would be the tumult experienced by much of the 'first world' in the 1960s. The 'hippie revolution' was a genuine social crisis, and a number of important social ideas took root which have caused permanent changes in areas such as business practices, healthcare, religion, treatment of the environment, attitudes towards women and tolerance of 'alternative' lifestyle choices, to name only the most important. But North American or European society after the changes was still recognizably the same as it was before. Historians in the future will look back and find plenty of continuities, and some of them will doubt the relevance of the term 'crisis', as do some historians of classical Athens; but anyone who lived through those times had no doubt that it was precisely applicable. Apart from anything else, dozens of young people around the world were legally killed by the authorities for trying to bring about these changes, so it should come as no surprise that the Athenian crisis, one aspect of which was also inter-generational conflict, could also prove deadly – as it did for Socrates, charged with corrupting the young.

Social crises do not occur unless there is a critical level of dissatisfaction with the way things are. Although there were rumblings as early as the 430s, when political divisions in Athens became sharper and gave aristocrats a focus for their discontent, 415 was the water-shed year, when all the latent tensions were brought out into the open and helped to queer the Sicilian expedition, which more or less ended Athenian hopes for a successful outcome to the war. The effect of the stresses was only accelerated by the realization that, unless the gods or Alcibiades could produce a miracle, defeat was assured. Apart from any of the other critical factors, imagine yourself an Athenian living, day after day, year after year, with the knowledge that before long you would become subject to your deadliest enemy.

But that was one of the few certainties of the time. What particularly characterizes the Athenian crisis is uncertainty, the inability to stay on track. Above all, the oligarchic coup of 411 is plain evidence of crisis. So are the extreme reactions that marred the wartime landscape: the massacres at Scione and Melos, the legitimizing in 410 of the death penalty for 'enemies of democracy', the witch-hunt of 415: even if there was a genuine threat to the constitution, panic was never going to be the best way to deal with it. These are clear signals from a society under stress.

The notorious 'fickleness' for which the critics castigated democracy was also a symptom of panic – of first over-reacting and then having to find ways to compensate. Within a day or two in 433 BCE, the Athenians voted first not to interfere in Corcyran affairs and then to do so – a decision that played a major part, as they knew, in provoking the Peloponnesian War. In 430 they deposed and impeached Pericles, only to reinstate him the following year. Within twenty-four hours in 428, they changed their minds about how severely to punish Mytilene. In 415, they were wholeheartedly committed to the Sicilian expedition, but after it had failed, they took no responsibility themselves: 'It was as if they themselves had never voted for the expedition: they were angry with the politicians who had recommended it, and with the oracle-experts, the seers and others whose divinations had encouraged them to expect to conquer Sicily.' They banished and cursed Alcibiades in 415, recalled him in 408, and banished him again a few months later; they felt he was dangerous, but this arbitrary treatment betrays weak-ness and a crisis of confidence: they were not sure they could contain him. They insisted that they had the right to try the Arginusae generals in 406, but a few days later they changed their minds and punished some of those who had insisted on the mass trial.

Another striking feature of Athenian politics is its amorality. The Mytilenean debate was couched only in terms of expediency, and in the

Melian dialogue the Athenians simply ruled out considerations of justice. The extension of this philosophy was the atrocious massacre at Scione. These two features of Athenian wartime politics – amorality and fickleness – are related: if all you are concerned about is your immediate good, you can easily be persuaded by a plausible appeal to that criterion to do things that under other circumstances would make you pause. This is one reason why Socrates emphasized that true morality has to be based on knowledge, because knowledge cannot be swayed, and it is also why he argued that, appearances notwithstanding, it is *moral* behaviour that is good for the agent.

MAJOR SOCIAL STRESSES

Two of the most dramatic and large-scale events that struck Athens were identified as stress factors by the historian Thucydides. In memorable passages, he described the effects of the plague on Athens in particular, and of warfare on societies in general. The first passage occurs as part of the historian's vivid description of both the medical and moral effects of the plague. Typhoid fever struck Athens in the summer of 430, at a time of sweltering heat, when the city was packed with those who had sought safety behind the city walls from the Peloponnesian invasions of the countryside. It lasted, intermittently, for the best part of four years (with a slighter recurrence in 410) and killed three hundred of the rich, 4,400 men of hoplite status, and countless others – peasants, women, children, slaves, foreigners – who rarely show up in ancient historians' statistics. It killed at least a quarter of Athens's population. It can hardly occasion surprise that its effects on the minds of a generation of Athenians were so powerful:

> People had fewer inhibitions about self-indulgent behaviour they
> had previously repressed, because they saw how rapidly fortunes
> could change – how those who were well off suddenly died and
> how those who had formerly been destitute promptly inherited
> their property. The upshot was that they sought a life of swift
> and pleasurable gain, because they regarded their lives and their
> property as equally impermanent. No one had the slightest
> desire to endure discomfort for the sake of what men held to be
> honourable, because they doubted whether they would live long
> enough to earn a reputation for honour. In fact, what was held to

be honourable and beneficial was whatever contributed to the pleasure of the moment, regardless of its source. Fear of the gods and human laws were equally ineffective as deterrents: the sight of the religious and the irreligious dying equally made people conclude that piety made no difference, and no one expected to live long enough to be taken to court and punished for his crimes.

There is a degree of exaggeration in this account – not everyone in Athens succumbed to lawlessness, and at a state level religious practices continued more or less unabated – but only to a degree. Things would not have got so out of hand if the moral order had not already been destabilized. Nor need the nihilism of people's reactions surprise us: in 1755 a major earthquake struck Portugal and Morocco, and the shocks, fires and tsunamis killed up to a hundred thousand people. The facts that most of the deaths were in Portugal, a devoutly Christian country, and that the earthquake struck on the day of a major Catholic festival led to widespread doubt in the existence of a benevolent deity and left an enduring legacy in the form of a weakening of Christian faith in Europe.

I hardly need to argue that war, and especially such a drawn-out war, stresses a society, and in the second passage Thucydides reflects on the effects of warfare, and especially civil war, on people's moral behaviour:

In times of peace and prosperity, states and individuals hold to better principles, because they are not forced by emergencies to act against their wills. But war is a harsh teacher: it denies easy access to daily necessities and makes most people adjust their temperaments to their circumstances . . . People claimed the right to change the usual meanings of words to fit in with the way they were behaving. So, for instance, irrational recklessness was described as loyal courage, while looking before you leap was seen as fair-seeming attempt to disguise one's cowardice; self-restraint was said to be a screen for the faint-hearted, and using intelligence to consider every aspect of a situation was said to make one incapable of any action at all. Impulsiveness was added to the qualities of true manliness, and taking thought for possible dangers was called a specious excuse for keeping out of danger. Ranting and raving was the mark of a man you could trust, and to contradict him was to make yourself an object of suspicion.

142

Intelligence was shown by successful intriguing, and even greater intelligence by sniffing out intrigues.

And he goes on to suggest how, in times of civil strife, family bonds are weakened, the most solemn oaths are pledged only because there is no other weapon to hand to wield against one's opponents, and illegal manipulation of assemblies is rife. It is a picture of utter amorality and of distortion of traditional values – and disturbingly reminds us of how Alcibiades too was prepared to redefine terms, so that patriotism became a quality one owed only to a state that already conformed to one's own political views. As Thucydides said, war is a harsh teacher. In one of his most devastatingly powerful plays, *Trojan Women*, produced in 415, Euripides showed how war forces people to betray their better selves and adopt double standards.

Apart from the long-drawn-out war and the plague, another major stress factor, not remarked by Thucydides, was economic. As a result initially of the sheer size of the population in the late 430s (over 335,000, on the latest estimate) relative to the amount of available land, and then of the dislocation of much of the peasant population from the countryside to the city during the war, the volume of foreign trade increased enormously and began to force the city's economy towards something recognizable as a market economy. As is common in pre-market societies, business relationships had been embedded in the structure of society; now they began to become disembedded, and the price or value of goods came to be dictated by market forces rather than by social factors such as reciprocity, ritualized barter and neighbourliness. Production began to change from being production for use (with the householding ideal of self-sufficiency) to production for gain. Commerce, rather than agriculture, was beginning to be the basis of economic life. These are major changes in a society: life would never be the same again.

THE GENERATION GAP

There was something Peter Pan-like about Alcibiades. The stories present him as an eternal youth, always challenging father-figures or authority in general, and rarely taking thought for the future. Many, in fact, saw the entire generation as in some sense immature and described the wealthy aristocrats of whom Alcibiades was the acknowledged champion as the 'young'. The inverted commas are there because the issue was ideological as much as it was factual; the actual ages of the people involved mattered less than the fact that traditional authority was being undermined. Every generation separates itself from the previous one, but in the 420s this process was exaggerated for the first time by wealth, better education and other social stresses. Comic and tragic plays of the period portray Alcibiades-like characters involved in situations which reflect both Athenian admiration for the energy of youth and their fear of it.

Aristophanes' *Acharnians* (produced in 425) includes a lament that the older generation, the Marathon-fighters, are having rings run around them in court by smart young whippersnappers; *Clouds* (423, in its original version) has a young man use what he has learnt from Socrates to justify beating up his father; *Wasps* (422) also pits son against father (the natural way for a playwright to portray inter-generational conflict) in a debate that is explicitly designed to show how ridiculous the older generation seems to the young man. Throughout, the old men are shown as the holders of the straight-forward values of past times, while the young follow all the modern fashions in dress and language and argument. Inter-generational conflict was a live issue in Athens in the last quarter of the fifth century, and especially from about 425 to 415. The youth culture not only accelerated certain cultural changes, but it also contributed to the social crisis.

In 423, in his play *Suppliant Women*, Euripides wrote:

> You were led astray by young men who enjoy being in the
> public eye and multiply wars with no regard for justice or for
> the citizens' deaths they cause. They do this for a number of
> reasons, one because he wants to lead an army, another in order
> to acquire power and abuse it, another for financial gain, without
> any concern whether the general populace is harmed by his
> treatment of them.

Eight years later, Nicias echoed these very words as he accused the Athenian people of being misled by 'the young' (especially Alcibiades) into wanting to invade Sicily. The common perception of the young was that they were warmongers. The ostracism of 416 was a critical moment, and Plutarch astutely remarks: 'Basically, the contest was between the younger generation, who wanted war, and the older generation, who wanted peace, with one side wielding the *ostrakon* against Nicias and the other against Alcibiades.' 'Young' was another way of saying 'adventurous', and after the Sicilian expedition 'rash'.

The young wanted political power too soon, it was thought, before they had the wisdom to wield it well; they frequented Socrates and other teachers, who showed them how to manipulate mass meetings, made them sceptical of religion, and taught them to disrespect their elders. When people are poor, scratching a living from the soil, as ninety per cent of fifth-century Athenians were, family values are paramount. Son succeeds father without question, and the family sticks together at all costs, younger looking after older in a rhythm as natural as the seasons. In archaic Athens even the rich lacked cushioning from the vagaries of fortune, and these values became deeply embedded at all levels of society. But imperial Athens was far better off, and wealth erodes the family. Sons who feel themselves sophisticated and educated may despise their fathers and their fathers' ways. It was a youth revolution of the kind witnessed in 1920s New York, or 1960s San Francisco. Aristophanes hilariously portrayed the conflict in the debate and the banter between 'Mr Right' and 'Mr Wrong' in *Clouds*; the dynamic, sophistic Mr Wrong defeats the old fogey Mr Right.

The young even had their own music and fashions. They wore their hair loose (as opposed to in a bun), a thing of the past in Athens, but of the present in Sparta. Spartan shoes were all the rage, and the aristocratic fashion for pederasty was also taken to be an imitation of Sparta. Alcibiades invented a type of footwear, led the way in the youthful preference for playing the lyre rather than the pipes, and started a craze for adorning the walls of one's home with colourful scenes from mythology. As for music, a number of poets catered to the tastes of the young for variety and excitement, for something to set them apart from their elders. Conservatives disapproved of the New Music for its promotion of 'sexual licence, barbarian emotionality, and vulgar excess', but the young loved it for precisely these reasons.

Alcibiades was, naturally, in the forefront of its promotion. It was not just that he was close friends with and possibly the lover of Agathon, one of the poets chiefly responsible for the new style of music, but also that when he made his triumphant, purple-splashed return to Athens in 408, he was piped into Piraeus by one of the foremost practitioners of it, on board his ship. In fact, there was no true musical revolution, and the New Music was a product of changes that had been developing for about a century, but it was *perceived* as subversive, just as rock-and-roll in the 1950s, though a product of older musical forms, was seen in certain quarters as the music of communism or the devil (or both). Athenian critics even wrote sophisticated attacks, assuming the ethical effects of music (the theory of which had been established a little earlier by Damon of Oa) and arguing that this new-fangled rubbish would corrupt the souls of the people. In the same way, a lot of the fear of popular music in the 1950s and 1960s was simultaneously moral and generational – the fear that children were liable to imitate the 'degenerate' icons of rock-and-roll rather than their parents.

So the Athenian young had different fashions and a different code of ethics (which seemed to the older generation to be no morality at all), and were in favour of war. Along with their imitation of aspects of Spartan culture, they were often suspected of oligarchic tendencies, of 'disdaining equality with the common people'. Despite the fact that many of the herm-mutilators were over thirty years old, it was apparently still plausible to think of it as a youthful prank. Both it and the profanation of the Mysteries were associated with the clubs, well-known venues for young, oligarchically inclined aristocrats.

But admiration or at least tolerance of youthful excess came to an end with the sobering Sicilian catastrophe; the impious scandals of 415 and the failure of the expedition discredited the policies and the lifestyle of the young set. Their heyday had lasted only a decade, but thereafter fathers were busy reclaiming social prominence from their sons and education from the so-called 'sophists'. The young had been allowed to take over for about a decade because the older men had been stupefied by the new rhetoric, disillusioned by Pericles' defensive strategy in the war and overwhelmed by the changes that threatened the old moral code. But now the call from all sides was for a restoration of 'the constitution of our fathers'.

THE INHERITED CONGLOMERATE UNDER STRESS

In the opening pages of his magisterial, wonderful *Republic*, the philosopher Plato held a mirror up to Athenian society in the throes of a moral crisis. The setting of this phase of *Republic* would make his readers think of some time in the 420s BCE. Cephalus of Syracuse (the father of the speech-writer, industrialist and democrat Lysias) explains the traditional view of justice, and when Socrates begins to probe, he walks away: to many people, it was simply unthinkable that the inherited conglomerate, the family-based perpetuation of the moral and religious code, should be questioned. There will always be those who think that, in the sphere of public morality, it is simple common sense just to say, 'It has worked for many years. Why rock the boat?'

The baton passes, in Plato's dialogue, to one of Cephalus's sons, and Socrates questions him with the intention of finding a firmer foundation for moral behaviour; ever the perfectionist, he does not accept that a moral code can work as long as it covers only the majority of cases, or that our focus, day by day, is on dealing with the complexity of particular cases as best we can, not with abstract principles or absolute ideals. He wants to find a loophole-free moral position. Then the orator Thrasymachus of Chalcedon, representative of the new education (Callicles in Plato's *Gorgias* and Alcibiades in Xenophon's *Recollections of Socrates* adopt similar positions), bursts in and sneers at all conceptions of justice: properly understood, justice is no more than the interest of the ruling party. In a democracy, the weak use justice to restrain the strong, and so, when faced with a choice between acting justly and acting to improve one's personal position, only a fool and a weakling would choose the former.

The inherited conglomerate naturally held that justice and all the virtues were good things – good for the community, and therefore good for the individual, since he was contributing towards the glue that bound the community together and kept him and all his fellow citizens safe and sound. If the community prospered, every individual citizen prospered. It was good, then, to pay your friends, enemies and deities what you owed them; it was good to display courage in fighting alongside your fellow citizens for your city; it was good to exercise self-restraint; it was good to be pious towards your human and divine superiors; it was good to channel your intelligence towards society's benefit as well as your own. But these generalizations overlook how hard it is to justify the idea that virtues are supposed to benefit their possessors, when they often cost the agent personal inconvenience or, in extreme cases, pain and distress. The immediacy of personal suffering, or even its prospect, tends to override abstract issues. In *Republic*, one of Socrates' interlocutors develops a thought-experiment involving the possession of a magical ring of invisibility, and concludes:

> There is no one who is iron-willed enough to maintain his morality and find the strength to keep his hands off what doesn't belong to him, when he is able to take whatever he wants from shops without fear of being discovered, to enter houses and sleep with whomever he chooses, to kill and release from prison anyone he wants, and generally to act like a god among men.

On this analysis, every human being is driven by the desire for self-gratification to seek pleasure and avoid pain.

All societies have to find a balance between co-operative and competitive values. They cannot afford to suppress the energy of individuality completely, but neither can they afford to let it destabilize the status quo. But, as the life of Alcibiades illustrates, in Athens in the last quarter of the fifth century, elite resentment of democracy had reached the point where some aristocrats insisted on the right to develop their own talents and follow their own predilections, even at the risk of offending their fellow citizens or transgressing the inherited moral code. Painters and sculptors began to portray their subjects with greater individuality; playwrights showed some of the difficulties with rampant individualism; in the middle of the 420s, after seventy-five years of restraint, tombs and their offerings abruptly began once again to be lavish, indicating a swing away from group-orientation to individuality and aristocratic competitiveness. Aristocrats resented the fact that the state had usurped many of their traditional paths to glory. There were a few arenas where they could gain prestige – politics, the courts, athletics – but even here the shine was taken off their glory by the fact that they were rewarded by democratic consensus. It seemed to them as though being a good citizen and being a true man were incompatible.

Ironically, recent Athenian history had itself provided the impulse to dispute the preferability of co-operation over competition. Athens had spent fifty years (roughly 480–430 BCE) building up a mighty economic empire. Naturally, this had entailed both diplomatic and military aggression in the pursuit of self-interest, and the city had benefited enormously. Athens made itself wealthy beyond the previous imaginings of the ancient Greek world (and so left us its legacy of faded glory in the ruined buildings on the Acropolis and elsewhere), and resisted all attempts from both inside and outside to instil moderation. Individual citizens, from the poorest to the richest, found themselves better off too. There was enough money for the democracy to pay the poor for various forms of service to the state, traders and bankers flourished, and the rich grew richer by buying land abroad or by financing commercial ventures at home or overseas. It seemed, then, as though in foreign policy competitive values did everyone good, while co-operation did no more than maintain the lesser status that had obtained in the past.

The question which served as a focus for enquiry into these matters was, simply, 'What is virtue?', meaning 'What does it take to be an outstanding human being?' The question was particularly poignant for Athenian aristocrats. It had previously been assumed, especially by them, that it was an easy question to answer: they were the best, and this was proved by the fact that the gods had granted them wealth and all the other blessings. Virtue was an innate and hereditary aristocratic gift, which brought with it certain necessary consequences, such as the ability to master other people, to rule. But what became of the old aristocratic virtues when egalitarianism was rampant, competition was suspected as often as it was admired, and the people not only had the power to make or break a man who partook in public life, but had effectively set themselves up as judges of what was and was not virtuous behaviour? How could one achieve the success of a Cimon, Themistocles or Pericles? The new politicians who achieved prominence from the 420s, in the wake of Pericles' death, were often not even from the old aristocratic class, and yet they took it upon themselves to rule. Was rulership not an innate quality, then? Was it something teachable, as Protagoras and others claimed, something anyone of any class or background could acquire?

The social crisis made these burning issues. The fabric of Athenian society was beginning to come apart at its most vulnerable seam, that of the tension between the elite and the ordinary citizens. Liturgy-avoidance is a test case. The liturgy system seemed perfect, a way to channel the competitiveness of the super-rich into service for the state. The rich were required to fund, at their own expense, either a festival liturgy (such as the training and financing of a chorus for a dramatic or choral festival, or the training of young horsemen for a torch-race) or a military liturgy (above all, maintaining a trireme for a year, before it was someone else's turn). The liturgist had to spend a certain minimum, of course, to get the job done (somewhere between one thousand

and four thousand drachmas – roughly £100,000 to £400,000 – depending on the liturgy), but he had discretion in how much more to spend, in order to outdo his rivals and win further goodwill from the people. It seemed, as I say, to be perfect: the state needed liturgists, and liturgists had a safe environment for their competitiveness.

In practice, towards the end of the fifth century, at least some of the wealthy came to resent their liturgies. After the Sicilian expedition and the revolt of its tribute-paying allies in the subsequent years, the city was extremely hard pressed financially, and the rich were being squeezed for more taxes just as their income was plummeting. At the same time, the fully fledged democratic system made it possible for politicians to win the people's favour by dispensing state funds to them, rather than by spending their own money: liturgy was no longer the main way to gain the required popularity and prominence for oneself and one's descendants; liturgists were no longer getting the return they wanted on their expenditure, and they felt exploited. In a paperless society such as classical Athens, it was easy to conceal one's wealth; there was no land registry, and it was easy to hide cash and other assets. The rich were allowed to assess the value of their own assets and submit the estimate to the Assembly; some of them began to lie.

Athenian democracy had institutionalized a number of ways to curb the competitiveness of the elite and exploit it for democratically acceptable purposes, while formerly aristocrats had largely been content to scale back their competitiveness for the good of the community and for the sake of concord. But now the elite were beginning to break free of these bonds and to return to their Homeric roots. That is why in the 430s Athenian politics became polarized between democrats and oligarchs: for the first time, the elite were dissatisfied with democratic values and needed slogans with which to identify their own interests. The conflict between competitive and co-operative values became highly charged and emotive – and so Alcibiades, in his desire to be a Homeric hero, was tarred with the brush of tyranny, since he clearly had little respect for the boundaries of collectivism or democracy.

The moral and social crisis in Athens was triggered by, among other things, the questioning of inherited values. Socrates, the great questioner, was of course instrumental in this. His image of himself as a horsefly, sent by the god to stir the somnolent city into wakefulness, is very precise. A horsefly swoops in, settles somewhere, bites and flies off again. Everywhere he settled – every individual he interrogated – is taken to represent the inherited conglomerate (the horse), not to be an individual whose irritation begins and ends with the individual himself. But Socrates was in a sense a conservative, in that he reacted against the fact that customs had been questioned without being replaced by anything constructive. He tried to teach his followers to question in a productive manner, in a way that would reveal underlying assumptions and help others to make moral progress. He felt he had something to offer Athens, even if at his trial the Athenians terminally rejected his vision of what makes a good citizen and what makes a good state.

CRITICS OF DEMOCRACY

There were those, especially among the 'young', who thought they had the cure for society's ills: get rid of democracy. There had been oligarchic stirrings earlier in the century, though we know little about them, and certainly not enough to estimate the level of their threat to the democracy. In any case, there was nothing as concerted or as articulated as in the last third of the fifth century. The polarization of oligarchy and democracy, and so the development of theoretical notions about them both, began when the realpolitik tension between Sparta and Athens became bound up with political issues, such that each state came to represent one of these two constitutions. This was the time when aristocratic instinct – the innate certainty that they were the natural rulers of Athens – hardened into something more political. The fundamental oligarchic argument was that they should have political power commensurate with their resources and their contributions to the state, but many understood this to mean exclusive power.

The attempt by Thucydides Melesiou (not to be confused with the historian, Thucydides Olorou) to unite his fellow aristocrats in opposition to Pericles, under this kind of elitist banner, ended in defeat and Thucydides' ostracism in 443. The next major phase of the clash came in the 420s with Cleon's rhetorical and fiscal attacks on the knights, which exacerbated the aristocrats' desire to protect their wealth against the erosive effects of the war. At the same time, they were united by a common enemy: the new breed of nouveaux riches populist politicians, stereotyped by the historian Thucydides' biased portrait of Cleon. At least Pericles had been 'one of us', an old aristocrat.

By the end of the 420s, the critics of democracy had begun to articulate their vague resentments into something resembling a political programme. It was not enough for them just to insist that democracy flew in the face of nature by promoting equality: Athenian democracy to a certain extent recognized inequalities, and found ways to channel the ambitions of the elite towards democratic ends. Nor was it enough for them to rely on slogans such as *eunomia* (the 'lawfulness' of a well-structured society) in response to democratic *isonomia* ('equality before the law'), or to insist on the naturalness of hierarchy ('proportionate equality') as opposed to the artificiality of absolute equality. A more sophisticated and elaborate response was needed.

The roll-call of contemporary critics of Athenian democracy, during its flourishing in the fifth and fourth centuries, is impressive. It includes not just men of action, such as Alcibiades and Critias, but just about all the intellectuals who come to mind: the playwrights, both comic and tragic (though their personal positions are more or less impossible to assess, since it is only their characters who voice opinions), the orators (occasionally, and usually just for tendentious purposes), the historian Thucydides, philosophers such as Socrates, Plato, Xenophon, Isocrates and Aristotle, and pamphleteers such as the anonymous author of *The Constitution of the Athenians* who is familiarly known as the 'Old Oligarch'. They had a limited number of points to make, and they made them more or less forcefully (Aristotle, for instance, was more concerned to imagine an ideal constitution than to criticize deviations from it), but the points they were making were essentially those that were repeated over the centuries and left Athenian democracy with a poor reputation up until the nineteenth century. There have always been many who agreed with Alcibiades that Athenian democracy was 'unequivocal folly'.

First, some argued that the masses were innately stupid and over-emotional, and remained so thanks to lack of education; moreover, since economic circumstances largely determined human behaviour, the fact that the masses worked made them less moral than the rich; therefore, democracy was the perverted rule of the morally inferior over the morally superior. Democracy was by definition the rule of the working class, whose members had neither the money nor the leisure nor the education to do the kind of long-term and objective thinking that government required. The idea that mass decision-making could be superior to individual wisdom was a joke. This is still a live issue in political philosophy: a recent book takes as its starting point the fact that 'Democracy is not naturally plausible. Why turn such important matters over to masses of people who have no expertise?' In ancient Athens, the problem was exacerbated by the fact that the elite felt that they *did* have such expertise, handed down from generation to generation ever since the good old days of aristocracy. For many Athenian aristocrats, oligarchy was not so much a political philosophy as a gut reaction.

Second, they felt that democracy was a kind of tyranny of the weak over the strong, a violation of the natural hierarchy, too egalitarian and open. Democracy made laws in its own interest (but even the critics acknowledged, wryly, that all political systems are self-serving) and gulled the credulous by calling this 'justice'. Democracy tended to confuse freedom with lack of restraint, lawlessness and anarchy, or at least promoted the sovereignty of the people rather than of the law, with attendant dangers. As a kind of tyrant, democracy favoured flatterers and yes-men, and exploited the wealth of others for its own purposes; it governed by whim, and the masses were therefore fickle and easily led by demagogues and self-interested speakers, especially into over-confidence or vindictiveness.

Third, democracy's preference for committees over individuals, and for the annual change of administrative positions, made it inefficient. It stifled initiative, favoured the average and failed to make use of experts in government. Democracy had too much power for its own good: elite fear of chastisement by the democracy made them less inclined to put their abilities in the service of the state. And in particular, democracy was hopeless at foreign policy: witness the follies and the final catastrophe of the Peloponnesian War. The masses were more likely than the elite to be belligerent, because the elite were linked by *xenia* to their peers abroad, had a better understanding of foreign affairs, and naturally wanted to protect their foreign estates.

Fourth, the people mishandled public money. This mismanagement manifested above all in paying the poor for public service in the courts and Assembly and for military service, and in an ambitious programme of enhancing the city with monumental buildings. As if these measures were not enough, the democracy had also taken the state into a cripplingly expensive war. The rich felt that they were forced to support these costly schemes, even though they disapproved of them politically.

Despite being somewhat of a ragbag, united only by distaste for the common enemy, these are powerful criticisms. It is obvious why Critias and the Thirty felt that what they were doing was a moral mission. All the same, the critics failed to acknowledge that one of the great advantages of living in the Athenian democracy was precisely that they could voice such criticisms with impunity. The very stability of the democracy was what gave it the self-confidence to foster relative freedom of thought and even criticism. Perhaps for this reason the critics were not generally revolutionaries, calling for the violent and immediate overthrow of democracy: they were intellectuals, constructing hypothetical alternatives, or even just hoping to temper democracy; at the most, we get the occasional hint of a policy of non-cooperation with the democracy.

Curiously, it would be hard to draw up a similar list of counter-arguments by democracy's supporters. Only a few isolated passages develop in a piecemeal fashion anything like a theory of democratic virtues, while others (such as Pericles' famous Funeral Speech in Thucydides) are too complacent to contribute much ammunition to any debate (it is eulogy of Athens, not political theory). Democracy was more performance than theory, and was constantly evolving. Nevertheless, various ideas and arguments crop up here and there: the egalitarianism of democracy, and the idea that the possession of common goals reduces discontent and increases concord, without any need for a hierarchy; the belief that almost every citizen has the mental capacities necessary for socialization and contribution to debate, so that there is such a thing as collective wisdom. Those in favour of democracy denied the equation of pluralism with anarchy, and claimed that accountability was self-evidently a good discipline for a community's officers to work under.

The debate was won by the democrats, not because they had the best arguments, but because their opponents had the worst track record. The scandals of 415, Alcibiades' arrogance and, above all, the brutality of the Thirty Tyrants were plain facts that needed no theoretician: if this was what oligarchy was like, democracy was clearly preferable. Oligarchs never fully recovered the moral high ground. Active dissent fizzled out in the fourth century and took with it much of the social crisis. After the rule of the Thirty, it was left to philosophers to formulate criticisms; the men of action had been silenced and democracy had been restored. There was only one loose end: Socrates.

TEN

Reactions to Intellectuals

Crises bring out the worst in people, not least because they look for someone to blame. In the closing third of the fifth century BCE, many Athenians picked on intellectuals. They were perceived, rightly or wrongly, to be the educators of the 'young', and what they taught them was subversive and dangerous nonsense – subversive because it undermined traditional views, and dangerous because in the days of the dominance of traditional views Athens had prospered, but now the gods had withdrawn their favour from the city and it was losing a disastrous war.

There are surprises here for those brought up with a rosy view of classical Athenian society. It is strange to think that those who were laying the foundations of the entire western intellectual tradition were not necessarily welcome in their time. Was democratic Athens not one of the most open and tolerant societies ever? What about Pericles' boast?

> Where our public lives are concerned, we live in the state like free men, and the same goes for the lack of suspicion with which we deal with one another in our daily pursuits. We do not react with anger if one of our neighbours indulges himself, nor do we put on the kind of ill-humoured expression which, for all its actual harmlessness, is bound to cause offence. Although we deal comfortably with one another in our private lives, in our public lives a deep respect stops us from doing wrong, because we obey the authorities and the laws.

For all that this generous view of Athenian tolerance was perpetuated uncritically by generations of scholars even well into the twentieth century, it can be maintained only at some distance from the facts. And though it is true that Pericles' speech is the greatest statement of Athenian perfection, it is also true that it was a Funeral Speech, designed to reconcile grieving families and concerned citizens to the losses they had already sustained in the war with Sparta, and to encourage them to face further losses with relative equanimity. Besides, Thucydides made no claim to absolute accuracy in the speeches he reports, and may have had his own agenda: creating a picture of Athenian perfection would, for instance, contrast nicely with the amorality of certain Athenian actions later in the war.

Education in classical Athens was limited: there were few teachers and not many students, and they were not required to do very much. Up until the age of six or seven, all children were raised at home by their mothers and slaves – especially, if the household had one, by a slave called a *paidagōgos* (literally a pedagogue, a 'child-leader'), whose job it was to mind the young master's manners and moral education at home, and to look after him when he was out of the home. During this period the child's education consisted largely of stories – exactly the same myths and legends with which we are still familiar today. Most children remained at home for longer, either because their parents could not afford or did not care to send them to school, or because their parents preferred to bring in a private tutor, or because they were girls, who scarcely needed educating. 'Suppose', imagines Xenophon's Socrates at one point, 'we want to entrust someone, after our deaths, with the education of our sons or with the guardianship of our unmarried daughters?' Sons might be educated, but daughters were to be protected until they were passed into someone else's care. Nevertheless, some girls were taught to read and write, and those boys who were destined for no more than their father's trade learnt the rudiments of arithmetic at home.

By the end of the fifth century, literacy in Athens had spread down to the artisan level, though the countryside remained largely unlettered. But by and large classical Athens functioned perfectly well without mass literacy. The uses to which writing was put – from letter-writing to legal documents such as wills and contracts, from the writing of literature to civic and political lists, from recording maritime loans to fixing magical curses – were usually things with which the masses were largely uninvolved. New laws and other civic information were posted in the Agora, but there was always someone around who could read them out to those who were illiterate, or educated slaves to write a letter. Even at the higher levels of society, ancient Athens was largely an oral culture: the literate tended to dictate letters rather than write them themselves, and to listen to a slave reading rather than read themselves. Reading as a pastime was virtually unknown; it was more common for men to gather in groups to hear a work being read out.

Schooling began in Athens around the beginning of the fifth century BCE, but schoolteachers remained few, underpaid and underrated in the classical period. Even in the fourth century Demosthenes taunted his rival Aeschines with being the son of a mere schoolmaster. Boys who were lucky enough to gain an education attended three kinds of school, each of which took in a dozen or so pupils. A *grammatistēs* taught them to read and write and do their sums, and made them study and even learn substantial amounts of the Homeric poems, for moral purposes. A *kitharistēs* taught them music, singing, dancing and the lyric poets, so that they would in due course be able to hold their own in the contests of the symposium. A *paidotribēs* supervised their physical education at a gymnasium or a palaestra (wrestling ground), to prepare them simultaneously for athletic contests and for warfare, since hoplite warfare required little skill, but only general fitness. Future knights were taught horse-riding at home. And that was it: education was upper-class indoctrination, not the development of critical, experimental or creative thinking.

A typical day involved attendance at the palaestra early in the morning, returning home for the late-morning meal, and then spending the early afternoon at one of the other schools. Schooling continued only until the early teens. There were no state-sponsored schools, and the state did not interfere if you did not send your son to school. The lax attitude towards education reflects two principles: that children were not highly regarded in their own right, but were seen as adults in waiting; and that the Athenians had supreme confidence in the ability of the inherited conglomerate to condition their children into traditional Athenian mores. Plato has Socrates' prosecutor Anytus express the opinion that 'any decent Athenian gentleman' made a better educator than the so-called professionals.

School education was seen as supplementary to the company of adults, at home or elsewhere, from whom one could learn the behaviour and patterns of thought that were expected of an Athenian. Homer and the lyric poets generally reflected a suitably upper-class ethos, and so in their more problematic ways did the tragedians. Attendance at the dramatic festivals was therefore another part of a boy's education – and perhaps one of the few parts that gave him some notion of critical thinking. Equally important, after the age of twenty, was attending to the decisions of the people in the Assembly and the law courts, to see what earned communal praise and what was blamed. A very few boys, only from the aristocracy, were further acculturated by being taken under the wing of an older lover.

THE SOPHISTS

A new breed of educators created a storm in this complacent world. The sophists (as they came to be called, though the single label disguises their differences) undermined the role of a boy's family in his education by offering their wares outside the family context, and their courses might require some kind of attendance for several months or even years; they placed considerably less emphasis on rote learning of poems and more on criticizing them, or even re-interpreting them as allegories; they implicitly denied that lineage or traditional Athenian education automatically made a man a good citizen, let alone fit for government, and offered to supplement his paltry education with other branches of study that would be of practical use in the modern world. No longer need a man take pride in being conspicuous for his military prowess, athleticism and good looks; all a man needed for success (in this culture where competition for the limelight was taken for granted) was the ability to speak well. Naturally, then, these new educators were suspect. Plato has Protagoras of Abdera say about himself: 'A foreigner who visits great cities and persuades the best of the young men to abandon the society of everyone else – family and friends, old and young – and to come to him instead for improvement has to be careful, because he is liable to a great deal of resentment, hostility and intrigue.'

Despite this resentment, these teachers did not *cause* changes, any more than the rash of eastern or eastern-inspired gurus of the 1960s and 1970s were 'brainwashing' young people from the first world; they came because there was a demand for them, because people needed to make sense of what was happening and to cope with a new world in the future. Athens was, relatively speaking, swimming in cash, and the leisured young were hungry for new horizons, and bored with the status quo. Moreover, an aristocratic young man was expected to enhance his own and his family's prestige by playing a part in the government of

Athens. But the Athenian democracy exercised such control over its officers that a politician's very life could depend on his ability to deliver a persuasive speech in the Assembly or law courts. So, of course, could his career: 'A man who has a policy but does not explain it clearly is in the same situation as one who has none in mind,' as Thucydides said. And greater sophistication, professionalism and clarity of thought were required to take charge of an empire, with all its financial, logistical and military responsibilities, and potential clashes of cultures. Every Greek city required a high level of involvement from those of its members who counted as full citizens, but none more so than democratic Athens. The issue was how to turn out competent statesmen: this was the need to which many of the new educators responded.

Sophists attracted pupils by giving displays, either as they travelled from city to city, or at international festivals where they could find large numbers already gathered. They offered to teach a vast range of subjects, from music and martial arts to government, with the balance on skills useful for government and manipulating the democratic system. Athenian democracy was a congenial environment, because, as Harvey Yunis describes it,

> Persuasion was built into the system: in the assembly individual citizens volunteered to engage in open, competitive debate before the voting, sovereign audience; in court litigants were compelled to speak for themselves before the same audience. Verbal combat in the assembly and courts could be intense: personal fortunes, political careers, lives, or the welfare of the community often hung in the balance.

Often, then, they were teachers of rhetoric and disputation (and hence of grammar, terminology, logic and other subjects that supported rhetoric and disputation). Most of them focused on the human sphere, social philosophy rather than highfalutin stuff, and approached issues empirically. They were very interested in *effects*: the effect of words on the human mind, the effect of music on the emotions.

This rudimentary higher education was designed only for the rich, since the sophists tended to charge exorbitant fees, but it was a step in the right direction, and they also gave displays of their learning or speechifying to wider audiences. Plato and Aristotle made 'sophist' a term of reproach, on the grounds that their arguments were often invalid (Aristotle) and that they were concerned only with winning arguments rather than improving people (Plato). But originally the word had more or less the same implications as our 'expert': sophists were clever men who were prepared, for a fee, to impart their skills, information or theories to others.

Many of the new educators focused less on doctrine than on method: how to use the right words, how to think, how to approach problems, how to argue. Some taught their students the ability to present either side of a case, especially by getting them to learn paired speeches with arguments and counter-arguments; they taught them to spot others' assumptions (especially invalid ones), by learning speeches that defended legendary criminals and miscreants against just such implicit assumptions. It was up to their students to apply or adapt the general principles and methods of argument contained within the model speeches to the particular circumstances of their culture. They perhaps glimpsed, then, the postmodernist idea that speech is a good way, and perhaps the only valid way, of describing and interacting with a multivalent world of ambiguity and cultural relativism. If some of the sophists come across as our contemporaries in some ways, that is because their legacy has proved hardy: there are still strong tendencies to favour empiricism over idealism, relativism over absolutism, humanism over transcendentalism, sociology over metaphysics, ethics over moral philosophy, everyday language over jargon, engagement in the 'real' world over ivory-tower wiseacring.

Rhetoric was not at this stage an abstract, literary art; it was the art of persuading live, mass audiences, especially for political purposes. Those sophists who focused on this sphere developed forensic and political rhetoric as a form of competition, and epideictic rhetoric as a form of display. The first was disturbing because it seemed that all one needed to win was the ability to argue well, whatever the facts of the case and whatever moral issues were involved; the second was disturbing because speech became the equivalent of actors' masks – a semblance, but where was the reality?

The Greek word *aretē* was traditionally applied to the canonical virtues: like the English word 'virtue' (from the Latin *virtus*), its root meaning is 'manliness'. But the *aretē* the sophists claimed to teach meant the skills that enabled a man to lead his community and to get the better of others in debate. It was above all Socrates who took the word out of this competitive context and made it refer to an inner state of morality. Protagoras is made by Plato to describe the 'virtue' he taught as 'the proper management of one's own affairs, or how best to run one's household, and the proper management of public affairs, or how to make the most effective contribution to the affairs of the city both as a speaker and as a man of action'. This was a direct attack on the aristocratic assumption that this kind of 'virtue' was their own privileged attribute, passed down from generation to generation. Politics became a subject that anyone with enough money and aptitude could undertake, never mind his family background. The sophists demonstrated for the first time in western history the sheer importance of education: it could enable people to improve themselves and rise in society. For the first time education itself became a subject deserving serious consideration: what should its content be, and to whom should it be made available?

The sophists were suspect for a number of reasons, then: for undermining ingrained assumptions, for seeming to talk without substance, for teaching the ability 'to make the morally weaker argument defeat the stronger'. They were feared as slick – as *deinos*, a word that simultaneously meant 'clever' and 'formidable'. The most famous orator of them all, Gorgias of Leontini, who came as an ambassador from his Sicilian city to Athens in 427 and became a superstar for his florid rhetorical style, did nothing to alleviate such concerns when he likened speech to a powerful medicinal drug that operated by means of a kind of deceit or bewilderment to stir or pacify emotions and change men's minds. As teachers of the ability to argue both sides of any case, they left most people, who held the naïve assumption that truth lay with one side or the other, fuming with frustration.

They were thought either to be frauds, teachers of 'nonsense and quackery', or, if there was substance to their teaching, to be corrupters of the young. 'It's plain to see', Plato has Socrates' prosecutor Anytus say, 'that sophists do nothing but corrupt and harm those who associate with them.' Above all, they were thought to have taught the young oligarchs, though in fact all they did was initiate discussion of politics at a theoretical level and so provide ammunition for champions of all constitutions, not just oligarchy. More important than any theory, however, was the confidence they gave the wealthy young men who could afford their services: since they could expect to win court cases by rhetorical means, some members of the elite began to wonder why they should submit any longer, why they should let the people be the arbiters of who received and who lost honour, rather than reclaiming that right for themselves. By pricing themselves beyond the reach of most Athenians, the sophists put a certain form of political expertise back in the hands of those who had once claimed a divine right to rule.

NATURE AND CONVENTION

The opposition developed in the fifth century BCE between 'nature' (*physis*) and 'convention' (*nomos*) has proved to be a robust and powerful tool of analysis; some of the sophists also used it to develop radical ideas about the relationship between an individual and his community. 'Nature' (by which the Greeks originally meant not the natural world, but the particular nature of anything) is whatever has not been interfered with by human beings, or even what *cannot* be affected by human interference; 'reality' or 'essence' are often good translations, while *nomos* is 'law', 'convention', 'custom', or 'social norms'. A great many important and perennial questions were raised in the context of this opposition in the course of the second half of the fifth century.

Did the gods exist in reality, or were they human inventions? If they did exist, were they really as the poets described them, and as tradition perpetuated them, or were such descriptions untrue to their natures? Was there such a thing as natural law and, if so, were its demands more binding on human beings than the demands of man-made law, especially since natural laws appear to be eternal and unbreakable, whereas men often change their laws? Laws and conventions also differ from culture to culture, so should a man follow the dictates of his nature or the dictates of his society? Which of these two sets of dictates will bring the greatest rewards? Is it not just stupid to believe that man-made laws are the only rules there are? Are some men natural slaves, or is slavery just a convention? Are *any* properties of *any* things natural, or are all conventional? Do words somehow express the essence of the things they refer to, or are they just arbitrarily made up? What, then, is the difference between reality and appearance, and can language do more than capture appearances? Are we in fact all equal, as far as our nature as human beings is concerned? Is it a natural law, which it is only realistic to recognize, that the stronger state or individual will rule the weaker, or should the strong restrain themselves, and curb their pursuit of self-interest, in accordance with conventional justice? But does this not make human law a kind of tyrant over certain individuals? Is one culture naturally superior to another, or are all equal, as human constructs? Even if cultures are human constructs, are they not of crucial importance, because without civilization humankind would long ago have been wiped out by wild animals and other natural forces? Is there, in fact, any such thing as 'natural justice' or is that an oxymoron?

Positions taken in these important debates varied from mild to offensive. While some held that *nomos* was hugely beneficial to human beings, both individually and collectively, Antiphon (possibly the same man as the mastermind of the oligarchy of 411) argued that we can judge nature's laws by seeing what causes us pleasure or pain, that indulging our natural capacities gives us the greatest pleasure, and that therefore this is what we should do – as long as we avoid unpleasant consequences, such as being spotted in a crime and punished. Writ large, this is precisely the logic of imperialism that Athens favoured. Alcibiades and others learnt from Antiphon that self-interest had as much right as social norms to motivate a person. In 423 Aristophanes brought such ideas to the attention of a mass audience in his *Clouds*; they were well known, and well known to be troubling.

Plato's Callicles argued that man-made laws were a means for the weak to defend themselves against the strong, but that a truly strong man would scorn conventions and set himself up as a despotic ruler, to give his appetites their head. Elsewhere Plato had Thrasymachus claim that conventional justice was for fools, weak in power and weak in mental ability, and a little later in *Republic* had a character argue that it was a fact of human nature that, if we could act with impunity, we would transgress every law in the world that obstructed the satisfaction of our desires, while in the Mytilenean debate Thucydides' Cleon insisted that the Athenians had to choose between acting as decent human beings and holding an empire. Democrats argued, in favour of co-operative virtues, that 'natural justice' and concord required equality among all citizens, but oligarchs now knew how to reply, in favour of competition, that 'natural justice' required that the strong and the intelligent ruled everyone else, and that this went not just for individual politicians but for states too: concord has to be imposed from above.

INTELLECTUALS UNDER ATTACK

The sophists' passion for extreme arguments made it easy for anyone so inclined to read them as subversive. At the same time, the other main intellectual trend of the period, the quasi-scientific explanation of the world, was widely regarded as equivalent to atheism, for its reliance on natural forces in explaining everything from the creation of the world to its tiniest phenomenon. There was no room for intervention by any supernatural entity, because there was nothing beyond nature and its principles.

Ancient atheism is hard for us to judge. Since the ancient gods are not our gods, we might even be inclined to admire the insights of those thinkers who espoused it or were working towards it, and to overlook how radical they actually were. It is worth repeating here that atheism threatened society, not religion as some abstract sphere, because religion was not a category separate from society. Atheism or any form of impiety angered the gods and turned them against the city. Thinkers had been developing more or less atheistic ideas for over a century, but atheists came under suspicion now because of the new argumentative tools that helped them to make their case stronger, and because Athens, the cultural centre of the Mediterranean world and the natural magnet for intellectuals of all stripes, was in the throes of a social crisis and needed someone to blame.

Intellectuals were suspect, then, but was this taken any further? The evidence for the prosecution of intellectuals before Socrates' trial is difficult to assess. There is quite a lot of it, and it is no worse or further removed in time than our evidence for other events of the fifth century, but some of it is plainly contaminated, as when we hear that Prodicus of Ceos was condemned to death by drinking hemlock – an obvious doublet of Socrates' death. Even the generalizations point both ways: on the one hand, Aristotle gives as an example of an argument the following syllogism: 'If the fact that generals are often put to death does not prove that they are worthless, neither does the fact that intellectuals are often put to death prove that *they* are worthless.' This looks like good evidence for the prosecution and even execution of intellectuals – but then, if authentic, Aristotle's later quip, that he was leaving Athens to stop the Athenians wronging philosophy for a second time, makes little sense, since it would not be the second time, but the fourth or the fifth or whatever – unless arrogant Aristotle was meaning to imply that only he and Socrates counted as true philosophers, or unless he was referring in the first place to the fate of intellectuals in other societies than Athens.

The first, vital piece of evidence is one of the hardest to assess. We are told that some time in the 430s a professional interpreter of oracles and politician called Diopeithes, who was nicknamed 'the mad' for his overblown speaking style, proposed and got passed in the Assembly a decree to the effect that 'anyone who did not pay due respect to divine phenomena or who offered to teach others about celestial phenomena should be impeached'. Our *only* source for the decree is Plutarch, writing some 530 years after the event, but he was a good researcher and a decree like this fits in with the general climate of the times. The omens just before the start of the Peloponnesian War, when this decree was probably passed, were ambiguous, to say the least. Diopeithes' decree may have been just one of a number of attempts to ensure the gods' goodwill towards Athens in the forthcoming conflict. Socrates was not tried under this decree, partly because its terms were not applicable to him, and partly because by the time of his trial decrees were no longer legally binding, but it lurks in the background as a sign of what was possible in classical Athens.

As Plutarch tells it, Diopeithes was also trying to get at Pericles, via his circle of intellectual friends. And so we hear of the prosecution of his common-law wife Aspasia of Miletus, the philosophers Anaxagoras of Clazomenae and Protagoras of Abdera, the sculptor Pheidias of Athens and the Athenian musicologist Damon of Oa. 'Pericles' educated friends . . . were seldom in the public eye and a liability when they were,' as Ober puts it. Of these, the evidence for Protagoras's trial is flimsy: two late writers tell us that he was banished from Athens after a trial, but Plato, a witness far closer in time, says that Protagoras was held in high repute throughout his life, without becoming liable to the standard calumnies. It is equally hard to be sure about Aspasia, since there is only one report of her trial for impiety (perhaps on the grounds that, as an alleged courtesan, she polluted shrines by entering them). The reporter, Antisthenes, was an early witness, since he was a follower of Socrates, writing in the fourth century; but like all the Socratic writers, what he wrote combined fact and fiction, and Aspasia was fast attracting the attention of anecdotalists.

Anaxagoras claimed that the sun and the moon, traditionally gods, were no more than lumps of burning rock, and wielded scientific reasoning against religious fears that a ram with only one horn was a terrible omen. But he was probably not taken to court for such views. Later writers said so, but the report on which they were all basing themselves was that of the fourth-century historian Ephorus of Cyme, who did not say that the Athenians actually prosecuted Anaxagoras for impiety, but that they 'tried' or 'wanted' to do so. But that is enough for our purposes: even if he was not brought to trial, it is clear that the notion of trying intellectuals was current before Socrates' trial, and there may be truth in the story that Anaxagoras was forced out of Athens, since he died some time in the 420s back in Asia Minor.

The musicologist Damon was almost certainly ostracized in the late 440s. The evidence is relatively profuse, and starts relatively early. A few *ostraka* have even been found in the Agora with his name – too few to prove much, except that he *was* considered the kind of undesirable power-possessor who was a candidate for ostracism. He was ostracized either because he was thought to be anti-democratic, and inclined to offer undemocratic advice to Pericles, or, just possibly, for trying to tamper with Athenian music, when music was recognized as a powerful force for education and acculturation.

Outside the Periclean circle, the evidence for harassment of intellectuals is less secure, or somewhat irrelevant. This in a sense makes the existence of Diopeithes' decree more plausible, since it might then have had the specific anti-Periclean purpose Plutarch assigned to it. We also hear that the natural scientist Diogenes of Apollonia was in danger of losing his life, but again this is an isolated and implausible report; at the most, perhaps he was unpopular, or ridiculed by comic poets (he is the unnamed source of quite a few of the ideas lampooned by Aristophanes in *Clouds*). We can be pretty sure that Diagoras of Melos fled into exile to avoid a trial, or was banished, but his crime was taking the Eleusinian Mysteries in vain, and there was a specific law on the statute books (so to speak) that criminalized such impiety, and so we can accept that Diagoras got into trouble without adding his case to the list of unusual actions against intellectuals.

FREEDOM OF THOUGHT

We can be fairly sure, then, that Socrates was not the first intellectual who got into trouble in Athens, but a couple of prosecutions do not add up to persecution, and Athens was still a more congenial culture for artists and intellectuals than Sparta and elsewhere. Even so, classical Athens was not as liberal as many have liked to think. The idealization of Athens in this respect was a deliberate construct, a highly successful piece of propaganda, started by Pericles in the section of the Funeral Speech I translated at the start of this chapter. But if the Athenians were intolerant of intellectuals, why did Athens continue to act as a magnet for them? Why did it retain its position as the intellectual and cultural centre of the Mediterranean world? Because intellectuals, along with everyone else, were taken to court only on those very rare occasions when they were felt to be *politically* undesirable.

What, then, of certain rights that any modern democracy deserving of the name takes to be inalienable, such as freedom of thought and the right of any individual to speak his or her mind? The Greeks had a far less developed sense of an individual's rights than we do today. The dividing line between 'public' and 'private' was different: our private lives extend a long way, but exactly the opposite was the case for an ancient Athenian citizen. Athenian perception of what was 'public' was so capacious that it was easy for a citizen to trespass on to public ground – and if what he was saying or doing could be construed as contrary to the public interest, he could become liable to censure or even prosecution. It never occurred to ancient Greeks that freedom from governmental interference might be an individual's right.

There is a lot of talk in Athenian speeches and dramas about every citizen's right to say what he wanted. The terms used are *isēgoria* and *parrhēsia*, the first meaning 'equality of public speech', and the second 'frank speech' or 'saying whatever you want'. At a couple of points Euripides suggested that the only alternative to Athenian *parrhēsia* was slavehood, and lines such as 'I pray that my family may flourish as free citizens with freedom of speech, dwelling in the far-famed city of Athens' were guaranteed to raise a cheer in the Theatre of Dionysus. Even the enemies of democracy recognized the centrality of this right to the democracy, and there was a state-financed ship called the *Parrhēsia*.

But *isēgoria* was the right of all citizens in good standing to voice an opinion in the Assembly; hence the discussion of every motion that came before the Assembly was prefaced by a herald crying the question: 'Who wants to speak?' And *parrhēsia* was not 'freedom of speech' as we understand it; it was not the right of every citizen to speak (and think) as he might wish under any circumstances, but the right to speak his mind in the Assembly. Likewise, when the term 'freedom of speech' first occurred in the English language, it meant 'the privilege of free debate belonging to members in parliament', and the same went for the fledgling United States of America: the original free speech clause in the US Constitution is Section 6, Article 1, guaranteeing freedom of speech 'in either House'. As Isocrates said in 355 BCE, *parrhēsia* was restricted to comic poets (who were taken to be politically engaged) and to speakers in the Assembly; he might have added the law courts, since they too were a political arena.

Nor was even this restricted freedom of speech considered inalienable. The comic poets were curbed on several occasions between 440 and 420, each time when a situation was considered so sensitive that drawing attention to it in the theatre might be inflammatory or otherwise politically inappropriate. And restrictions were in place which applied to all public speakers: there was a long-standing law against slandering the dead, and another (dating from around 420) against unsupported accusations of crimes for which an individual could lose his status as an Athenian citizen. The law against slander was beefed up in the 390s to attempt to restrict slander of magistrates in office, but in the fifth century, at any rate, comic poets could get away with transgressing these laws, because they were sanctioned by the Athenian people, who were more powerful than any of the abused individuals, and because the festivals at which their plays were produced were regarded as times when normality was, to a degree, suspended.

In any case, talk of 'rights' can seem anachronistic: it is a useful tool of historical analysis, but it was not a major aspect of the ancient Athenian political universe, as it is of ours. If anything was going to bring up the issue of rights, it was the harassment of intellectuals; but this pivoted not on infringement of rights, but on whether or not they had harmed the community. In his defence speech Socrates did not protest: 'What about my right to think and speak as I choose?' He argued that his thoughts and words were not subversive of the established moral code and did not harm the city. Ancient Athenians simply took for granted that the state had a more pressing claim than any individual.

The only way they could counter the pervasive presence of the state was by appealing to a higher authority: thus both Sophocles' fictional Antigone and the historical Socrates appealed in their moments of crisis to higher religious claims – Antigone by preferring certain 'unwritten laws' to those of the state, Socrates by claiming that his mission was god-given. A fully fledged concept of rights had to wait until larger entities – the state or the gods – were dethroned. Until then, they held all the cards: serving the state or worshipping the gods was an absolute good. Until an individual's rights relative to the state were recognized, until a degree of relativity began to undermine the absolutism, citizens' rights were attenuated. Ancient political theorists did not couch their theorizing in the kind of terms we might expect, of balancing the demands of individuality against the demands of citizenship: they tried to imagine perfectly functioning societies, and the citizens of these societies often appear to be little more than cogs in a machine.

THE CONDEMNATION OF SOCRATES

ELEVEN

Socratic Politics

Nowadays, those of us who are concerned about such things assume that the quest for moral goodness is, to a large extent, a private affair: I deploy my inner resources to avoid doing harm and to do good. But just as, towards the end of the previous chapter, we saw how the ancient Greek conception of the public domain impinged on areas that we would take to be private, so another surprise is in store: in Socrates' day, almost all Greek thinkers assumed or argued that the polis was the correct and only environment for human moral flourishing – that a good community *created* goodness in its citizens.

So Plato occupied himself in *Republic* with imagining an ideal state in which all members of society would be good to the best of their abilities, while for Aristotle education in moral goodness was a product of the right constitutional environment, and his *Politics* is expressly a continuation of his *Nicomachean Ethics*: thorough ethical enquiry entails also describing the state that will best allow its citizens to find and retain goodness. As a moral philosopher, Socrates was also concerned with the circumstances that would allow his hopes and aspirations for people to be fulfilled. Plato was not being untrue to his mentor when he had him divide statesmen into two classes – those who aim for the moral perfection of their fellow citizens and those who aim merely to gratify them.

If political thought starts with the consideration of three factors – how power should be exercised in the community, how power should be limited and controlled in the community, and what the goals are of wielding power in the community – then, as far as our evidence goes, Socrates contributed to the first and the third of these questions, but failed to address the middle one. That is, he was sure that power should be given to the wise, and he was sure that the point of political power was the moral improvement of every citizen, but it is not clear how he thought the wise were to achieve this, or what steps he thought should be taken to educate and control the power-possessors and ensure that the goal of moral improvement was not diverted into other channels, or where he stood on the pros and cons of collectivism versus pluralism – which is to say that it is not clear to what extent he had mapped out and thought through at least some of the issues Plato came to address in *Republic*.

Though Socrates never worked out a political programme, we can be sure that it would have been based on reason. Socrates believed that all of us are, essentially, rational creatures; he even, controversially, went so far as to claim that all errors are intellectual errors, as if we could never be swayed by emotion. Any reforms that were to be put in place, then, would be rationally thought out and, more importantly, rationally presented to the citizens, because as a wholehearted intellectualist, Socrates denied the gap between a person's realizing that something is correct and his acting on that realization. A great part of a true statesman's job would simply be education. Reasoned reflection – certainly not passive acceptance – would lead his fellow citizens to see that the statesman's laws were rationally justified, or at least would lead them to trust that he had their best interests at heart. If there was something they did not like about their community, they could either leave or try to influence the legal code to suit them better. The successful Socratic statesman need never use tricks, coercion, or even mere habituation. This may sound naïve (as it did first to Plato and Aristotle), but Socrates pursued this vision for at least thirty years. Visionaries often seem naïve to their successors.

Some readers might already be puzzled by the idea of a politically engaged Socrates, remembering that, according to Plato, his little supernatural voice discouraged him from playing an active part in democratic politics. But he was not altogether aloof: from 449 BCE, when he became eligible for public service, he did his duty as a soldier (three times, and one of those was an extended campaign), on the Council (once) and probably also as a dikast (more than once). We have no way of knowing whether this amount of service was more or less than usual, and in any case, since both membership of the Council and empanelment as a juror were subject to a lottery, even definite statistics would still leave room for doubt, though both involved first volunteering for the job. When Plato's Socrates says that he has never taken part in the political life of the city, he means high office, of the kind that might have enabled him to push through reforms more quickly.

Socrates' decision not to play a major role in Athenian politics should not be taken to mean that he thought that politics was pointless, but that he himself would be ineffective on the public stage, that society was too corrupt for effective political action, and that he would risk death if he exposed himself in this way. We may regret that Socrates did not protest against some of the injustices that were performed by Athens during his lifetime, but despite this all our sources agree that Socrates was a person of the utmost moral integrity, by which I mean that he spent his entire life, devoted his entire being, to reducing injustice and promoting justice. This led him not just to disdain death, but even to avoid a certain amount of political activity; even as a high-ranking official of the Athenian democracy, he could never have promoted his vision without compromising it, which to a person of integrity is the same thing as giving up. And so he paradoxically practised politics in private, by helping others to become the kind of politicians that he wanted to see.

SOCRATIC POLITICAL THOUGHT

The attempt to reconstruct Socrates' political views brings us as sharply up against a source problem as did the attempt to reconstruct his views on religion. If there was anything in Socratic thought on these matters that could have had a negative construction put upon it by Socrates' accusers or by their readers, would Xenophon and Plato not have found ways to obscure matters? But Xenophon and Plato believed that Socrates' political views were broadly right, and while this coincidence may make it impossible to disentangle what they attribute to Socrates completely from their own beliefs and opinions, it does also mean that they reflect Socrates' political views. If there were significant differences between the political views Plato ascribes to Socrates and those to be found in Xenophon's works, we would have no way to say which of them, if either of them, was being true to his mentor; but in fact the views they ascribe to Socrates in this respect complement one another perfectly.

Socrates approached political philosophy via the question 'Who should rule?' He took rulership to be a profession: the ruler should not be partisan, but just an expert ruler. And he argued that professional rulership meant improving the lot and especially the moral behaviour of the citizens:

> We found that all the other results which one might attribute to statesmanship – and there are many of these, of course: provision

of a high standard of living for citizens, for example, and freedom, and concord – are neither good nor bad. We decided that, if as a result of statesmanship the citizen body was to be benefited and happy, it was crucial to make them wise and knowledgeable.

Wisdom and knowledge were, for Socrates, either identical with moral goodness or its necessary conditions.

Socrates' political views start from a single, fundamental premise, shared by all his followers: 'Socrates said that it was not those who held the sceptre who were kings and rulers, nor those who were elected by unauthorized persons, nor those who were appointed by lot, nor those who had gained their position by force or fraud, but those who knew how to rule.' And he believed that leadership qualities were the same whatever the scale of the domain – a city, an army, a household. It may seem innocuous, even obvious, that only experts should undertake the difficult task of government, but Socrates drew conclusions from this premise that were radical in their time. The single sentence just quoted dismisses in turn the claims of monarchy, oligarchy, democracy and tyranny as legitimate constitutions, in favour of government by experts, however many there may be.

The incompatibility between the Athenian democracy and government by Socratic experts is brilliantly imagined by Plato, in an extended ship-of-state metaphor:

Imagine the following situation on a fleet of ships, or on a single ship. The owner has the edge over everyone else on board by virtue of his size and strength, but he's rather deaf and short-sighted, and his knowledge of naval matters is just as limited. The sailors wrangle with one another because each of them thinks that he ought to be the captain, despite the fact that he's never learnt how. They're for ever crowding closely around the owner, pleading with him and stopping at nothing to get him to entrust the helm to them. They think highly of anyone who contributes towards their gaining power by showing skill at winning over or subduing the owner, and describe him as an accomplished seaman, a true captain, a naval expert; but they criticize anyone different as useless. They completely fail to understand that any genuine sea-captain has to study the yearly cycle, the seasons, the heavens, the stars and winds, and everything relevant to the job, if he's to be properly equipped to hold a position of authority in a ship.

In fact, they think it's impossible to study and acquire expertise at how to steer a ship or be a good captain. When this is what happens on board ships, don't you think that the crew of such ships would regard any true captain as nothing but a windbag with his head in the clouds, of no use to them at all?

The idea of government by experts was also Pythagorean. Pretty much all we know about Pythagorean politics is that for about fifty years, from somewhat before 500 to around 450 BCE, a number of cities in southern Italy were administered by members of the school, and that this administration was far from democratic. And Socrates was close to a number of Pythagoreans. Plato's *Phaedo*, his moving portrait of Socrates' last day on earth, consists of a frame dialogue in which a Pythagorean associate of Socrates from the town of Phleious, near Argos, asks Phaedo for an account of the conversation which Socrates had in prison with, among others, two prominent Pythagoreans from Thebes.

If someone was an expert and was recognized as such, people would willingly obey him, Socrates believed, because they would see that he had their best interests at heart and that there was no one more effective than him at doing them good. 'This I know,' he said, 'that to do wrong and to disobey my superior, whether god or man, is bad and disgraceful' – and the reason he felt certain of this was that it was just obvious: naturally, all of us would obey someone we recognized as an expert, just as we do what the doctor tells us. The Socratic citizen is not finally and completely virtuous (though his leaders ideally would be), but is receptive to words of wisdom framed in an appropriate form of rhetoric; and he is receptive in this way because he appreciates that his leaders have his welfare in mind. In this way, political concord – the elusive goal of all statesmen – would be assured.

The obedience of the majority to their wise rulers is not coerced: Socrates does not envision a totalitarian state. Were there to be a Socratic leader, his first purpose would be the persuasion, by rational argument, of as many of the citizens in his care who had ears to hear, that the focus of their lives should be on improving their souls, and his second purpose would be the establishment of the correct legislative apparatus for achieving this goal. Even if Socrates never elaborated a detailed political programme, there is nothing in his political outlook that would limit the improvement of citizens to personal contact or improving rhetoric: the city could be equipped with sufficient legislative machinery, as long as the laws promoted an environment of justice within which individuals could flourish as moral beings.

The only qualification on his call for true statesmen was his belief that perfect wisdom is unavailable for any human being, in any sphere of activity. Above all, we cannot see the future, and so we have to pray to the gods that the consequences of our actions turn out well. The unattainability of perfect knowledge does not undermine his search for expertise. 'A man's reach should exceed his grasp,' as Robert Browning said: ideals are worth striving for, and Socrates always held out the possibility of the existence of true moral experts, who knew what justice was and therefore had a reliable standard by which to see to its instantiation in the world. And if Athens was to be where such experts arose, under Socrates' guidance, then Athens was going to have to change to accommodate them.

NEITHER DEMOCRAT NOR OLIGARCH

Socratic leaders rise to the top simply by demonstrating their expertise to a receptive audience, or by being trained by already existing experts. There would be no point to the democratic lottery, and Socrates inveighed against it. He used to say that just as it would be nonsense to use a lottery to choose athletes to represent the city at the games, or to choose public doctors, or any other kind of expert, so it would be equally nonsensical to expect the lottery to produce competent politicians. But the lottery was fundamental to Athenian democratic egalitarianism; elections were used rarely, only when it was felt to be essential to favour those with specific abilities. A Socratic principle was that if something could be tackled by human intelligence, that was the instrument best used; only if something is completely incomprehensible, like the future, should one resort to the gods (by prayer or divination). But the use of the lottery in the Athenian democracy was equivalent to turning to the gods – to praying, so to speak, for the right leaders. Socrates countered this: if there are competent statesmen, use them.

Socrates likened a good statesman to a herdsman, whose job it is to look after his flock. The image has become a comfortable cliché, but that should not disguise the fact that it is fundamentally undemocratic: democratic officers did not have the unchecked power of a herdsman.

Just as Socrates was explicitly opposed to the lottery, so, in the case of genuinely talented politicians, he was implicitly opposed to many of the democratic safeguards, such as annual elections and many-headed committees, which served to check the power of individuals.

Socrates did not shrink from the corollary to his call for expertise in government: the contention, familiar from the critics of democracy, that democratic government puts power into the hands of the ignorant masses – that the 'mass wisdom' on which democratic procedure was predicated was an oxymoronic fiction. On the contrary, because of their ignorance the masses are easily misled by speakers who aim to flatter and persuade rather than to educate, as a true statesman would. In keeping with this, Socrates believed that deliberation with oneself or with just a few others was the best means for reaching the truth, not public, mass deliberation. Not that mass deliberation is by its very nature doomed to failure, but reaching the truth requires freedom from the pressure of time or partisan interests, both of which are more likely to play a part in public meetings than in a small group.

But the masses, in the mass, are a source of corruption and are riddled with false values. One can acquire virtue only under the right conditions, and manual work is a major impediment. Such snobbery about work was typical of upper-class Greeks, but we should not be too quick to judge. Before the days of universal education, the condition of the poor was in many respects benighted, and the sentiment lingered long: even in the eighteenth century, the Scottish philosopher David Hume opined that 'poverty and hard labour debase the minds of the common people'. Socrates, anyway, thought the cobbler should keep to his last – that butchers, bakers and oil-lamp makers were generally equipped only to recognize the value of a true leader, and otherwise should stick to their areas of expertise, leaving politics to dedicated political experts, on the bizarre principle, later taken up by Plato, that each person properly has one and only one job to do. This is why Plato admits that for Socrates the Spartan and Cretan constitutions were models of good government, because these societies were highly structured. If Plato went on to develop political views based on a stratification of society into workers and experts, he was hardly breaking away from his mentor.

Plato also has Socrates criticize the most eminent democratic politicians of Athens's past as useless: 'Pericles made the Athenian people idle, work-shy, garrulous and mercenary . . . There's never been a good statesman here in Athens . . . These men from Athens's past made the city bloated and rotten.' In short, democracy is a case of the morally bankrupt leading the intellectually incompetent. Plato has Socrates describe himself as the only true politician, because he was the only one who was concerned with the moral education of his fellow citizens, which should be the primary task of all statesmen.

Despite his misgivings about democracy, Socrates still chose to spend his life in Athens. Does this not show that in fact he preferred the democracy to other constitutions? Socrates himself addressed this issue, but the reason he gave for staying in the city was not that he *preferred* its constitution, but that he was obliged to respect its laws: by the accident of having been born and having grown up in democratic Athens, he had, as someone who was committed to the rule of law, taken on this obligation. This forms part of his explanation of why he did not defy the court ruling and escape from prison as he could have. We may guess that another reason for his having stayed in Athens was that it gave him the freedom to pursue his life's work. He stayed, not because he was satisfied with Athenian democracy as a political system, but because he was allowed (for a long time, anyway, before the special circumstances of his trial) to pursue his vision.

It will not do to argue, as several influential commentators have, that, even if Socrates was no democrat, he still thought democracy better than the alternatives – that he did not really believe that moral/political experts would ever be found, and so did not really believe that there was a viable alternative, and limited himself to a little constructive criticism of democracy. His criticisms are too fundamental for that. And was his lifelong search for experts no more than a gesture, from someone who never expected to find them? Socrates believed that a small group of even somewhat imperfect political experts was preferable to democracy, with its reliance on the lottery and on the illusion of mass wisdom. Besides, the people of Athens clearly saw Socrates as an enemy of democracy; if Socrates was even tepid about democracy, we can legitimately wonder why, given that he stayed in Athens during the rule of the Thirty, those murderous creatures did not put him to death and the relatively benign democracy did.

It is irrelevant that Socrates counted among his lifelong friends the 'loyal democrat' Chaerephon. Most of us are, and all of us should be, open-minded enough to have friends with different political views from our own. In any case, the way that Socrates introduces

Chaerephon in Plato's *Apology* points in entirely the opposite direction. Socrates says that not only was Chaerephon a loyal democrat, but that 'he also shared your recent exile and restoration'. The reference is to the period when the Thirty were in charge of Athens – when democrats fled the city (or were put to death) and were restored only after the nasty little civil war. And Socrates admits his distance from these events: he does not say 'our' recent exile and restoration, but 'your' – as he must, because it was well known that he had stayed in Athens during the regime of the Thirty.

Is this not sufficient evidence on its own to prove that Socrates was some kind of oligarch? Far from it, because pretty much the same reasons that make Socrates no democrat make him no oligarch either. Oligarchy is the rule of the few – a greater or lesser number in different states, but always defined as those with certain property and/or birth qualifications. But – logically, at least – Socratic rulers are not necessarily wealthy or high-born; they are simply those with the requisite knowledge. Socrates *inclined* more towards oligarchy, because philosopher-kings (we might as well use the Platonic term, since, as thoughtful scholars recognize, in *Republic* Plato describes a political system with which Socrates would have felt comfortable) were bound to be few, and because the rich were the only ones with the leisure to acquire the kind of expertise he demanded of his rulers; but Socrates could not have approved of any existing oligarchy, which would strike him as government by the ignorant just as much as democracy. It was not a wealth or birth elite he was interested in, but an educated elite; he wanted a literal 'aristocracy' – 'rule by the best people', who were equipped to rule not by breeding, nor by money, nor by eloquence, but by their ability to know the good and how to make it happen. Socrates was not interested in this or that constitution, only in seeing that Athens, or some version of it, was the right kind of moral environment. Perhaps his failure to come up with detailed political provisions was due to his hope that a reformed Athens would have considerably less need of legal and judicial apparatus.

SOCRATES' MISSION

What of the inescapable fact of Socrates' remaining in Athens during the regime of the Thirty? The Thirty made Athens an exclusive zone: 'All those who were not on the list [of the Three Thousand] were forbidden to enter the city.' This presumably means to enter the city for political purposes, since it is hard to see how the regulation would have been enforceable at the city gates, and of course shopkeepers and everyone else needed to enter to do business. So in what sense did Socrates remain in the city? Did he live there? His ancestral deme, Alopece, lay not far south of the city walls, but that proves nothing: very many people lived away from their ancestral demes. It is hard to picture Socrates outside of the centre of Athens, where he could continue to accost people and talk to them and his circle of admirers, even during the regime of the Thirty. Otherwise, Xenophon's claim that their ban on teaching the 'art of words' was aimed specifically at Socrates makes no sense at all. It may be an implausible claim in itself – the ban looks like a prohibition of rhetorical training rather than of Socratic teaching methods – but it still makes no sense for Xenophon even to suggest it unless Socrates remained active in Athens during the time of the junta. Socrates undoubtedly stayed in Athens in the only important sense; it does not matter where he slept at night, but he continued to go about his work there.

Socrates' remaining in Athens demands attention, especially since it is ignored by more philosophically inclined commentators, following the lead of Plato and Xenophon. What *was* Socrates' relationship with the Thirty? Xenophon did his best to defend Socrates by making out that they tried to curb him by legislation, and went on to retail a conversation in which Socrates disputed the matter with both Critias and Charicles, and widened the rift between him and them. Plato communicated the same message by telling how the Thirty tried to involve Socrates in their schemes by getting him, along with four others, to arrest a wealthy and distinguished Athenian citizen called Leon of Salamis (a known democrat), so that they could kill him and confiscate his assets; Socrates flatly refused and just went back home instead, leaving the others to get on with the nasty job.

If these are attempts to whitewash Socrates, they are scarcely convincing. The conversation with Critias and Charicles looks fictional, and the story about the arrest ends with a significant whimper, not a bang: if Socrates saw Leon's arrest as illegal or immoral, why did he not protest? He did nothing more than return home – hardly a courageous moral stand. Both Plato and Xenophon skate over the significance of the fact that Socrates chose to remain in Athens. Whether or not he was one of the select Three Thousand deemed worthy of citizenship in the New Model Athens (and he may well have been), he still chose to stay. His affiliations reached right to the very top, with Critias and Charmides and Aristotle of Thorae his pupils and friends, with his half-brother Patrocles and other students on the margins of the Thirty, and with views that the oligarchs could well have taken to be compatible with their own.

Pretty much everyone of any importance in Athens took sides, and those who could not tolerate the Thirty left Athens for elsewhere, even if not actively to participate in rebellion. It was a time of wretched chaos, with people moving into and out of Athens with as many possessions as they could carry. The refugees leaving the city had either been dispossessed of their property or were fleeing for their own and their family's safety. Those who stayed chose to stay, in the sense that any of them could have joined the exodus and found temporary accommodation elsewhere; it cannot be argued, then, that mere residence was neutral. Socrates would have been welcome in oligarchic Thebes, where he had close associates among the Pythagoreans who flourished there, and which had already taken in other exiles, including Thrasybulus.

All those who remained after the eviction were regarded as sympathizers; this is proved by the fact that, after the restoration of the democracy, they were all offered the opportunity to leave Athens and take up residence in the oligarchic enclave of Eleusis, where most of the Thirty had already fled. Lysias wrote his *Defence against the Charge of Subverting the Democracy* for a man who had, like Socrates, remained in Athens during the regime of the Thirty; a lot of it consists of a fairly desperate attempt to argue that residence in Athens at the time was *not* a sign of allegiance to the Thirty. Socrates must at the very least have known that his remaining in Athens, with his friends and associates in power, would look like approval, and that since he was a figurehead his actions would be noticed and assessed; and until the Leon episode, which Plato implies occurred towards the end of the regime (because the Thirty had no time to put him to death), he had done nothing to distance himself from them. So it was either approval, or stupidity, or inappropriate indifference.

Things were only made worse by the intentions of the Thirty to turn Athens into a Spartan-style society and by Critias's published eulogies of Sparta. Socrates and his followers had long been known or at least widely reputed to be attracted to Sparta. Not that they wanted to decamp and live there, but they liked the sound of a more structured society, if not also its oligarchic regime. How could Socrates not have seemed a sympathizer? It did not take great intelligence or sensitivity to see what kind of people the Thirty were; it did not take Thrasybulus and hundreds of others long to see what was going on, and we should not rate Socrates' intelligence or sensitivity as less acute than theirs. Socrates must have been attracted to the Thirty at least to the extent that he was prepared to give them time, to see if their intentions for Athens coincided with his own.

We do not have to look far to see what the attraction was: Critias was promising the moral reform of Athens; he wanted to purge the dross and leave only the gold of a few good men and true, who would manage a now-virtuous city. This crusade is so close to Socrates' political ideal that some must have wondered whether Socrates was actually Critias's adviser. No doubt Socrates soon became disillusioned when it became clear that Critias's means of implementing his fine-sounding policy included mass executions and expulsions, and no doubt that is why he refused to help them when they asked him to arrest Leon (who was indeed killed without trial), but by then it was too late: he had already become tainted by association with the Thirty. Even great philosophers can be naïve.

Socrates was caught by his desire to see the moral regeneration of Athens. In *Apology* Plato has him undertaking this task single-handedly, while throughout *Recollections of Socrates* Xenophon has him trying to educate others to become moral leaders of the city:

> On another occasion, Antiphon asked him how it was that he expected to make others good at politics when he himself did not take part in politics . . . Socrates retorted: 'Which would be the more effective way for me to take part in politics – by doing so alone, or by making it my business to see that as many people as possible are capable of taking part in it?'

He advised people first to set their own houses in order; only when they could control themselves (the foundation of all morality) could they hope to take control of some larger entity, such as the state. Socrates' task was to teach his students how to search for justice, so that they could exercise moral leadership. For most people, it would take a lifetime to learn how to discipline their appetites and emotions and thinking, and that would be enough; they would never turn to politics. But there were a select few who Socrates clearly hoped would develop into the kind of gifted and moral rulers he wanted to see. Xenophon even reports him as saying, in a conversation set in 407 BCE, that as a result of the social crisis Athens was now ready for moral regeneration.

I feel no qualms in attributing to Socrates a somewhat millenarian frame of mind as regards Athens's future. Anyone with any sense could see that radical changes were likely, and perhaps inevitable. The old citizen-state ideal was one of self-sufficiency, to guarantee its autonomy and freedom from external influences. This ideal, however, was far more realistic when it was formulated, some two hundred years before Socrates was born; by the middle of the fifth century, it was well out of date. Short of a radical austerity drive and a drastic culling of the population, Athens was never going to be self-sufficient again. The simplest of economic factors – shortage of grain, timber and minerals – had driven the city to acquire a maritime empire, and the bell could not be un-rung. The empire had not only caused scores of Greek states to think of themselves as less than independent, but it had also forced a similar network on to Athens's enemy, Sparta. And the rewards of empire, or even just of interdependence, were self-evident in Athens's enormously increased wealth. If Athens no longer had an empire, someone else was going to. Others were forming confederacies or leagues, a process that was accelerated by the scale of the new kind of warfare, in which a citizen militia no longer sufficed: states needed allies, and money to hire professional soldiers. It was the last possible moment in Greek history for Socrates' political ideal, the last time when states such as Athens would be small enough to make it realistic to think of a select group of statesmen steering the state towards moral perfection.

The increasing internationalism of political life meant that the city-state was rapidly becoming a dinosaur. No one can accurately predict the next phase of evolution of anything as complex as a society, but it is possible to predict that evolution is bound to take place. The only secure bridge between the past and the future is principle; the ways in which principles are applied must be left up to future citizens. Socrates dug beneath the formulations of Athenian morality to see what principles underlay and underpinned them; these were what he wanted his students to carry through to the next generation. Those who lacked this insight, however, or who chose to hide their heads in the sand,

185

could see Socrates' questioning only as an attempt to undermine the foundations. The general culture of a city was held to educate its citizens, and conservative Athenians thought their city had done a pretty good job: they had defeated the Persians, gained control over an empire, enriched themselves, made Athens the glory and the cultural centre of Greece. They accused Socrates of rocking the boat, without realizing that the boat was already rocking of its own accord.

ALCIBIADES' ROLE

There is a distinct and easily observable pattern, in both Plato's and Xenophon's works, to Socrates' dealings with talented young men with political aspirations. First, he flirts with them, letting them understand that he can satisfy their ambitions; then he exposes their failings, by demonstrating either that they lack personal morality ('How can you expect to take control of the state when you cannot even control your-self?') or that they lack the expertise to shine in their chosen field. Finally, having shown them their defects, he may agree to take them into his select circle.

In Plato's *Alcibiades* we see Socrates working on his star pupil. Socrates claims to have had his eye on Alcibiades for some time, but now at last his little internal voice has let him approach him. Alcibiades' natural advantages – he is the best-looking young man in Athens, from the greatest family of the greatest city in Greece; he is well connected and wealthy – have led him to treat all his other suit-ors with disdain. Socrates expects to do better. Why? Because he is aware that Alcibiades (despite being aged only nineteen at the time) wants to be the leading statesman not just in Athens, not just in Greece, not just in Europe, but in the entire known world. Socrates is the only one who can help him attain this ambition, but Alcibiades must curb his arrogance and submit to his questions.

It turns out that Alcibiades knows nothing that will help him ful-fil his ambitions: his knowledge, based on a standard upper-class Athenian upbringing, is either politically irrelevant, or inferior to that of experts. The chief topic on which Alcibiades is ignorant, but which he needs to know if he is to be a competent statesman, is the nature of justice. He acts as if he knows what it is, but he does not, and the inher-ited conglomerate has failed to teach him this as it fails in other respects too, wherever an issue is complex or disputable. Perhaps, Alcibiades suggests cannily, a politician does not need to know justice, but only what is expedient. But Socrates aggressively exposes his ignorance of the nature of expediency as well.

Under Socrates' probing, Alcibiades becomes aware of his crippling ignorance of vital matters. In Aeschines of Sphettus's version of this conversation, Alcibiades is so overcome by this awareness that he bursts into tears, lays his head on Socrates' lap, and begs him to become his teacher; but Plato's Socrates has not yet finished. It is no consolation, he goes on, that almost all other Athenian politicians are equally ignorant; that does not excuse Alcibiades' ignorance. If he is to play a major part on the world stage, not just in Athens, he is bound to come across a better class of rival.

Having deflated Alcibiades, Socrates introduces a constructive suggestion: above all, Alcibiades needs self-knowledge, if he is to be a competent statesman, capable of creating concord in the city. Knowing oneself is caring for one's self, but what is the self? The true self is not the body, which is no more than an instrument, but the soul or mind (and Socrates cannot resist adding that this is what makes him Alcibiades' only true lover, because he loves him for his soul, not for his body). But the soul can know itself only by looking, as in a mirror, at goodness, either in another soul or in the divine realm. Until we know ourselves, we cannot know the good, and cannot know what is good for ourselves, or for others, or for a state. Without such knowledge, a politician is likely to do more harm than good; he must impart his own goodness (characterized as justice and self-control) to his fellow citizens, and plainly he cannot do so unless he is good himself. Until he has gained this condition of virtue, a man should not take up politics, but should apprentice himself to someone better than himself. Alcibiades is converted, and promises to stick as closely to Socrates in the future as Socrates has to him in the past.

But the very last words of the dialogue are pessimistic: 'I hope you do persevere in this,' Socrates says, 'but I have my doubts. I don't doubt your natural abilities, but I can see how powerful the city is, and I'm afraid it might defeat both of us.' This is Plato's way of signalling that Alcibiades did *not* turn out the way Socrates had wanted, and he does the same, somewhat more subtly, in *Symposium* too. Xenophon adds that Alcibiades was initially attracted to Socrates because he thought he could help him to achieve his political ambitions, and that Socrates was the only one who could tame him, but that Alcibiades was soon corrupted away from Socrates by the lure of beautiful women and powerful friends. Worldly success came easily to him, and so he felt he no longer needed Socrates' guidance. This became the standard story of the relationship between the odd couple in the later Platonic tradition. But Aeschines of Sphettus included the poignant rider that Socrates had expected the strength of his love to enable him to reform Alcibiades, even though doing so would be 'as difficult as getting milk and honey from a dry well'.

Socrates could see that Alcibiades had the energy, the talent and the position to go far in any field. Socrates wanted to produce one or more philosopher-kings to see Athens over its period of crisis and to revitalize the city's moral life; this is what he had in mind for Alcibiades. It may well be also what he had in mind for others among his students who showed similar potential: Charmides, Euthydemus Dioclou and Critobulus of Alopece, the son of Socrates' old friend Crito, all appear in this kind of role in Xenophon's *Recollections of Socrates* – and we should add Critias as well, except that for obvious reasons no Socratic writer showed Socrates grooming the future mass murderer for political life. The list should probably contain the name of Xenophon himself, since, when serving abroad, he showed a strong inclination to set himself up as king or tyrant of an overseas colony. And in the dialogue *Theages* (included in Plato's corpus, but written by an unknown contemporary), Theages is introduced to Socrates as the teacher best able to satisfy his desire for political power. The brief dialogue ends inconclusively, with Socrates saying that he will take the young man on if his supernatural voice lets him, but it confirms that Socrates was remembered for helping ambitious and talented young men become expert statesmen.

As for Alcibiades, when Socrates looked back on the career of his brightest hope, he must have thought to himself, 'What a waste!' Perhaps he even voiced this opinion aloud to some of his disciples, because Plato perfectly summarized the point, in the context of explaining why philosopher-kings, those who combine ability to rule with ability to do their communities good, were so thin on the ground. A naturally talented young man will be courted and flattered by others for their own purposes:

'What do you imagine he'll do in this situation,' I [Socrates] asked, 'especially if he happens to come from a wealthy and noble family within a powerful state, and is also good-looking and well built? Don't you think he'll be filled with unrealizable hopes, and will expect to be capable one day of managing the affairs not only of Greece, but of the non-Greek world as well? In these circumstances, won't he get ideas above his station and puff himself up with affectation and baseless, senseless pride?' – 'He certainly will,' he [Adeimantus] said. – 'Now, suppose someone gently approaches him while he's in this frame of mind and tells him the truth – that he's taken leave of his senses and won't get them back, as he should, without working like a slave for it – do you think it's going to be easy for the message to penetrate all these pernicious influences and get through to him?' – 'No, far from it,' he said. – 'And,' I went on, 'supposing his innate gifts and his affinity with the reasonableness of what's being said do in fact enable him to pay attention, and he is swayed and attracted towards philosophy, what reaction would you expect from those others, when they think they're losing his services and his friendship? Won't they do and say absolutely anything to stop him being won over? And as for the person who's trying to win him over, won't they come up with all kinds of private schemes and public court cases to stop him succeeding?'

And a few pages earlier, he attributed 'horrendous crimes and sheer depravity' to just such a person, someone who is brilliant but has been corrupted by pandering to the people's whims. No one doubts that these passages refer, without naming names, to Alcibiades and, at the very end of the quoted excerpt, to Socrates' trial. In the context of a discussion about philosopher-kings, it confirms Socrates' aspirations for Alcibiades – and his regret in *Republic* about the corruption of Alcibiades is pointed, since *Republic* sketches an ideal state of a kind that the historical Socrates might have wanted Alcibiades to play a major part in. Socrates' followers were almost as obsessed with Alcibiades as their master himself was; one of the central questions addressed by Plato in *Republic* was precisely how to get a person who is motivated by desire for prestige and honour to devote himself to philosopher-rulership.

Some time during the three-year siege of Poteidaea, Socrates went into a trance for the best part of twenty-four hours. What was he doing? Was he a mystic who had penetrated the cloud of unknowing?

Was he thinking? Was he cataleptic? In any case, twenty-four hours is a very long time to spend in motionless contemplation (whether rational or mystical), and attests to Socrates' remarkable powers. The only other significant aspect of the episode is that on coming to himself Socrates offered a prayer to the sun, which was then rising, and went on his way. The literary sun of northern Greece in the late 430s is the only certain light that can be shed on this episode, but it was surely extraordinary enough to represent some kind of turning point in Socrates' life – a new beginning, the start of a new day. I want to suggest, somewhat fancifully, that the turning point had to do with Alcibiades, with whom Socrates was spending a great deal of time during the campaign – that during these twenty-four hours Socrates first conceived the political dimension of his mission, to take this boy in hand and train him as a philosopher-king, and to find others too.

Socrates could see that the long-feared world war was about to begin; he knew that it would be vital, whatever the outcome, for Athens to emerge from the other side of the war with men of principle in charge, and so he decided to focus on teaching the young, and especially on training them in morality and politics. Hence Plato portrays his first question, on returning from Poteidaea, as a concern for the attainments or promise of the young men of the city – and it is Charmides, who was to become one of his select group of politically promising young men, to whom he is introduced. Pericles had Damon, Protagoras and Anaxagoras to help him form his policies and present them; the sophists in general often had the aim of turning out competent statesmen; Socrates wanted to play the same role, in his way, for the next generation of Athenian statesmen. It was a momentous decision, and he paid for it with his life.

TWELVE

A Cock for Asclepius

Xenophon preserves a tidy story. After the trial, as Socrates was being taken off to prison to await execution, he was accompanied by a few of his followers, some of whom were deeply distressed. One of them said that what he found particularly hard to bear was that Socrates had done nothing to deserve such a death. Socrates replied with a laugh: 'Would you feel better if I *did* deserve it?'

The story may be faintly amusing, but it overstates its case. Even his most devoted followers must have recognized that their mentor was sailing close to the wind. We may even wonder why condemnation had not happened earlier. Condemnation or acquittal in the Athenian legal system often depended more on whether or not the defendant was perceived or suspected of un-Athenian activities, than on whether or not he had committed the crime. And the weight of the un-Athenian activities that Socrates was either involved in or was suspected of being involved in is impressive.

He was a clever arguer and taught young men to be clever arguers; he usurped their fathers' roles in education and in general was perceived to be subversive of inherited values; he was either a sophist or indistinguishable from one; in his youth he had dabbled in atheistic science and even now his religious views were highly unconventional; he was suspected of being the leader of a weird cabal; he had irritated many prominent Athenians with his interminable, aggressive questioning; he had taught Alcibiades, the mocker of the Mysteries, the most corrupt of a corrupt generation, oligarch and possibly would-be tyrant, a pro-Spartan traitor who was widely held to be responsible for the loss of the war; he was close to others who had either mocked the Mysteries or desecrated the herms; he was close to Critias, the ideologue of the brutal Thirty, and others of that circle; his political views were elitist and smacked of the same programme of moral regeneration of Athens by 'enlightened' leaders that Critias had attempted to instigate; he was thought to be in favour of a Spartan-style constitution; he had stayed in Athens during the regime of the

Thirty; at his trial, he was defiant and openly hostile to the democratic courts and the inherited conglomerate. Iconic historical moments, such as Socrates' trial, will always be hijacked by partisan interests, but to try to make the trial depend on any single issue is a serious distortion of the facts.

Worst of all, he surrounded himself with men whom he presumably infected with these same views. Both Plato's and Xenophon's Socratic works are peopled by undesirable characters; anti-democrats outnumber the non-aligned or the pro-democrats by a considerable factor. Of the fifteen interlocutors that Plato shows conversing with Socrates whose political affiliations we know, five are democrats and the rest are villains and traitors. Socrates was known to have taught and loved Alcibiades and Charmides; he taught Critias and Euthydemus, who was Critias's beloved; another of the Thirty, Aristotle of Thorae, was at least in the Socratic circle, as was Cleitophon, who helped to prepare the ground for the oligarchy of 411 and was on the margins of the oligarchy of 404; at least seven of those who fled into exile as a result of the scandals of 415 were close associates; Xenophon was a student, and he was banished in the 390s from Athens for his anti-democratic and pro-Spartan leanings; in general, Socrates moved in the circles of those who were or were suspected of being oligarchs, and was close to the politically suspect Pythagoreans. Socrates could have been condemned just on the strength of his unfortunate associates and students, by those dikasts who knew nothing of his political and religious views.

But Socrates had been irritating people with his questions since about 440, was known to be the teacher of arrogant young men by the end of the 430s (his first mention in an extant comic fragment), and, whether or not my speculation about a conversion moment at Poteidaea is right, seems to have been committed to a political path for at least thirty years before his trial. To judge by the references to Socrates in the comic poets, his heyday was in the 420s and 410s, and he had somewhat dropped out of the limelight for at least a decade before his trial. It was twenty-four years since Aristophanes and Ameipsias had made him the most notorious atheist and subversive intellectual in Athens. Why take the elderly philosopher to court just then, in the spring of 399 BCE?

Like other intellectuals, Socrates became a target only once he was perceived as a threat to public order. His links to the Thirty changed his status from harmless eccentric to undesirable. He had been living on borrowed time ever since the defeat of the Thirty in 403. This is not to say that the charge of impiety was, in some Stalinist sense, just a cover for a political trial: religion and society were so intimately connected that to charge Socrates with impiety was already to accuse him of being socially undesirable. The corruption charge was also implicitly political, since everyone would immediately have thought of the 'young' – Alcibiades, Critias and the oligarchic set of the 420s and 410s. There had been dark mutterings about the influence of Socrates over these baneful characters.

The general atmosphere was not at all conducive to Socrates' acquittal. The main topic of serious conversation after the fall of the Thirty was 'How did we come to this?' All the controversial figures and events of the previous thirty years were being rehashed and mined for significance; and the arguments about where they went wrong, and how they could have let the empire slip out of their grasp, often came back to the part Alcibiades had played in their downfall, or the part he might have played in restoring the city's fortunes, had he been allowed to, or had he been a little less . . . less Alcibiades. And the people looked on Socrates differently because of his association with the Thirty. As one who had stayed in Athens during their regime, Socrates had already been offered the opportunity to leave Athens and take up residence in Eleusis. He had refused; for a figurehead, a trial was the logical next step.

THE PROSECUTION TEAM

We now have the context to speculate about the motives of Socrates' prosecutors – Meletus of Pitthus, Lycon of Thoricus and Anytus of Euonymon. There were several men called Meletus within the relevant time-frame, but we know so little about them that we cannot even be sure how many there were. It is attractive to think that the Meletus who prosecuted Socrates is the same as the Meletus who had prosecuted another high-profile case of impiety, against Andocides, a few months earlier; this would give us a consistent picture of a religious conservative with the democracy at heart. But Plato has Socrates describe his Meletus as 'young and unknown', an unsuitable description for the prosecutor of Andocides, once one of the wealthiest men in Athens and a notorious anti-democrat.

There was also a Meletus who was involved in the arrest of Leon of Salamis during the regime of the Thirty. Since Socrates refused to take part in this arrest, his posthumous defenders would have made a lot of the involvement of one of his prosecutors; and besides, if this Meletus were our Meletus, Socrates could hardly have said that Meletus was unknown to him. But we know from Andocides' defence speech that the Meletus who prosecuted him was also the one who took part in the arrest of Leon. In that case, our Meletus, Socrates' Meletus, is left out in the cold. His father may have been a writer of tragedies, of no great distinction. His obscurity makes it plausible to think that he was little more than a front man for the other two prosecutors, Anytus and Lycon, who were far more prominent figures in Athenian public life. This is confirmed by Socrates' words after the guilty verdict: 'There cannot be the slightest doubt that if Anytus and Lycon had not stepped up to prosecute me, Meletus would have become liable to the thousand-drachma fine for not having obtained a fifth of the votes.' The weight of Lycon and Anytus tipped the scales against Socrates – and it should come as no surprise that it was political weight.

We know very little about Lycon, except that he achieved some prominence as a democratic politician in the 400s, but the most plausible conjecture for his hostility towards Socrates is that he associated him with the Thirty, who had murdered his son. Lycon (if it is the same Lycon) features in Xenophon's *Symposium*, set in 422 BCE, when he was apparently on cordial terms with Socrates. But many years had passed since then, and the death of his beloved son may have turned his mind.

The most ominous of the accusers was Anytus. His political ascent is lost to us, and he first appears at the top of the tree, as a general, in 409. Pylos, on the south-western tip of the Peloponnese, had been in Athenian hands since 425, but had just been retaken by the Spartans. Anytus was entrusted with the task of recovering this important bridgehead. Bad weather prevented him from doing so and, as they so often did with unsuccessful generals, the Athenians decided to prosecute him, but he was acquitted – thanks to bribery, apparently.

At the end of the Peloponnesian War, Anytus was initially a supporter of the Thirty, or at least of Theramenes, but when ideology became more important than friendship he fled into exile to join Thrasybulus's resistance movement, abandoning his valuable business to the rapaciousness of the Thirty. He rapidly became one of the leaders of the resistance, to be mentioned in the same breath as Thrasybulus himself. He was equally prominent after the civil war, especially as one of the architects of the attempt to reconcile democrats and oligarchs and promote social concord. In a dialogue set in 402, Plato said that the Athenian people were choosing Anytus for the most important positions in the state. He was plausibly described as one who served the democracy well, and as a man of power in the city.

His career after 399, however, is obscure. In popular tradition, the Athenian people regretted killing Socrates and took it out on the prosecutors, with various stories giving various versions of their gruesome ends. None of these moral tales is trustworthy. In any case, we are not now concerned with what happened to the prosecutors after the trial. The point is that two prominent democrats, one of whom was a hero of the revolution against the Thirty and still an eminent democratic politician, prosecuted Socrates; Socrates was undoubtedly being tried for his association with Critias. And this is precisely what we find that Athenians themselves believed: some fifty years later, in 345 BCE, Aeschines cited the case of 'Socrates the sophist', saying that he had been executed for teaching Critias.

After 403, Athenians wanted to stabilize the democracy, to prevent further oligarchic coups. This mood was so prevalent that, barring strong opposing reasons, the trial of a man such as Socrates, by these prosecutors, would inevitably be seen as politically motivated. With hindsight, we identify 404–403 as a great watershed in Athenian history, but hindsight must not blind us to the fact that Athenians at the time did not know that they had defeated the forces of tyranny and narrow oligarchy once and for all (or at least until the democracy was overwhelmed by an external power); they thought they were still fighting these internal enemies, shoring up the democracy. There had been an interval of seven years between the oligarchy of 411 and that of 404, so the relatively peaceful passage of a mere four years up to 399, or only two years since the final defeat of the oligarchs at Eleusis, would not seem to be grounds for complacency. Moreover, the Thirty had been imposed on Athens by Sparta, with the help of Persia, and neither of these two influences on Athenian events had evaporated. If it is true that Anytus was known as one of the architects of post-war concord, he had, for the sake of the democracy, to make an exception in the case of Socrates.

ANYTUS'S PROSECUTION SPEECH

There was an incredible amount of circumstantial and anecdotal evidence stacked up against Socrates. Just from this alone we could draw up a list of things we might reasonably guess that the prosecutors might have said, but we do not have to resort entirely to guesswork, since at least some of the content of their speeches can be gleaned from three sources. The first two of these are the defence speeches written by Plato and Xenophon, since from time to time they appear to be responding to points that had been raised by the prosecution speeches; the third, and the most important, is a pamphlet published by Polycrates in 392.

Polycrates was an Athenian rhetorician, best known for writing paradoxical pieces defending famous villains or attacking famous heroes. None of his work survives, but some of it is reflected by others. His defence of the legendary Egyptian king Busiris, for instance, who had the nasty habit of slaughtering visitors to his country, met with an extended response from Isocrates. His other famous work was the *Prosecution Speech against Socrates*, which purported to be the speech Anytus had delivered at the trial. Its purpose was to advertise Polycrates' wares as an aspirant to the speech-writing profession and to express support for the democracy. It met with responses from both Xenophon and, centuries later, Libanius of Antioch (and presumably from unknown others in between).

Polycrates' pamphlet has long been sidelined as a way to reconstruct Anytus's speech, because most scholars believe that, since the end of the civil war in Athens, there had been a general amnesty that forbade reference to any crimes or alleged crimes committed before 403. Since Polycrates' pamphlet plainly contravened such an amnesty (for instance, by charging Socrates with having been Alcibiades' teacher), it seemed safe to ignore it. But we now know that there was no blanket amnesty. Socrates' prosecutors could have said pretty much anything they wanted at his trial (as they could have done even if there had been a blanket amnesty, as long as they did not refer specifically to pre-403 people and incidents; but that would have seriously weakened their case), and so there is nothing in what is recoverable of Polycrates' *Prosecution Speech against Socrates* that debars it from genuinely reflecting Anytus's actual speech. And this is what Xenophon suggests too: early in his *Recollections of Socrates*, when he refers to Polycrates' work, he attributes the arguments to 'the prosecutor' (or 'the accuser'), which looks very like a reference to Socrates' trial and to one of his three prosecutors.

The very nature of Polycrates' writing points in the same direction. Like his more illustrious predecessor Gorgias of Leontini, he was known for writing paradoxical pieces, designed to display rhetorical skill in an unlikely cause. The name of the game was not the truth, but rhetorical display. But neither Gorgias's nor Polycrates' repertoire was restricted to paradox. If the *Prosecution Speech against Socrates* were mere entertainment, Xenophon would not have bothered to respond to it, since no one would have taken it seriously. There is a good possibility that Xenophon's 'accuser' is in fact Anytus, and so that we do know at least a little of what Socrates' prosecutors said in their speeches.

The basic tactic of a prosecution speech in the Athenian courts was to admit personal involvement, attempt to convert private to public anger by claiming to be acting in the public interest and by pointing out the defendant's criminal record and depraved, anti-democratic character, and argue that the preservation of the city depended on a guilty verdict. It is likely, then, that Anytus began with some such generalizations, before proceeding to the meat of his speech. Little of what follows is fanciful, though I have of course written it up myself; otherwise, it is based on the various later writings that seem to reflect the prosecution speeches.

Gentlemen, I will not take up much of your time. My friend Lycon, whose record on behalf of the city is known to you all, has yet to speak. Besides, you have already heard Meletus speak, and demonstrate that this man before you, Socrates of Alopece, is an out-and-out atheist, the leader of a weird cabal, and a sophist who teaches young men corrupt and subversive skills – teaches them to bypass honest citizens such as their fathers and their family friends in favour of his new-fangled, impious and immoral notions. He is no true citizen, but an acolyte of a god not recognized by the state. But I will say no more about the charge of impiety, so ably covered by my colleague, and will focus on the charge of corruption.

I do not need to take up your time because in all likelihood you already know what kind of man Socrates is; you have seen him in the Agora, surrounded by a gaggle of effeminate, lisping young men, and a scattering of emaciated older men. He also hangs out in the gymnasia, but I doubt many of you have seen him there, because you have better things to do with your time than ogle boys' bodies. And what does he do? What show does he put on for his audience? He latches on to one of you and forces you to submit to his questions. And these are not innocent questions. No, he does not ask you the time of day or the way to Taureas's wrestling-school. To the great amusement of his disciples, he ties you up into sophistic knots and shames you, claiming to demonstrate that none of us knows what goodness is. He cleverly gives the impression that he himself does have such knowledge, though no one has ever heard him say what it is.

He supports his slippery arguments by reference to anti-democratic poets, and by these means he claims to show that our inherited values, which have nursed our fair city to greatness, are so riddled with inconsistencies as to be worthless. He perverts the ideas of our most noble poets, making out that Hesiod claimed that one should commit crimes in order to make a living, while our forefather Homer made Odysseus out to be a thief, said that the very Trojan War was a form of theft, and encouraged the thrashing of poor people – of you, the honest citizens of Athens. Well, let me remind him of what the great Hesiod said: 'Often all the citizens of a community suffer as a result of one bad man.'

And there can be no doubt that this man has harmed our community. Our city is founded on the values handed down by our fathers – yet Socrates teaches young men to ignore their fathers as useless, as incapable of teaching virtue, and encourages them to despise the laws and traditions. He feels himself to be so far above the city's morals that he would not stoop to teach others to lie and steal, and to do these things himself. His students typically think of themselves as smarter than their uneducated fathers – and where did they get that notion from? Socrates says that clever sons should restrain their ignorant fathers, in case their ignorance leads them to harm themselves. He equates ignorance, as a form of mindlessness, with insanity, and so calls you all insane!

The only true friend, he says, and the only true parent, is one who knows what is right – right, that is, by Socrates' private standards – and can explain it to others and guide them towards it. But he says this only to make himself appear the greatest friend to his students, and so to drive a wedge between them and their families. How can anyone take the place of a father, who has given his children the gift of life? It is hardly going too far to say that this man was solely responsible for the inter-generational

*conflict that so afflicted our city a few years ago. He and he
alone plunged the city into the crisis from which it is only now
recovering. We must make sure that he does nothing to undermine
this recovery.*

*It is well known that he mocks, and teaches others to mock, the
lottery, the basis of our democratic egalitarianism and token of
our trust in the gods. As if he were a loyal citizen, he says that
the lottery actually harms the city. He wants to see a few men of
knowledge in charge of the city – and what would we call that,
if not oligarchy? He has long been known to favour Sparta and
Spartan practices, which brings us back again to the elitist
pederasty that he perpetuates. He is so far from encouraging his
followers to play a part in the public life of our city, that by his
very example as well as his words, he gets them to prefer idleness
to undertaking their civic duties.*

*So far I have spoken in general about his followers. Let me
now be more specific. Socrates was the teacher of Alcibiades and
of Critias. I scarcely need to remind you of Alcibiades' deeds.
This was a man who aspired to tyranny himself, instigated the
oligarchic coup twelve years ago, profaned our most sacred
Mysteries and may well have desecrated the herms. This was
a man who aided both the Spartans and the Persians in their
military efforts against us, when he could and should have put
his undeniable talents towards helping us to win the war. This was
a man who was cursed and banished, as a monster of impiety,
and who had scarcely been restored by you, in your lenience, to
our city, when his tyrannical ambition again raised its vile head
and you rightly saw fit to banish him once more. Alcibiades was
responsible for almost all the terrible things our city suffered
during the war.*

*As for Critias, the terrible events he masterminded are too
recent for you to need any reminders. He wanted to turn us into a
satellite of Sparta; he wanted to wipe the slate clean of democracy
and start again. In pursuit of this vision, he mercilessly killed
fifteen hundred citizens or loyal metics, and stole the property
of many more, whom he sent into exile. All Athenians of sound
hearts and minds rose up in rebellion against him. What did
Socrates do? He stayed in Athens; he stood by and watched as
Critias drove Athenians out of the city, stole their property and*

murdered their kinsmen. And why did he stay? Because Critias was one of his pupils – as were Charmides and Aristotle, men of scarcely less evil repute. Indeed, it would probably not surprise you to learn that many of Critias's ideas were gleaned from his master.

He will tell you that he is no teacher, and so that he never taught Alcibiades and Critias. He will call on his famous poverty to witness that he has never accepted money for teaching – when it proves only his utter eccentricity. He will tell you that a teacher should not, in any case, be blamed for his students' views. He will tell you that his views are not subversive or atheistic – and in fact that there is no one in Athens more moral and upright than him, a claim that I will not even bother to address. But is it just a coincidence that Alcibiades and Critias held views that were so similar to those of their master? Did they pluck them out of thin air? Everyone believes that teachers – not teachers of facts, but teachers of opinions, as he was – are responsible for their students' opinions. If he denies this, it is just another example of his contempt for what we, the common people, believe.

Along with the rest of the Three Thousand, he was offered the chance to retire to Eleusis, with no further retaliation for his wickedness. He did not have the common decency to take up the offer and avoid this trial; since he chose to stay and to appear in court, he deserves the death penalty. If you do not kill this man, you connive at the moral malaise that has gripped our fair city and which we are now doing our best to combat, and you will fail to deter future oligarchic revolutions, masterminded by this man himself or yet others of his circle. Look, even now he counts among his followers at least one relative of Critias, young Plato. It is up to you to protect our youth, the future of the city, by condemning this man to death.

Something like this is what Anytus seems to have said. Since he was focusing on the corruption aspect of the charge, he naturally emphasized how Socrates widened the gap between fathers and sons. Accustomed as we are nowadays to trying to bring up our children to be independent, their own men and women, Anytus might seem to be over-emphasizing a relatively trivial issue, but it was the single most important aspect of the charges against Socrates. It was not just that he was impious and irreligious, but that he taught young men to be so too. Mogens Hansen was only slightly overstating the case when he said:

> Sokrates was not charged with being an atheist, but with being a missionary . . . A trial of a person who had his own views about the gods was rare, and a trial of a person who criticized the democratic institutions is unique. The presumption is that Sokrates was not put on trial for having such views, but rather for having propagated them to his followers every day, year in, year out.

The generation gap seemed to threaten the very future of the city, since the continuity of the city was assumed to depend on the perpetuation of the values on which the fathers' generation had been reared, and of course simply on the sons' willingness to take up the reins of demo-cratic government, which Socrates appeared to undermine. So it was up to Anytus, the driving force behind the prosecution, to address the corruption charge, and so also the majority of the explicit or implicit comments in our sources for Socrates' trial are concerned to rebut the idea that he misled the youth of Athens. Plato simply denied that Socrates was a teacher, a transmitter of information, and spent much of his life as a writer perpetuating an image of a Socrates who disap-pears so thoroughly behind a mask of irony and questioning that it is all but impossible to attribute views to him. At the most, Plato says, certain young men imitated Socrates' method of questioning.

Xenophon's tack was different. His Socrates is a fully fledged teacher, full of wise advice for all and sundry, and not slow to admit that he is an educational expert. In *The Education of Cyrus*, an idealized, fic-tional (and often tedious) account of the upbringing of Cyrus the Great, the founder of the Persian empire, Xenophon tells a transparent fable. Tigranes, the son of the king of Armenia, was very fond of 'a certain sophist'. Cyrus had observed this, and one day asked Tigranes what had happened to this man. He was astonished to hear that the king had put the man to death, and asked why. 'According to my father, he was cor-rupting me,' replied the prince, and went on: 'But you know, Cyrus, that teacher of mine was such a paragon of virtue that even when he was just about to die, he called me over and said: "Don't be angry with your father for putting me to death, Tigranes. It's not malevolence, just igno-rance, and I for one am sure that no one ever *intends* to make ignorant errors." ' The Armenian king happened to overhear Cyrus's question to his son, and explained that he had killed the teacher 'because it seemed to me that, under his influence, my son was looking up to him more than me'.

The moral is as plain as Xenophon meant it to be, and has long been recognized. The wise teacher, identifiable as Socrates by his voicing a core Socratic belief (that no one does wrong on purpose), was killed because he made Alcibiades, or the *jeunesse dorée* of Athens in general, prefer him to the state, represented in the story by the Armenian king. His condemnation was a direct response to the social crisis.

A SCAPEGOAT

Socrates was taken to court as a figurehead – precisely as Plato suggested by identifying as his most potent enemies the 'old accusers', who had made Socrates a figurehead. He was punished for the intergenerational conflict, which was caused by social factors rather than by individuals, and certainly not by a single individual; he was punished as a morally subversive teacher, when there were others who could equally have had this odd charge pinned on them; he was punished as a critic of democracy, when he was far from alone; even Critias and Alcibiades were products of the time rather than of his teaching. Socrates was put to death because the Athenians wanted to purge themselves of undesirable trends, not just of an undesirable individual.

At the end of the war, the Athenians could look back on a record of moral uncertainty, which had led them to episodes of ruthless brutality. They also knew that from time to time they had behaved with the utmost stupidity – in their treatment of the Arginusae generals, for instance, or in turning down respectable peace offers from Sparta. But over and above these human faults, there was the divine. In a society so thoroughly permeated and cemented by religious sentiment, catastrophe could only be seen as a sign of the gods' displeasure. Athens had just lost a war; the gods were clearly not on the city's side.

Since the gods were motivated by reciprocity, the removal of their goodwill towards the city proved that the Athenians had let them down somehow, and deserved to be punished. In other words, there was a vein of impiety in the city, which the gods were punishing. The easiest way to deal with such a trend was to make it particular, to attribute it to a single individual. This mental leap was facilitated by the Greek concept of pollution, which was seen as a kind of pernicious vapour that could spread from even a single individual and infect an entire community. Punishing a murderer was as much a religious as a legal obligation, since his miasma had to be prevented from spreading. Even animals and inanimate objects that had 'caused' a human death could be 'tried' and, once found guilty, killed or banished beyond the city's borders.

But since it was impossible to guarantee that all sources of pollution had been dealt with, once a year, in the month of Thargelion (the eleventh month of the Athenian calendar, roughly equivalent to our May), two people, one representing the men of the community and wearing a necklace of black figs, the other representing the women and wearing green figs, were driven out of the city. Much remains obscure about this ritual, known as the Thargelia (the month was named after it). Both the scapegoats were paupers or criminals, and once they were outside the city walls, they were flogged. The festival lasted for two days, with the expulsion on the 6th of the month, and then feasting and enjoying the good things the expulsion had made possible on the following day.

The usual Greek words for 'scapegoat' (the English word derives from the ancient Judaic practice of using a goat rather than a human) were *katharma* ('scouring') or *pharmakos*, which is closely related to *pharmakon*, meaning 'medicine' or 'remedy': the scapegoat carried away the city's ills (somehow symbolized in Athens by dried figs) and cured it. In fact, the ritual probably started as an attempt to prevent or cure disease; hence it was sacred to Apollo, the god of disease. The flogging, and the symbolic death of expulsion from the community, diluted the ancient practice of actually killing the scapegoat. Voluntary scapegoats were far more propitious than unwilling ones, and there would always be criminals available who preferred a ritual flogging and expulsion to whatever fate the courts had decreed for them.

There are issues here that were still vital for Socrates' contemporaries in Athens, not just because the annual ritual was still carried out, but also because all Athenians were constantly being reminded of the importance of self-sacrifice for the good of the city. The Parthenon, the temple of Athena on the Acropolis, was completed in 438, and its sculptures by 434. On the interpretation of the frieze that I prefer, the story it told was one of the main Athenian foundation myths, the legend of King Erechtheus and his daughters. Faced with a barbarian invasion, Apollo told the king that he would have to sacrifice one of his three daughters to save the city, and in order to spare him the impossible choice, all three chose to die.

We are faced with a number of strange coincidences, on which it might be hazardous to construct much of an edifice. But Apollo was not only the god of the Thargelia and of the legendary king's daughters' self-sacrifice; he was also Socrates' god, the one who had prompted his mission in Plato's story, the one whose moral maxims (such as 'know yourself') Socrates felt himself to be perpetuating and, as the god of divination, the one who was probably the source of his little voice. Perhaps most astonishingly, 6 Thargelion, the first day of the scapegoat festival, was Socrates' birthday – or so the tradition had it. But even if this is a fabrication or a guess, it suggests that someone made a connection between Socrates and the Thargelia.

I like to think that Socrates, the devotee of Apollo, accepted his death, as a voluntary scapegoat. He had failed to see his vision for Athens become a reality, and no doubt if he were still free he would think that the continuation of his mission was the best chance Athens had for regeneration. But that was in the past. If, even in a temporary fit of post-war zeal, the Athenians thought it would take the death of a troublesome thinker to heal the rifts in the city and to create the concord that all politicians appeared to be committed to, and that he himself had worked for in his own way, so be it. Rather than escape, as he easily could, he let himself be killed.

Socrates' last words, uttered to his old friend Crito from his deathbed in prison as the poison took hold of his body, were: 'Crito, we owe a cock to Asclepius. Please make sure you pay the debt.' Asclepius was the healing god, whose worship had been introduced into Athens less than thirty years previously. These famous and mysterious words have attracted numerous interpretations. I would like to add one more. Playing on the close link between *pharmakos* and *pharmakon*, 'scapegoat' and 'cure', Socrates saw himself as healing the city's ills by his voluntary death. A thanks offering to the god of healing was due.

Glossary

Agora: a combination of central city square, marketplace and administrative centre.

Archon: literally, 'leader'. The term was used to describe various high officials of Athenian government at different points of its history. In the classical period, there were nine annually selected archons: the Eponymous Archon (who gave his name to the year), the King Archon, the Polemarch (war-leader), and six *thesmothetai* (originally responsible for law and order).

Deme: Cleisthenes' reforms in 508 included the assignment of all Athenian citizens, and their future descendants, to one of 139 demes ('villages', 'parishes'), for constitutional and identificatory purposes. The registration of eighteen-year-olds in their ancestral deme constituted their entry into Athenian citizenship. A deme, then, was an Athenian citizen's ancestral parish, whether or not he still lived there, and was used for personal identification: Socrates Sophroniscou [son of Sophroniscus], of [the deme] Alopece.

Dēmos: the common people. For a democrat, the word meant every citizen irrespective of wealth and other social markers; for a member of the elite, it meant everyone except other members of the elite, i.e. 'the masses'.

Dikast: a member of an Athenian jury, which combined the functions of judge and jury.

Ephor: literally, 'overseer'. The name of a high official in Sparta – and, temporarily, in Athens in 404.

Helot: an agricultural serf in Laconia and Messenia, which had been conquered by Sparta.

Hetaireia: a club or association of like-minded men, usually aristocrats; formed originally for social reasons, but capable of becoming politicized.

Hoplite: a heavy-armed footsoldier, armed, typically, with a helmet, a corselet with a short protective skirt, bronze greaves for the shins, and above all a large, round, concave shield, about 90 cm in diameter, made of bronze-covered wood with a rim of bronze. He carried a long thrusting spear with an iron head, and an iron sword.

Klepsydra ('water-stealer'): a water-clock.

Kōmos: a revel, in which a boisterous party, typically of aristocrats who had already drunk deeply at a symposium, paraded through the city, still dressed as symposiasts and still singing and joking, in search of another house where they could prolong the evening.

Liturgy: a public service imposed on wealthy Athenians: they had to fund a warship for a year, or finance a religious festival (for instance, by providing a chorus for a playwright to put on a play or plays at one of the festivals of Dionysus).

Metic: a non-Athenian resident in Athenian territory, from the Greek *metoikos*. The term was used not only for domiciled foreign residents, but for temporary residents who stayed for a minimum of a month at a time. Metics were liable to a special metic tax, and in general had fewer rights than Athenian citizens; they could not normally own land, for instance.

Ostracism: the process whereby each year the Athenian people had the right to send a prominent public figure into exile for ten years, though with no loss of property rights. A minimum of six thousand votes had to be cast for all the candidates, and the one who was exiled was the one with the most votes against him. A vote was an *ostrakon* – a piece of broken pottery with the appropriate politician's name inscribed or painted on it. The process fell into disuse after 416, while remaining as a theoretical possibility.

Palaestra: literally, a 'wrestling-ground', but in practice a small gymnasium. Events might be held there, but on a daily basis it was a place for training and for the schooling of upper-class children.

Panhellenic: pertaining to all Greeks, wherever they lived – and they inhabited coastlines from southern France to northern Africa, southern Italy and Sicily, the west, north and south Turkish littoral, and of course the Balkan peninsula.

Pnyx: the usual meeting-place for the popular Assembly at Athens, on a low hill to the west of the Acropolis.

Polis: the 'city' or 'state'. Each of the many hundreds of Greek poleis from around the Mediterranean and Black Sea consisted of an urban centre and more or less surrounding territory. Since what distinguishes poleis, whatever form of government they had, is a high degree of involvement by citizens in government, the most accurate translation of the word 'polis' is the rather cumbersome 'citizen-state'.

Proxenia: see *Xenia*.

Prytany: a thirty-six- or thirty-seven-day period of the year when the fifty Councillors from one of the ten tribes of Athens were in charge of daily governmental functions; hence they were called the *prytaneis*, 'the executive'.

Satrap: a governor of a province of the Persian empire. Satraps were viceroys, ultimately answerable to the Persian king, but they had immense power and wealth, and ruled their provinces like kings or princelings.

Sophist: an educator or intellectual. The word is no more than a noun formed from the Greek word for 'clever', and just as educators and intellectuals come in all guises, so the sophists taught different subjects and used different methods. Except in the reaction they met from conservatives and rivals, they were far from being a unified school or movement.

Stoa: a building consisting chiefly of a long, covered colonnade. The reconstructed Stoa of Attalus II (third century BCE) in the Athenian Agora gives the best impression.

Sycophant: a kind of blackmailer, who threatened prosecution in the Athenian courts as a way to make money.

Talent: the largest unit of Athenian currency (worth, say, about £500,000): 36,000 obols = six thousand drachmas = sixty mnas = one talent.

Thetes: the lowest of the four Solonic property classes in Athens.

Trierarch: the man responsible for financing a trireme for a year, and for supervising its crew.

Trireme: a Greek warship, propelled by three banks of oarsmen on each side. Its precise design is in many respects extremely uncertain.

Tyrant: a sole ruler who seized power by unconstitutional means, or inherited such power, though he was not necessarily a despot.

Xenia: a binding, hereditary relationship, often translated 'guest-friendship', that cut across all other social systems; in a time of war, for instance, it would not cross the minds of *xenoi* in opposing camps that their relationship would be damaged in the slightest; or again, *xenoi* trusted one another with money and other resources in ways that circumvented normal political and economic channels (and so could seem to outsiders like bribery). But *xenoi* had taken an oath of obligation to each other; they had a religious duty to each other that transcended more mundane sentiments such as patriotism. *Xenia* facilitated communication in a number of important areas, such as trade and diplomacy. *Proxenia* was an extension of *xenia*, whereby a whole community became, so to speak, a person's *xenoi*; a *proxenos*, then, was the representative of a foreign community within his home community.

References

PREFACE

xii *groused enough*: see especially my 'Xenophon's Socratic Mission', in Christopher Tuplin (ed.), *Xenophon and His World* (Stuttgart: Steiner, 2004; = *Historia* Einzelschrift 172), 79–113.

ONE

4 *complained . . . about the time restriction*: Plato, *Apology* 19a, 37a–b.

4 *the smallest jury we hear of*: ps.-Aristotle, *The Athenian Constitution* 53.3.

5 *'This indictment . . . penalty demanded is death'*: Diogenes Laertius, *Lives of Eminent Philosophers* 2.40.

6 *If Plato is to be trusted*: Plato, *Phaedo* 59c–61c.

6 *Socrates asked them not to*: see Plato, *Crito* 44b ff.

7 *harm the city, he said*: Plato, *Crito* 49a–50a.

7 *thanks to . . . Enid Bloch*: 'Hemlock Poisoning and the Death of Socrates', in Brickhouse and Smith (eds), *Trial and Execution*, 255–78. A shorter version of this paper first appeared online in March 2001, in the *Journal of the International Plato Society*: http://www.nd.edu/~plato/bloch.htm.

7 *as Plato described them in . . . Phaedo*: *Phaedo* 117a–118a; a peaceful death is also implied by Xenophon, *Apology* 7.

8 *how Meletus understood the charges*: see Plato, *Apology* 26b.

8 *speaking off the cuff . . . doing no wrong*: Plato, *Apology* 17c; Xenophon, *Apology* 3 (see also *Recollections of Socrates* 4.8.4).

10 *One of the most famous episodes*: Plato, *Apology* 20e ff. It was famous even in antiquity. See, for instance, ps.-Lucian, *Amores* 48 (second century CE), which humorously gives the story an erotic spin: Socrates is wisest because of his attraction towards young men.

10 *famous in comedy*: e.g. Aristophanes frr. 539, 573 Kock, *Birds* 1296, 1564; Alexis fr. 210 Kock (fr. 214 Arnott); Antiphanes fr. 197 Kock.

10 *started around 440 BCE . . . by the end of the decade*: Plato, *Laches* 187d–188a. The earliest comic fragment mentioning Socrates, datable to before 430, is fr. 12 Kock (Giannantoni I A2) of the poet Callias, in which he has a character accuse Socrates of making people arrogant. Clearly, young men had already begun to imitate his questioning of others, as a means of making themselves feel superior to others.

11 *a mention in Xenophon's Apology*: 14.

12 *as Moses Finley once remarked*: *Aspects of Antiquity*, 62. On other Socratic apologies, see Trapp, 'Beyond Plato and Xenophon', in Trapp (ed.), *Socrates from Antiquity to the Enlightenment*, 51–63.

12 *Maximus of Tyre*: Oration 3 in Michael Trapp, *Maximus of Tyre: The Philosophical Orations* (Oxford: Oxford University Press, 1997).

12 *started perhaps late in the fourth century*: we would not know about this tradition, were it not for the chance preservation of a papyrus fragment containing part of a Socratic dialogue, in which Socrates is asked why he did not mount a defence. The fragment is PKöln 205 (in Michael Gronewald, *Kölner Papyri*, vol. 5 (Opladen: Westdeutscher Verlag, 1985), 33–53); it is summarized by Jonathan Barnes in *Phronesis* 32 (1987), 365–6.

12 *Plato claims . . . and Xenophon to have heard about it*: Plato, *Apology* 38b; Xenophon, *Apology* 10.

14 *a specific reference*: Plato, *Apology* 19b–c; see also Xenophon, *On the Management of an Estate* 11.3.

14 *in two later plays*: Aristophanes, *Birds* 1280–4, 1553–6 (produced 414); *Frogs* 1491–9 (produced 405). See also other comic fragments collected by Giannantoni in his section I A.

14 *taken an interest in current scientific ideas*: specifically those of Anaxagoras of Clazomenae (according to Plato, *Phaedo* 96a–99d), perhaps mediated by Anaxagoras's pupil Archelaus, a native Athenian; see Geoffrey Kirk, John Raven and Malcolm Schofield, *The Presocratic Philosophers* (Cambridge: Cambridge University Press, 1983), 385–6. It seems also to be an implication of Xenophon, *Recollections of Socrates* 4.7.1–6 that at some point Socrates had acquired expertise in such matters; at any rate, his attitude towards them does not seem to be the product of ignorance. Some claim that Xenophon, *Recollections of Socrates* 1.6.14 suggests even that Socrates taught such matters, but I cannot find evidence of this.

15 *imitated . . . by Xenophon*: *Apology* 19–21.

15 *the 'inherited conglomerate'*: Murray, *Greek Studies* (London: Oxford University Press, 1946), 67.

16 *'If a mere . . . acquitted'*: Plato, *Apology* 36a.

17 *A late biographer*: Diogenes Laertius, *Lives of Eminent Philosophers* 2.42.

17 *he addressed . . . as true dikasts*: Plato, *Apology* 39c.

18 *a few more or less trivial details*: both writers have Socrates claim that those who are about to die gain prophetic powers, and that the indications from his supernatural voice were that he would benefit from the trial; both writers attribute the part of the indictment that mentioned new gods to this supernatural voice; both writers have Socrates insist that he has never wronged anyone.

18 *raised a hubbub*: Socrates asks for quiet or anticipates such interruptions at Xenophon, *Apology* 15; Plato, *Apology* 17c–d, 20e, 21a, 27a–b, 30c, 31d–e.

18 *defiance and arrogance*: 31d–e; 28a–b; 24e–25c; 20e–21b, 28e–29a; 34c–35d (see also *Crito* 48c–d); 37a–b; 38d–e; 28e–29a, 35d; 36d–e.

18 *Xenophon's express purpose*: *Apology* 1.

19 *as recent scholars have argued*: 'Sense can be made of the *Apology* only if Socrates is seen as attempting to secure his acquittal in a manner consistent with his principles' (Brickhouse and Smith, *Socrates on Trial*, 210). Reeve describes Plato's *Apology* as 'part of a reasonable and intelligible defense compatible with his [Socrates'] deepest principles, and it establishes his innocence' (*Socrates in the* Apology, 185).

19 *he has Socrates say . . . and on another occasion . . .*: Plato, *Gorgias* 521e (see also 486a–b, 522b); *Theaetetus* 174c.

TWO

20 *he ruefully agreed*: ps.-Aristotle, *The Athenian Constitution* 9.1.

21 *personal motives*: Plato, *Apology* 23e: Meletus championed the poets, Anytus the politicians, Lycon the orators.

21 *'Extant evidence . . . public actor'*: Allen, *World of Prometheus*, 39–40.

25 *'Athenian rhētores . . . move a proposal'*: Yunis, *Taming Democracy*, 10.

28 *the oath taken by dikasts*: see especially Demosthenes 24.149–51 (*Against Timocrates*).

28 *as law-makers, rather than as law-interpreters*: e.g. Demosthenes 56.48 (*Against Dionysodorus*); Lysias 14.4 (*Against Alcibiades* I).

28 *'The prosecutor in one action . . . by turning prosecutor'*: Ober, *Mass and Elite*, 144–5.

28 *Written laws were idealized as equalizers*: e.g. Euripides, *Suppliant Women* 430–4.

29 *not always obliged*: in his speech *Against Aphobus* (27.40–1) Demosthenes complained that his opponents refused to produce in court a will that would have corroborated a point he was making.

31 *'The Athenians' criteria . . . firmly drawn'*: Wallach, *Platonic Political Art*, 97.

THREE

32 *Aristotle . . . quipped*: the story is preserved in Aelian, *Miscellany* 3.36 (first/second centuries CE).

33 *the scholarly consensus*: e.g. Hansen, 'The Trial of Sokrates', 165; Schofield, 'I. F. Stone and Gregory Vlastos', 285.

33 *the prosecution speech that survives*: the speech is preserved as Lysias 30 (*Against Nicomachus*).

33 *'a surprisingly high proportion . . . strong political agenda'*: Todd, *Shape of Athenian Law*, 308.

36 *both Xenophon and Plato*: Xenophon, *Recollections of Socrates* 1.1.5; Plato, *Apology* 26c.

37 *Protagoras . . . expressed his agnosticism*: fr. 4 Diels/Kranz.

37 *Prodicus of Ceos*: fr. 5 Diels/Kranz.

37 *Democritus of Abdera*: e.g. A74, A75 Diels/Kranz; but see the fuller set of relevant testimonia in Christopher Taylor, *The Atomists: Leucippus and Democritus* (Toronto: University of Toronto Press, 1999), 138–41.

37 *Thrasymachus of Chalcedon*: fr. 8 Diels/Kranz.

37 *as Aristophanes called Socrates*: *Clouds* 830 (423–414 BCE).

37 *long remembered*: e.g. Aristophanes, *Birds* 1058 ff. (produced 414), *Frogs* 320 (produced 405).

37 *a garland-seller complain*: Aristophanes, *Thesmophoriazusae* 450–1.

37 *In some famous lines*: from Euripides' *Sisyphus* (produced 415). Some ancient sources attribute these lines to a lost play by Critias, and so it commonly appears as Critias, fr. 25 Diels/Kranz, and is assigned to Critias in the standard text (James Diggle, *Tragicorum Graecorum Fragmenta Selecta* (Oxford: Oxford University Press, 1998)), but most scholars now believe it to be a Euripidean fragment.

38 *Nor do Euripidean characters stop there*: e.g. frr. 286 and 292 Nauck (both from *Bellerophon*), *Trojan Women* 987 ff.; and then see all the other fragments and lines collected and discussed by Yunis, *A New Creed*.

39 *'Everyone could see . . . altars of the state'*: Xenophon, *Recollections of Socrates* 1.1.2; see also Xenophon, *Apology* 11, Plato, *Euthydemus* 302c.

39 *no more than outline*: Xenophon, *Recollections of Socrates* 4.3.7; see also 1.4.

39 *'Since the god is good . . . and not attributed to the god'*: Plato, *Republic* 379c.

39 *Homer . . . has Zeus complain*: *Odyssey* 1.32–3.

40 *Socrates himself wonder out loud*: Plato, *Euthyphro* 6a (cf. 6b–c).

40 *a number of admired writers*: rationalizing criticism of myths and conceptions of the gods may be found in Xenophanes of Colophon, Heraclitus of Ephesus, Solon of Athens, Pindar of Cynoscephalae, Hecataeus of Miletus, Euripides of Athens, and Prodicus of Ceos – let alone the extraordinary Derveni Papyrus. See also Plato, *Phaedrus* 229c–d.

40 *'I cannot believe . . . debased tales of poets'*: Euripides, *Heracles* 1341–6; see also, e.g., *Iphigeneia among the Taurians* 385–91, which concludes, Socratically: 'In my opinion, no deity is bad.'

40 *as Plato has Socrates come close to suggesting*: *Euthyphro* 15a.

41 *reduce piety to vulgar trading*: Plato, *Euthyphro* 14e.

41 *'Socrates prayed . . . those of the good'*: Xenophon, *Recollections of Socrates* 1.3.2–3.

41 *Close to the start of* Republic: Plato, *Republic* 331b.

41 *'Revere the gods . . . rules and regulations'*: Isocrates 1.13 (*To Demonicus*).

41 *on Homer's authority*: see Homer, *Iliad* 9.497–501, with Plato, *Republic* 364b–365a.

42 *'Dear Pan . . . by himself'*: Plato, *Phaedrus* 279b–c.

43 *'double causation'*: see e.g. Michael Clarke, *Flesh and Spirit in the Songs of Homer* (Oxford: Oxford University Press, 1999), 277–82.

43 *perfectly acceptable within Greek religion*: e.g. Euripides, *Electra* 890–2.

43 *'not doing away with . . . traditional ways'*: Isocrates 7.30 (*Address to the Areopagus*).

44 *the gods were inscrutable*: Xenophon, *Recollections of Socrates* 4.7.6;

Plato, *Euthyphro* 4e; in general, Plato, *Apology* 23a–b on the paltriness of human wisdom, and Socrates' lifelong campaign against false claims to knowledge.

44 *mystical cabal . . . guru*: e.g. Aristophanes, *Clouds* 140–3, *Birds* 1553–6; Plato too presents Socrates, especially in *Symposium* and *Phaedrus*, as an enlightened person, capable of showing others the way to transcendent experiences.

44 *as one scholar has recently*: Bussanich, 'Socrates the Mystic', and 'Socrates and Religious Experience'.

44 *Pythagoreans . . . trances*: in *Phaedo*, Plato has two known Pythagoreans present with Socrates in prison on the last day of his life; at *Symposium* 175a–b and 220c–d he tells us a little about Socrates' trances; the latter one lasted at least twenty hours, and was in public view.

46 *'supernatural alarm'*: the most important passages are Xenophon, *Apology* 12–13, *Recollections of Socrates* 1.1.2–5, 4.3.12–13, 4.8.1, 4.8.5–6, 4.8.11, *Symposium* 8.5; Plato, *Apology* 31c–d, 40a–b, 41d, *First Alcibiades* 103a–b, 135d, *Euthydemus* 272e, *Republic* 496c, *Phaedrus* 242b, *Theaetetus* 151a; ps.-Plato, *Theages* 128d–130e. For later antique reflection on the phenomenon, see Plutarch, *On Socrates' Personal Deity*.

46 *they both agree*: Xenophon, *Apology* 12, *Recollections of Socrates* 1.1.2; Plato, *Euthyphro* 3b.

46 *Aristophanes had a character condemn*: *Frogs* 888–91.

46 *apparently well known*: Plato, *Apology* 31c; Xenophon, *Recollections of Socrates* 1.1.2.

47 *'Such things are easily misrepresented to the masses'*: Plato, *Euthyphro* 3b.

47 *Some scholars*: e.g. Brickhouse and Smith, *Socrates on Trial*, 69–87; Smith and Woodruff, *Reason and Religion*, 3–4.

FOUR

51 *'Hello, Socrates . . . bearded chin now'*: Plato, *Protagoras* 309a.

51 *Alcibiades and philosophy*: Plato, *Gorgias* 481d.

51 *'I might as well . . . elder brother'*: Plato, *Symposium* 219d; Alcibiades' speech about Socrates runs from 214e–222b, but can be fully appreciated only in the context of the book as a whole, since it is full of echoes of earlier speeches.

52 *Socrates took part*: Plato, *Apology* 28e. On Delium, see Plato, *Laches* 181a–b, *Symposium* 221a–c; on Poteidaea, see the beginning of Plato's *Charmides*, with Christopher Planeaux, 'Socrates, Alcibiades, and Plato's τὰ Ποτειδεατικά: Does the *Charmides* Have a Historical Setting?', *Mnemosyne* series 4, 52 (1999), 72–7.

52 *said to be still attracted to Socrates*: Plato, *Symposium* 222c.

52 *Xenophon tried to convince*: *Recollections of Socrates* 1.2.12–16, covering both Alcibiades and Critias.

53 *five of the immediate followers*: Plato, Aeschines of Sphettus, Antisthenes, Euclides and Phaedo. In addition to these dialogues called *Alcibiades*, he plays a minor role in Xenophon's *Recollections of Socrates*, and features in

Plato's *Protagoras* and of course *Symposium*; he also features prominently in Phaedo's *Zopyrus* (the name of Alcibiades' childhood tutor). See Nicholas Denyer, *Plato: Alcibiades* (Cambridge: Cambridge University Press, 2001), 5.

54 *already being referred to by comic poets*: in Aristophanes' *Banqueters* (produced in 427), a fashionable young man uses a neologism that his father attributes to Alcibiades (fr. 198 Kock). Another early Aristophanic reference is *Acharnians* 716 (produced in 425). He was already known as a womanizer to Pherecrates (fr. 155 Kock, which is undatable with certainty, but belongs to the early 420s).

54 *a later wit*: Bion of Borysthenes (third century BCE), as reported by Diogenes Laertius, *Lives of Eminent Philosophers* 4.49. There are numerous stories about or references to Alcibiades' voracious sexual appetite: see, for instance, Plutarch, *Life of Alcibiades* 3–5, 8.5, 39.5; Athenaeus, *The Learned Banquet* 220c (= Antiphon fr. 67 Thalheim), 534f–535a, 574e (= Lysias fr. 5 Thalheim; this story has Alcibiades visiting Abydus with his dissolute uncle Axiochus); Xenophon, *Hellenica* 3.3.1–4; ps.-Andocides 4.10, 14 (*Against Alcibiades*). But almost all these stories are untrue, deriving either from comic fantasy or from hostile political pamphlets. The only element that is certainly correct is that Alcibiades did have a prodigious sexual appetite.

54 *even tragedians*: see Bowie, 'Tragic Filters', and e.g. Strauss, *Fathers and Sons*, 115, but especially works in the bibliography by Vickers.

54 *despite later fabrications for tourists*: in the second century CE, visitors to Athens were shown a sculpted representation of the Graces, and a Hermes, which were attributed to Socrates (Pausanias, *Guide to Greece* 1.22.8) – but then for centuries Athenian tourist guides were notorious for linking all their famous artefacts indiscriminately with all their famous personalities, so that during the Turkish regime the Temple of Olympian Zeus, for instance, was regularly pointed out as the Palace of Hadrian (or even of Theseus). And there is still a cell on Philopappou Hill in Athens which is marked, erroneously, as Socrates' prison.

55 *recognized signs*: ps.-Aristotle, *Physiognomics* 808a.

57 *consistently portrayed*: see Plato, *Charmides* 154b ff., *Lysis* 204b ff., *Republic* 403b, *Symposium*, *Phaedrus*; Xenophon, *Symposium* 4.26, 8.12, 8.32, *Recollections of Socrates* 1.2.29, 1.3.8–13; see also Plato, *Laws* 636a–c, 836c–841e, though these sentiments are not put into Socrates' mouth.

57 *'Just then . . . I was in ecstasy!'*: Plato, *Charmides* 155d.

57 *his name was especially linked*: Plato, *Symposium* 222b.

58 *his father had become connected*: Plato, *Laches* 180e.

58 *A later tradition*: preserved in Plutarch, *Life of Aristides* 27, who refers to various unreliable authors, but also, hesitantly, to Aristotle; see also Diogenes Laertius, *Lives of Eminent Philosophers* 2.26 and Athenaeus, *The Learned Banquet* 555d–556a.

58 *'one a stripling . . . the others still children'*: Plato, *Apology* 34d.

59 *'because it is hard . . . with long hair'*: Aristotle, *Rhetoric* 1367a.

60 *'Even a poor man . . . receives a eulogy'*: Plato, *Menexenus* 234c.

64 *date from the fourth century*: Demosthenes 54.16 ff. (*Against Conon*).

64 *'Charicles and Critias and their club'*: Lysias 12.55 (*Against Eratosthenes*).

65 *two set-piece speeches*: Thucydides, *The Peloponnesian War* 6.16–18, 6.89–92.

66 *certainly the leader of a club*: Isocrates, 16.6 (*On the Team of Horses*).

FIVE

67 *Some scholars have speculated*: see Brunt, 'Thucydides and Alcibiades'.

67 *'Alcibiades . . . downfall of the city'*: Thucydides, *The Peloponnesian War* 6.15.

73 *Thucydides dramatized*: *The Peloponnesian War* 3.37–48.

77 *like Oscar Wilde*: Wilde is reputed to have said to André Gide: 'I have put my genius into my life, whereas all I have put into my work is my talent.'

77 *plenty of stories*: see especially Plutarch, *Life of Alcibiades* 2–9.

77 *a punch-up with a rival impresario*: ps.-Andocides 4.20 (*Against Alcibiades*). The prestige attached to performing this liturgy made it a highly competitive and emotional occasion; at any rate, Demosthenes too had a fist-fight with a rival under similar circumstances: see his Speech 21, *Against Meidias*. See Peter Wilson, 'Leading the Tragic *Khoros*: Prestige in the Democratic City', in Christopher Pelling (ed.), *Greek Tragedy and the Historian* (Oxford: Oxford University Press, 1997), 81–108.

78 *According to Thucydides*: *The Peloponnesian War* 5.43–46.

80 *'It was a grandiose scheme . . .'*: Gomme, *Historical Commentary*, 4.70.

81 *'That may be so . . .'*: Plutarch, *Life of Alcibiades* 15.3.

83 *Thucydides cast the negotiations*: *The Peloponnesian War* 5.84–113.

SIX

85 *'The 44 . . . account for 25 of them'*: Davies, *Wealth*, 100–1. Ancient sources that pinpoint ownership of horses as a sign of great wealth include Aristotle, *Politics* 1289b; Lysias 24.10–12 (*On the Refusal of a Pension to an Invalid*); ps.-Demosthenes 42.24 (*Against Phaenippus*); Aristophanes, *Clouds* 14–16, 25–32.

86 *a later historian records*: Diodorus of Sicily, *Library of History* 13.74.

86 *or possibly third*: fourth, Thucydides, *The Peloponnesian War* 6.16.2; third, Isocrates 16.34 (*On the Team of Horses*), and the Euripidean ode in Plutarch, *Life of Alcibiades* 11.2. At *Life of Demosthenes* 1.1 Plutarch records a tradition that this surviving ode was not actually by Euripides.

86 *in a speech the following year*: Thucydides, *The Peloponnesian War* 6.16.

87 *led others to claim*: as ps.-Andocides did, 4.27 (*Against Alcibiades*). The dating of this speech is controversial: good starting points are the relevant articles by Prandi and Raubitschek in the bibliography.

87 *rumours of tyranny*: reported already for the year 415 by Thucydides, *The Peloponnesian War* 6.15.4, and ps.-Andocides 4.24, 27 (*Against Alcibiades*); see also Isocrates 16.38 (*On the Team of Horses*).

REFERENCES

88 *kinky sex*: Lysias, fr. 5 Thalheim.

88 *within a generation . . . rumours*: Antisthenes, fr. 29 Caizzi.

88 *Aristophanes was mocking*: Wasps 488–507 (produced in 422), *Birds* 1074–5 (produced in 414). For other contemporary passages where 'tyrant' is used as a more or less meaningless term of abuse, see Douglas MacDowell, *Aristophanes: Wasps* (London: Oxford University Press, 1971), n. to 345.

89 *According to Thucydides*: The Peloponnesian War 6.15.2, 6.90.2; the ambition is attributed both times to Alcibiades.

89 *dreams of western conquest lingered*: e.g. references to Sicilian wealth in Euripides' *Cyclops* (423 BCE) and Aristophanes, *Peace* 93–4 (421 BCE).

89 *'to help the Segestans . . . further Athenian interests'*: Thucydides, *The Peloponnesian War* 6.8.2.

91 *Thucydides says*: The Peloponnesian War 6.27.1.

91 *'in case a herm-basher catches sight of you'*: Aristophanes, *Lysistrata* 1093–4.

92 *a very striking . . . vase*: Musée cantonal d'archéologie et d'histoire, Lausanne, Inv. no. 3250 (Beazley Archive no. 352524). It is the cover image for Furley's *Andokides and the Herms*.

92 *Another vase*: Louvre, Paris, Inv. no. 1947 (Beazley Archive no. 202393).

93 *One of the informants . . . one of the defendants*: Andocides 1.37, 52 (*On the Mysteries*).

93 *'part of a conspiracy . . . subvert the democracy'*: Thucydides, *The Peloponnesian War* 6.27.3.

93 *'They did not assess . . . on the evidence of bad men'*: Thucydides, *The Peloponnesian War* 6.53.2.

94 *he asked his dikasts*: Andocides 1.36 (*On the Mysteries*).

94 *One of those accused later claimed*: Andocides 1.67 (*On the Mysteries*).

95 *linked in a single sentence*: Isocrates 16.6 (*On the Team of Horses*).

95 *five or six occasions*: at the house of Poulytion (Andocides 1.11–13; Andromachus's deposition), at the house of a certain Charmides (1.16; Agariste's deposition), at the house of Pherecles (1.17–18; Lydus's deposition), at the house of Alcibiades (Plutarch, *Life of Alcibiades* 22.3), at the house of 'a metic' (Diodorus of Sicily, *Library of History* 13.2.4, unless this just refers to Poulytion), and at an unnamed location (Andocides 1.15; Teucrus's deposition).

95 *'one of the most sensational events in an uncommonly sensational year'*: Wallace, 'Charmides, Agariste and Damon', 333.

97 *feature in a number of literary works*: see Nails, *People of Plato*, 242.

98 *'supposedly loyal democrats at the time'*: Andocides 1.36 (*On the Mysteries*).

98 *in a speech to the Spartans*: Thucydides, *The Peloponnesian War* 6.89.6.

98 *'that what had happened . . . the investigation should continue'*: Andocides 1.36 (*On the Mysteries*).

99 *Alcibiades of Phegous*: Andocides 1.65 (*On the Mysteries*).

100 *Demosthenes mistakenly said*: 21.147 (*Against Meidias*).

100 *'an oligarchic and tyrannical conspiracy'*: Thucydides, *The Peloponnesian War* 6.60.1.

100 *'I'll show them I'm alive'*: Plutarch, *Life of Alcibiades* 22.2.

100 *'stood facing west . . .'*: ps.-Lysias 6.51 (*Against Andocides*). The nice story (Plutarch, *Life of Alcibiades* 22.4) that one priestess refused to take part, on the grounds that she was 'a priestess for prayers, not for curses', is probably fictional, because a priestess was a state official: the Athenian people ordered priests and priestesses to do any cursing that was required in a political situation such as this, and there was little room for dissent.

101 *the speech in which he persuaded*: Thucydides, *The Peloponnesian War* 6.89–92.

101 *evidence . . . not of an especially convincing kind*: from the biographer Satyrus, of the third century BCE, quoted by Athenaeus, *The Learned Banquet* 534b. The hint is speculatively developed by Westlake, 'Alcibiades, Agis, and Spartan Policy'.

102 *'While King Agis . . . rule over the Spartans'*: Plutarch, *Life of Alcibiades* 23.7.

102 *'the . . . surprising availability . . . extra-marital sex'*: Paul Cartledge, *Agesilaos and the Crisis of Sparta* (London: Duckworth, 1987), 113.

SEVEN

105 *which found its way into Thucydides' narrative*: *The Peloponnesian War* 8.50–1. The whole story is unbelievable: Phrynichus wrote to Astyochus, accusing Alcibiades of not acting in Sparta's best interests, but Astyochus told the Athenian leaders on Samos about the letter. Phrynichus wrote to Astyochus again, offering to betray the Athenian cause. But, first, Alcibiades was already under sentence of death from the Spartans, so the news that he was not acting for Sparta was irrelevant; and, second, why would Phrynichus, an intelligent man, write a second time to Astyochus after the Spartan had already betrayed him? And if Phrynichus had been in treacherous contact with the Spartans, Peisander would not have resorted to the lesser charge of letting down the rebel Persian satrap Amorges, in order to get rid of Phrynichus (8.54.3).

106 *'a different form of democracy'*: Thucydides, *The Peloponnesian War* 8.53.1; see also 8.53.3 on a 'more moderate' form of government.

109 *'downright democracy'*: Thucydides, *The Peloponnesian War* 8.92.11.

110 *Thucydides calls Alcibiades' restraining . . .*: *The Peloponnesian War* 8.86.4–5.

111 *the most helpful enemies*: Thucydides, *The Peloponnesian War* 8.96.5.

111 *'The elite . . . had proven unable . . . Athenian political society'*: Ober, *Mass and Elite*, 94.

112 *'And suppose . . . their past errors'*: Aristophanes, *Frogs* 689–91.

116 *in his play* Baptae . . . *Eupolis*: frr. 76–98 Kassel/Austin; see Ian Storey, *Eupolis: Poet of Old Comedy* (Oxford: Oxford University Press, 2003), 94–111.

116 *'. . . having his way with my sea'*: Xenophon, *Hellenica* 1.6.15.

116 'greatest sea battle ever fought by Greeks against Greeks': Diodorus of Sicily, *Library of History* 13.98.5.

117 'it was intolerable not to let the people do what they wish': Xenophon, *Hellenica* 1.7.12.

118 'We are in command now, not you': Xenophon, *Hellenica* 2.1.26; Plutarch, *Life of Alcibiades* 37.1.

119 'People thought . . . freedom for Greece': Xenophon, *Hellenica* 2.2.23.

119 *made famous by Xenophon*: in his *Anabasis*. See *Xenophon: The Expedition of Cyrus*, translated by Robin Waterfield, with introduction and notes by Tim Rood (Oxford: Oxford University Press, 2005), and Robin Waterfield, *Xenophon's Retreat: Greece, Persia and the End of the Golden Age* (London: Faber and Faber, 2006).

120 *a sordid tale of adultery*: see Plutarch, *Life of Alcibiades* 39.5.

120 *Thucydides distributed blame*: see pp. 67–8.

120 'that he alone was responsible . . . be initiated by him alone': Xenophon, *Hellenica* 1.4.17.

120 *as it has been called*: by Strauss and Ober, in their *Anatomy of Error*.

121 'They miss him . . . pander to his moods': Aristophanes, *Frogs* 1425, 1431–2.

EIGHT

124 'art of words': Xenophon, *Recollections of Socrates* 1.2.31.

126 *We hear that in all fifteen hundred people were illegally killed*: ps.-Aristotle, *The Athenian Constitution* 35.4, with other references in Rhodes's note on this passage.

126 *hostile sources*: e.g. Xenophon, *Hellenica* 2.3; since Xenophon himself had, as one of the knights, probably helped the Thirty police the city, he was trying to distance himself from the atrocities.

127 'an amateur among philosophers, and a philosopher among amateurs': Proclus, *Commentary on Plato's Timaeus*, on 20a.

127 *named after his grandfather*: Critias appears in anodyne roles in Plato's *Charmides* (where, however, he is shown to be confused about the virtue of self-control) and *Protagoras*. Though the unfinished dialogue *Critias* is named after our Critias's grandfather, I suspect that Plato teases us to a certain extent, since grandfather Critias in certain respects resembles what we know of his grandson: he is learned in the same way, and promotes an idealized society.

127 *Xenophon's efforts*: *Recollections of Socrates* 1.2.12–38.

127 'to purge the city . . . to goodness and justice': Lysias 12.5 (*Against Eratosthenes*).

127 *whoever wrote the seventh Platonic Epistle . . . says*: at 324c–d.

128 'the best possible state': Xenophon, *Hellenica* 2.3.34. On Athenian admirers of Sparta in general, see Cartledge, 'The Socratics' Sparta'.

128 'The Fatherland . . . time for scruples': quoted in Cees Nooteboom, *Roads to Santiago*, trans. Ina Rilke (New York: Harcourt, 1997), 108.

129 *thought . . . to be a trimmer*: Xenophon, *Hellenica* 2.3.31 and 33.

129 *'as though this number . . . all the good people'*: Xenophon, *Hellenica* 2.3.19.

129 *Diodorus of Sicily's account*: *Library of History* 14.5.1–3.

130 *'This is a memorial . . . the accursed Athenian populace'*: Scholiast on Aeschines 1.39.

132 *Thrasybulus was remembered*: Pausanias, *Guide to Greece* 1.29.3.

132 *'democracy would only benefit . . . died there'*: Xenophon, *Hellenica* 3.1.4.

133 *Other trials too almost explicitly offered*: e.g. Lysias 13.80–1 (*Against Agoratus*). Other speeches that refer copiously, but not exclusively, to crimes or alleged crimes committed by the Thirty or during their regime include Isocrates 20 (*Against Lochites*) and Lysias 26 (*On the Scrutiny of Evandros*) and 31 (*Against Philon*).

133 *'Peace was never final . . . period of unrest'*: Wolpert, *Remembering Defeat*, 138.

135 *'It was deliberately made difficult . . . men of thirty and over)'*: Rhodes, 'Athenian Democracy after 403 BC', 306.

135 *Concord . . . was the new watchword*: see e.g. Andocides 2.1; Demosthenes 19.298; Dinarchus 1.99; Lysias 2.13, 17.24; Aeschines 3.208.

NINE

139 *some historians of classical Athens*: see e.g. Paul Cartledge, 'The Effects of the Peloponnesian (Athenian) War on Athenian and Spartan Societies', in David McCann and Barry Strauss (eds), *War and Democracy: A Comparative Study of the Korean War and the Peloponnesian War* (New York: Armonk, 2001), 104–23; and John Davies, 'The Fourth-century Crisis: What Crisis?', in Walter Eder (ed.), *Die athenische Demokratie im 4. Jahrhundert v. Chr.* (Stuttgart: Steiner, 1995), 29–36.

140 *'It was as if . . . to conquer Sicily'*: Thucydides, *The Peloponnesian War* 8.1.1.

141 *'People had fewer inhibitions . . . punished for his crimes'*: Thucydides, *The Peloponnesian War* 2.53.

142 *'In times of peace . . . sniffing out intrigues'*: Thucydides, *The Peloponnesian War* 3.82.2–8.

143 *Alcibiades too was prepared to redefine terms*: Thucydides, *The Peloponnesian War* 6.92.2–4.

143 *Euripides showed . . . double standards*: see my paper 'Double Standards in Euripides' *Troades*', *Maia* 34 (1982), pp. 139–42.

143 *on the latest estimate*: Moreno, *Feeding the Democracy*, 31.

144 *'You were led astray . . . treatment of them'*: Euripides, *Suppliant Women* 232–7, echoed by Nicias in Thucydides, *The Peloponnesian War* 6.12.2–13.1. See Strauss, *Fathers and Sons*, 141–2, for the echoes, and Dover, *Greek Popular Morality*, 105, for further passages linking youth with warmongering.

144 *'Basically . . . against Alcibiades'*: Plutarch, *Life of Nicias* 11.3.

145 *it was thought*: e.g. Thucydides, *The Peloponnesian War* 6.38.5; Eupolis frr. 100, 121 Kassel/Austin; Cratinus fr. 283 Kassel/Austin.

REFERENCES

145 *Aristophanes . . . in* Clouds: 889–1114.
145 *'sexual licence, barbarian emotionality, and vulgar excess'*: D'Angour, 'New Music', 273.
146 *'disdaining equality with the common people'*: Thucydides, *The Peloponnesian War* 6.38.5.
146 *it was apparently still plausible*: see Thucydides, *The Peloponnesian War* 6.28.1.
147 *Callicles . . . and Alcibiades*: Plato, *Gorgias* 483b–484a; Xenophon, *Recollections of Socrates* 1.2.45.
148 *'There is no one . . . god among men'*: Plato, *Republic* 360b–c.
150 *His image of himself as a horsefly*: Plato, *Apology* 30e–31a. Plato must also have been thinking of the disturbing effects on the inherited conglomerate of Socratic questioning when he wrote *Republic* 538c–539a.
151 *we know little about them*: Plutarch, *Life of Aristeides* 13.1, on an attempted coup in 479 BCE, and Thucydides, *The Peloponnesian War* 1.107.4–6, on oligarchic intrigue in 457.
152 *'proportionate equality'*: the phrase 'proportionate' or 'geometrical equality' may have been an oligarchic slogan, borrowed perhaps from the elitist Pythagoreans. See Dodds's note on Plato, *Gorgias* 508a (where the phrase first occurs): Eric Dodds, *Plato, Gorgias* (London: Oxford University Press, 1959), 339–40.
152 *'unequivocal folly'*: Thucydides, *The Peloponnesian War* 6.89.6.
152 *a recent book*: David Estlund, *Democratic Authority: A Philosophical Framework* (Princeton: Princeton University Press, 2007).
154 *the occasional hint*: e.g. ps.-Xenophon (the 'Old Oligarch'), *The Constitution of the Athenians* 2.20. This is the foundational text for oligarchic criticism of democracy, most likely written some time between 424 and 414. See especially Osborne's edition of the pamphlet, and Ober, *Political Dissent*, 14–26.
154 *Pericles' famous Funeral Speech*: Thucydides, *The Peloponnesian War* 2.35–46.

TEN

155 *Pericles' boast*: Thucydides, *The Peloponnesian War* 2.37.
156 *made no claim to absolute accuracy*: Thucydides, *The Peloponnesian War* 1.22.
156 *'Suppose . . . our unmarried daughters'*: Xenophon, *Recollections of Socrates* 1.5.2.
157 *Demosthenes taunted . . .*: 19.249 (*On the Embassy*).
157 *'any decent Athenian gentleman'*: Plato, *Meno* 92e.
158 *'A foreigner . . . hostility and intrigue'*: Plato, *Protagoras* 316c–d.
159 *'A man who has a policy . . . who has none in mind'*: Thucydides, *The Peloponnesian War* 2.60.6.
159 *'Persuasion was built . . . hung in the balance'*: Yunis, 'Constraints of Democracy', 230.
161 *'the proper management . . . man of action'*: Plato, *Protagoras* 318e–319a.

REFERENCES

161 *'to make the morally weaker argument defeat the stronger'*: this is the formulation of Plato, *Apology* 18b–c, following the lead of Aristophanes, *Clouds* 112–15.

161 *Gorgias . . . did nothing to alleviate such concerns*: In Praise of Helen 8–14.

161 *'nonsense and quackery'*: Isocrates 15.197 (*On the Exchange*), defending himself against the kind of charges brought by Xenophon in the final chapter of *On Hunting* 13.1–5. See also Isocrates' defence in his *Against the Sophists*.

161 *'It's plain to see . . . who associate with them'*: Plato, *Meno* 91c.

163 *Antiphon*: see especially Gerard Pendrick, *Antiphon the Sophist: The Fragments* (Cambridge: Cambridge University Press, 2002).

163 *in his* Clouds: Aristophanes, *Clouds* 1071–82. Mr Wrong argues that virtue involves self-denial, and that with sophistic training anyone can indulge himself and use clever argument to escape the consequences.

163 *Plato's Callicles argued*: in *Gorgias* 483b–484c. I believe Callicles to be a real person, but at any rate he reflects fifth-century attitudes. Further references in this paragraph: Plato, *Republic* 336b–344c (Thrasymachus); Plato, *Republic* 358e–360d (Glaucon); Thucydides, *The Peloponnesian War* 3.37–40 (Cleon).

164 *difficult to assess*: more or less opposite conclusions are reached, for instance, by Dover ('The Freedom of the Intellectual') and Robert Wallace ('Private Lives and Public Enemies').

164 *Prodicus of Ceos . . . death by drinking hemlock*: Suda, s.v. Prodicus. The Suda is a Byzantine encyclopedia of the tenth century CE.

164 *'If the fact that . . . are worthless'*: Aristotle, *The Art of Rhetoric* 1397b25–7, a neglected piece of evidence.

164 *Aristotle's later quip*: preserved in Aelian, *Miscellany* 3.36 (first/second centuries CE).

165 *'anyone who did not pay due respect . . . impeached'*: Plutarch, *Life of Pericles* 32.1.

165 *as Ober puts it*: Ober, *Mass and Elite*, 90.

165 *two late writers . . . but Plato . . .*: Diogenes Laertius, *Lives of Eminent Philosophers* 9.52 and 54; Sextus Empiricus, *Against the Professors* 9.56. The former was probably writing in the third century CE, and the latter towards the end of the second century CE. The Plato reference is *Meno* 91e.

165 *only one report*: Antisthenes fr. 35 Caizzi.

165 *the sun and the moon . . . a ram*: Hippolytus, *Refutation of All Heresies* 1.8.6 (summarizing Aristotle's pupil Theophrastus of Eresus); Plutarch, *Life of Pericles* 6.2.

165 *Ephorus of Cyme*: fr. 196 Jacoby, with the discussion of Yunis, *A New Creed*, 67.

166 *relatively profuse, and starts relatively early*: it starts in the fourth century with ps.-Aristotle, *The Athenian Constitution* 27.4 (the text says 'Damonides' rather than 'Damon', but this is a confusion of Damon with his father), continues with Plutarch, *Life of Aristeides* 1.7, *Life of Nicias* 6.1, *Life of Pericles* 4.3, and ends, for what it is worth, with Libanius 1.157 (*Defence of Socrates*).

221

166 *isolated and implausible*: Demetrius of Phalerum fr. 107 Stork, van Ophuijsen and Dorandi.

167 *'I pray that my family . . . in the far-famed city of Athens'*: Euripides, *Hippolytus* 421–3; the contrast with slavery occurs at *Ion* 670–2 and *Phoenician Women* 391–2. For a fourth-century example, see Demosthenes 60.26 (*Funeral Speech*). Many other passages could be cited: see the references in e.g. Sara Monoson, *Plato's Democratic Entanglements: Athenian Politics and the Practice of Philosophy* (Princeton: Princeton University Press, 2000), chapter 2.

167 *Even the enemies of democracy*: ps.-Xenophon, *The Constitution of the Athenians* (the 'Old Oligarch') 1.2, 1.6; Plato, *Republic* 557b, *Gorgias* 461e.

167 *when the term 'freedom of speech' first occurred in the English language*: in Sir Edward Coke's *Institutes of the Laws of England* (1628–44); I owe this reference to Arlene Saxonhouse, *Free Speech and Democracy in Ancient Athens* (Cambridge: Cambridge University Press, 2006), 19.

168 *As Isocrates said in 355 BCE*: 8.14 (*On the Peace*).

ELEVEN

173 *expressly a continuation*: Aristotle, *Nicomachean Ethics* 1179b–1181b.

173 *Plato . . . had him divide statesmen into two classes*: *Gorgias* 502e–503b.

174 *his little supernatural voice discouraged him*: Plato, *Apology* 31d–32a, 36b–c.

174 *soldier . . . Council . . . dikast*: Plato, *Apology* 28e, 32b, 35a. The last is a little uncertain, but is a reasonable deduction from Socrates' words: 'I have personally often seen such people on trial . . .'

175 *'We found . . . wise and knowledgeable'*: Plato, *Euthydemus* 292b–c.

176 *'Socrates said . . . knew how to rule'*: Xenophon, *Recollections of Socrates* 3.9.10; see also especially 3.6–7, and Plato, *Crito* 47a–d, *Apology* 25b. But for a convincing argument that the call for expertise in politics is vacuous, see Renford Bambrough, 'Plato's Political Analogies', in Peter Laslett (ed.), *Philosophy, Politics, and Society* (Oxford: Blackwell, 1956), 98–115 (repr. in Renford Bambrough (ed.), *Plato, Popper and Politics* (Cambridge: Heffer, 1967), 152–69; and in Gregory Vlastos (ed.), *Plato: A Collection of Critical Essays*, vol. 2 (Garden City, NY: Doubleday, 1971), 187–205).

176 *believed that leadership qualities were the same*: Xenophon, *Recollections of Socrates* 3.4.6–12. Plato agreed (*Statesman* 258e–259c) and so did Xenophon (*On the Management of an Estate* 21); Aristotle disagreed (*Politics* 1252a). Protagoras of Abdera may have agreed too, if Plato is reflecting his views at *Protagoras* 319a.

176 *'Imagine . . . of no use to them at all'*: extracted from Plato, *Republic* 488a–489a; the 'windbag with his head in the clouds' is of course Socrates, who was described that way by Aristophanes in his *Clouds* (225–34).

177 *Socrates believed*: this emerges more clearly from Xenophon's works than from Plato's, especially *The Expedition of Cyrus*, *The Education of Cyrus the Great* and *On Cavalry Command*. Two shorter passages are *Hiero* 8–11 and *On the Management of an Estate* 21.

177 *'This I know . . . bad and disgraceful'*: Plato, *Apology* 29b.

178   *The only qualification . . .*: see especially Plato, *Apology* 20c–23b and, for
      ignorance of consequences and the necessity of calling on the gods,
      Xenophon, *Recollections of Socrates* 1.1.7–9.
178   *'A man's reach should exceed his grasp'*: Robert Browning, 'Andrea del
      Sarte', 97.
178   *He used to say . . . competent politicians*: Xenophon, *Recollections of
      Socrates* 1.2.9, 3.1.4; Aristotle, *The Art of Rhetoric* 1393b.
178   *if something could be tackled by human intelligence*: Xenophon,
      Recollections of Socrates 1.1.7–9.
178   *Socrates likened a good statesman to a herdsman*: Plato, *Republic* 342a–e,
      345c–e; Xenophon, *Recollections of Socrates* 1.1.32 and 3.2.
179   *'mass wisdom' . . . an oxymoronic fiction*: Plato, *Hippias Major* 284e,
      Laches 184e, *Apology* 25b, *Crito* 47c–d; Xenophon, *Recollections of
      Socrates* 3.7.5–7.
179   *riddled with false values*: Plato, *Apology* 29d, 31c–32a, *Crito* 48c.
179   *manual work is a major impediment*: Plato, *Alcibiades* 131a–b; Xenophon,
      On the Management of an Estate 4.2–3, 6.4–9; see also Aristotle, *Politics*
      1328b, 1337b.
179   *David Hume*: quoted by Guthrie, *Sophists*, 128.
179   *Plato admits*: Plato, *Crito* 52e; see also Xenophon, *Recollections of
      Socrates* 3.5.20, where there is a hint of nostalgia for the pre-democratic
      Athenian constitution.
179   *'Pericles made . . . bloated and rotten'*: extracts from Plato, *Gorgias*
      515e–519a; cf. *Meno* 93a–94e.
180   *Plato has Socrates describe himself as the only true politician*: *Gorgias*
      521d. Socrates also describes himself as skilled at politics at *Meno*
      99e–100a, on which see Christopher Taylor, *Socrates*, 52.
180   *Socrates himself addressed this issue*: Plato, *Crito* 51c–52d.
180   *several influential commentators*: especially Vlastos, 'The Historical
      Socrates and Athenian Democracy', and Kraut, *Socrates and the State*.
180   *'loyal democrat'*: Plato, *Apology* 21a.
181   *thoughtful scholars*: 'The whole intellectual project of *Republic* is a
      Socratic project – an attempt to think through how Socrates might have
      conceived of an ideal political system': Malcolm Schofield, *Plato* (Oxford:
      Oxford University Press, 2006), 315–16. See also Kraut, *Socrates and the
      State*, 10 ('The *Republic* describes the sort of state he [Socrates] would
      have infinitely preferred to all others'), and Ober, *Political Dissent*, 10 (in
      Republic, Plato sought to 'establish a city in which "Socratic politics"
      might flourish'). And from there it is only a short step to argue, as
      Christopher Rowe has done, that Plato's *entire* political project, right
      up to his latest works, is Socratic in inspiration: 'The *Republic* in Plato's
      Political Thought', in Giovanni Ferrari (ed.), *The Cambridge Companion
      to Plato's* Republic (New York: Cambridge University Press, 2007),
      27–54.
181   *'All those . . . were forbidden to enter the city'*: Xenophon, *Hellenica* 2.4.1.
182   *Xenophon's claim*: *Recollections of Socrates* 1.2.30–9.

182 *ignored by . . . commentators*: for instance, the most influential paper on Socrates' attitude towards the Athenian democracy – Vlastos, 'The Historical Socrates and Athenian Democracy' – fails to mention even once that Socrates chose to stay in Athens during the rule of the Thirty.

182 *Leon of Salamis*: Plato, *Apology* 32c–d; see also Xenophon, *Recollections of Socrates* 4.4.3. The only difference is that in Plato Socrates refused because of the immorality of the arrest, while Xenophon stresses its illegality.

183 *widely reputed*: e.g. Aristophanes, *Birds* 1281–2: 'Everyone was mad about Sparta in those days – growing their hair long, starving themselves, never washing, Socratizing.'

184 ' "*On another occasion . . . taking part in it?*" ': Xenophon, *Recollections of Socrates* 1.6.15; see also especially 2.1 and 3.1–7. Socrates is less pessimistic than Plato: Socrates wanted to remodel society, but Plato thought one would have to start again from scratch (*Republic* 501a).

185 *now ready for moral regeneration*: Xenophon, *Recollections of Socrates* 3.5.5.

187 *In Aeschines of Sphettus's version*: fr. 9 Dittmar (= Giannantoni VI A51). The loss of Aeschines' Socratic writings is especially regrettable; some of the fragments of his *Alcibiades* are translated in G. C. Field, *Plato and His Contemporaries*, 2nd edn (London: Methuen, 1948), 146–52, or in Trevor Saunders (ed.), *Plato: Early Socratic Dialogues* (Harmondsworth: Penguin, 1987), 377–9.

187 *Xenophon adds . . . Socrates' guidance*: *Recollections of Socrates* 1.2.24–5, 39.

188 *Aeschines . . . included the poignant rider*: fr. 11c Dittmar (= Giannantoni VI A53).

188 *Charmides, Euthydemus . . . and Critobulus*: Xenophon, *Recollections of Socrates* 2.6 (Critobulus), 3.7 (Charmides), 4.2–3, 5 (Euthydemus); 3.1–6 are also relevant.

188 *Xenophon . . . as king or tyrant*: Xenophon, *The Expedition of Cyrus (Anabasis)* 5.6.15–18, 6.4.1–7, 6.4.14, 6.6.4, 7.1.21.

188 *the dialogue* Theages: on which see Mark Joyal, *The Platonic* Theages (Stuttgart: Steiner, 2000). We happen to know, from Plato, that Theages was expected to make his mark as an Athenian politician, but suffered from some illness that, fortunately, turned him to philosophy instead (*Republic* 496b–c) but, unfortunately, killed him young (*Apology* 34a).

188 ' "*What do you imagine . . . stop him succeeding?*" ': Plato, *Republic* 494c–e; the whole brilliant passage 487b–502c should be read.

189 *a few pages earlier*: Plato, *Republic* 491e.

190 *Was he cataleptic?*: mystic: Bussanich (above, n. to p. 44); thinking: most commentators; catalepsy: Bertrand Russell, *A History of Western Philosophy* (London: George Allen and Unwin, 1946), 109 – and note that in Russell's day catalepsy was usually taken to be a symptom of mental illness. In any case, they are all interpreting the remarks of Plato at *Symposium* 220c–d.

190 *his first question*: Plato, *Charmides* 153d.

TWELVE

191   *a tidy story*: Xenophon, *Apology* 28.

192   *at least seven of those who fled into exile*: see the list in Nails, *People of Plato*, 18, which includes Phaedrus, Eryximachus, Acumenus, Axiochus, Charmides, Critias and Alcibiades. See Nails also for brief essays on the people I listed in this paragraph as Socrates' unfortunate associates: the evidence is their occurrence, especially as Socratic interlocutors, in either or both of Plato's and Xenophon's works.

192   *his first mention in an extant comic fragment*: see above, note to p. 10.

193   *'young and unknown'*: *Euthyphro* 2b.

194   *from Andocides' defence speech*: 1.94 (*On the Mysteries*).

194   *'There cannot be the slightest doubt . . . fifth of the votes'*: Plato, *Apology* 36a–b.

194   *bribery, apparently*: see ps.-Aristotle, *The Athenian Constitution* 27.5.

194   *mentioned in the same breath*: Xenophon, *Hellenica* 2.3.42–4.

194   *Plato said . . . important positions in the state*: *Meno* 90b; see also Xenophon, *Apology* 29.

195   *He was plausibly described*: Andocides 1.150 (*On the Mysteries*); Isocrates 18.23 (*Against Callimachus*).

195   *various stories giving various versions*: Diodorus of Sicily, *Library of History* 14.37.7, has both Meletus and Anytus executed by the Athenians without trial; Diogenes Laertius, *Lives of Eminent Philosophers* 2.43, has only Meletus put to death, with Anytus banished – only to be banished again as soon as he arrived at the city where he had chosen to see out his exile. Further references in Chroust, *Socrates, Man and Myth*, n. 1184.

195   *'Socrates the sophist'*: Aeschines 1.173 (*Against Timarchus*).

196   *response from Isocrates*: Isocrates 11 (*Busiris*).

197   *later writings that seem to reflect the prosecution speeches*: Xenophon, *Recollections of Socrates* 1.1 and 1.2 are both expressly defences of Socrates against the charges of, respectively, irreligion and corrupting young men; 1.2.9–61 responds to 'the accuser'. Libanius's *Apology of Socrates* contains a few passages that are useful in this regard. Other incidentally relevant passages are Isocrates, *Busiris* 5; Plato, *Meno* 90b–95a (the conversation with Anytus); and several places in both Plato's and Xenophon's versions of Socrates' defence speeches which seem to respond to the prosecution speeches – e.g. Plato, *Apology* 24d–28a and Xenophon, *Apology* 19–21 (the dialogues with Meletus); Plato, *Apology* 33a on Socrates' denial that he was a teacher; Plato, *Apology* 29c and 33a on Anytus calling for the death penalty. The scholar who has done the most to reconstruct Polycrates' pamphlet is Chroust, in *Socrates, Man and Myth*.

198   *'Often all the citizens of a community suffer as a result of one bad man'*: Hesiod, *Works and Days* 240.

201   *'Sokrates was not charged . . . year in, year out'*: Hansen, 'The Trial of Sokrates', 160–1.

201 *Plato simply denied that Socrates was a teacher*: *Apology* 19d–20c, 33a–b, and in general his regular disavowal of knowledge (and even *need* for a teacher: *Laches* 201a). These features are not to be found in Xenophon's Socrates.

201 *young men imitated Socrates' method*: Plato, *Apology* 23c, 33c, 37d.

201 *not slow to admit*: Xenophon, *Apology* 20.

201 *a transparent fable*: Xenophon, *The Education of Cyrus* 3.1.14, 38–40.

202 *long been recognized*: see the reference to Jean Brodeau's 1555 commentary on *The Education of Cyrus* by Gera, 'Xenophon's Socrateses', 39, n. 18.

202 *'old accusers'*: Plato, *Apology* 18a ff.

203 *Much remains obscure about this ritual*: see Parker, *Polytheism and Society*, 481–3 for the most important texts, and for discussion Parker, *Miasma*, ch. 9, and Bremmer, 'Scapegoat Rituals'.

203 *the ancient Judaic practice*: Leviticus 16:20–2.

203 *the interpretation of the frieze that I prefer*: Joan Breton Connelly, 'Parthenon and *Parthenoi*: A Mythological Interpretation of the Parthenon Frieze', *American Journal of Archaeology* 100 (1996), 53–80.

204 *he was also Socrates' god*: see C. D. C. Reeve, 'Socrates the Apollonian?', in the Smith and Woodruff collection *Reason and Religion in Socratic Philosophy*.

204 *felt himself to be perpetuating*: Plato, *Alcibiades* 124a, *Charmides* 164e–165a; Xenophon, *Recollections of Socrates* 3.9.6, 4.2.24.

204 *Socrates' birthday*: Diogenes Laertius, *Lives of Eminent Philosophers* 2.44, on the authority of Apollodorus of Athens, a chronographer of the second century BCE.

204 *the best chance Athens had for regeneration*: see Plato, *Apology* 30a, 31a, 36c–d.

204 *Socrates' last words*: Plato, *Phaedo* 118a.

204 *numerous interpretations*: the most recent paper on the subject known to me (Peterson, 'An Authentically Socratic Conclusion') helpfully lists no fewer than twenty-one. The most widely accepted is the attractive idea that Socrates has been 'cured' from the sickness of life.

Bibliography

In this book, I have attempted to pull together into a single tale a large number of strands of ancient Athenian society, history, politics, personalities and culture. My reading has been equivalently wide and varied, and has consisted of more articles and chapters than whole books. This is by way of apologizing to lay readers for the abstruse nature of some elements of this bibliography, and for its extent. No one can claim to have read exhaustively in this period of ancient Athenian history, but I have read, re-read or dipped into countless books and articles in the course of my research. Many of the works I have read disagree with one another, but in order to make the stories told in this book accessible to as wide a readership as possible, and in order to keep the book short, I have omitted most of the caveats scholars normally include. This means that I have included in this bibliography more, and more scholarly works than is usual in a popular history book, so that anyone wishing to pursue the controversies I have glossed over, and to see how different reconstructions might be possible, has sufficient material to begin with. What follows, then, should be regarded as what I consider to be the best, in terms of some combination of relevance, quality, importance, controversy and readability (up to the middle of 2007, when research on this book effectively ended). I have focused on English-language material, and marked with an asterisk those secondary works which seem to me to be both reasonably accessible and of considerable importance to the topics covered in this book. The primary texts are of course *all* of fundamental importance.

HISTORY

The most important ancient texts are Thucydides, *The Peloponnesian War*, which is best read in the edition of Robert Strassler, *The Landmark Thucydides* (New York: Simon & Schuster, 1996), with its revised version of Richard Crawley's 1874 translation; Xenophon, *Hellenica*, translated as *A History of My Times* by Rex Warner (Harmondsworth: Penguin, 1979); and pseudo-Aristotle, *The Athenian Constitution*, translated by Peter Rhodes (Harmondsworth: Penguin, 1984). The relevant parts of Diodorus of Sicily's *Library of History* (books 12 to 14, available

BIBLIOGRAPHY

in the Loeb Classical Library, published by Harvard University Press) sometimes offer alternative traditions. The plays of Aristophanes (most easily available in the Penguin Classics series) provide fascinating but often ambiguous insights into social history. Among the orators, speeches by Andocides, Lysias and Isocrates are the most significant for this book, and are available either in the Loeb Classical Library or, increasingly, in good translations published by the University of Texas Press in the series 'The Oratory of Classical Greece'.

SOCRATES

The most important ancient texts are the early dialogues of Plato and Xenophon's Socratic works. They are available in good translations, of which I would recommend the following: Trevor Saunders (ed.), *Plato: Early Socratic Dialogues* (Harmondsworth: Penguin, 1987); Hugh Tredennick and Harold Tarrant, *Plato: The Last Days of Socrates* (London: Penguin, 1993); Hugh Tredennick and Robin Waterfield, *Xenophon: Conversations of Socrates* (London: Penguin, 1990); Robin Waterfield, *Plato: Meno and Other Dialogues* (Oxford: Oxford University Press, 2005). Each of these volumes contains introductions and notes, as well as the translations. Many relevant texts are translated in Thomas Brickhouse and Nicholas Smith (eds), *The Trial and Execution of Socrates: Sources and Controversies* (New York: Oxford University Press, 2002); William Calder (ed.), *The Unknown Socrates* (Wauconda, Ill.: Bolchazy-Carducci, 2002); and John Ferguson (ed.), *Socrates: A Source Book* (London: Macmillan, 1970).

ALCIBIADES

The most important ancient texts are Plutarch, *Life of Alcibiades*, translated by Robin Waterfield, with introduction and notes by Philip Stadter, in *Plutarch: Greek Lives* (Oxford: Oxford University Press, 1998); Plato, *Alcibiades I*, translated by Douglas Hutchinson, in John Cooper (ed.), *Plato: Complete Works* (Indianapolis: Hackett, 1997); Plato, *Symposium*, translated, with introduction and notes, by Robin Waterfield (Oxford: Oxford University Press, 1994). Among the orators (available as above), pseudo-Andocides 4, Isocrates 16, and Lysias 14 and 15 are the most relevant. Finally, there is Cornelius Nepos's brief Life, available in Gareth Schmeling's translation, in *Cornelius Nepos: Lives of Famous Men* (Lawrence, Kan.: Coronado, 1971).

POLITICAL THEORY

Many of the texts already mentioned are relevant, but others too. Translations of Greek tragedies may readily be found in the familiar Penguin Classics and Oxford World's Classics series. The most relevant Platonic dialogues are *Gorgias*, translated, with introduction and notes, by Robin Waterfield (Oxford: Oxford University Press, 1994); *Republic*, translated, with introduction and notes, by Robin Waterfield (Oxford: Oxford University Press, 1993); *Statesman*, translated by Robin Waterfield, with introduction and notes by Julia Annas (Cambridge: Cambridge

228

University Press, 1995); and *Laws*, translated, with introduction and notes, by Trevor Saunders (Harmondsworth: Penguin, 1970). For Aristotle's *Politics* I prefer Trevor Saunders's revision of Thomas Sinclair's original (Harmondsworth: Penguin, 1981). The 'Old Oligarch' is best studied with the help of Robin Osborne (ed.), *The Old Oligarch: Pseudo-Xenophon's Constitution of the Athenians* (2nd edn, London: London Association of Classical Teachers, 2004). Many early texts can be also found in Michael Gagarin and Paul Woodruff, *Early Greek Political Thought from Homer to the Sophists* (Cambridge: Cambridge University Press, 1995).

SOPHISTS

There are several good translations of all the fifth-century sophists, or at least their most important fragments and testimonia: John Dillon and Tania Gergel, *The Greek Sophists* (London: Penguin, 2003); Rosamond Kent Sprague (ed.), *The Older Sophists* (Columbia: University of South Carolina Press, 1972); Robin Waterfield, *The First Philosophers: The Presocratics and the Sophists* (Oxford: Oxford University Press, 2000).

Adeleye, Gabriel, 'Theramenes and the Overthrow of the "Four Hundred" ', *Museum Africum* 2 (1973), 77–81.
—, 'Critias: Member of the Four Hundred', *Transactions and Proceedings of the American Philological Association* 104 (1974), 1–9.
—, 'Theramenes: The End of a Controversial Career', *Museum Africum* 5 (1976), 9–22.
—, 'Critias: From "Moderation" to "Radicalism" ', *Museum Africum* 6 (1977–8), 64–73.
Adkins, Arthur, *Moral Values and Political Behaviour in Ancient Greece* (London: Chatto & Windus, 1972).
—, 'Αρετή, Τέχνη, Democracy and Sophists: *Protagoras* 316b–328d', *Journal of Hellenic Studies* 93 (1973), 3–12.
Ahbel-Rappe, Sara, and Rachana Kamtekar (eds), *A Companion to Socrates* (Oxford: Blackwell, 2006).
Akrigg, Ben, 'The Nature and Implications of Athens' Changed Social Structure and Economy', in Robin Osborne (ed.), *Debating the Athenian Cultural Revolution: Art, Literature, Philosophy, and Politics 430–380 BC* (Cambridge: Cambridge University Press, 2007), 27–43.
Allen, Danielle, 'Imprisonment in Classical Athens', *Classical Quarterly* n.s. 47 (1997), 121–35.
—, *The World of Prometheus: The Politics of Punishing in Democratic Athens* (Princeton: Princeton University Press, 2000).
Anderson, Daniel, 'Socrates' Concept of Piety', *Journal of the History of Philosophy* 5 (1967), 1–13.
Anderson, Mark, 'Socrates as Hoplite', *Ancient Philosophy* 25 (2005), 273–89.
Andrewes, Antony, 'The Generals in the Hellespont 411–407 BC', *Journal of Hellenic Studies* 73 (1953), 2–9.
—, 'The Arginousai Trial', *Phoenix* 28 (1974), 112–22.

Avery, Harry, 'Critias and the Four Hundred', *Classical Philology* 58 (1963), 165–7.

*Balot, Ryan, *Greek Political Thought* (Oxford: Blackwell, 2006).

—, 'Socratic Courage and Athenian Democracy', *Ancient Philosophy* 28 (2008), 49–69.

Beck, Frederick, *Greek Education, 450–350 B.C.* (London: Methuen, 1964).

Beckman, James, *The Religious Dimension of Socrates' Thought* (Waterloo, Ontario: Wilfred Laurier University Press, 1979).

Bett, Richard, 'The Sophists and Relativism', *Phronesis* 34 (1989), 139–69.

—, 'Is There a Sophistic Ethics?', *Ancient Philosophy* 22 (2002), 235–62.

Bloedow, Edmund, *Alcibiades Re-examined* (Wiesbaden: Steiner, 1973; = *Historia* Einzelschrift 21).

—, ' "Not the Son of Achilles, but Achilles Himself": Alcibiades' Entry on the Political Stage at Athens II', *Historia* 39 (1990), 1–19.

—, 'On "Nurturing Lions in the State": Alcibiades' Entry on the Political Stage in Athens', *Klio* 73 (1991), 49–65.

—, 'Alcibiades: "Brilliant" or "Intelligent"?', *Historia* 41 (1992), 139–57.

Blumenthal, Henry, 'Meletus the Accuser of Andocides and Meletus the Accuser of Socrates: One Man or Two?', *Philologus* 117 (1973), 169–78.

Blyth, Dougal, 'Socrates' Trial and Conviction of the Jurors in Plato's *Apology*', *Philosophy and Rhetoric* 33 (2000), 1–22.

*Boedeker, Deborah, 'Athenian Religion in the Age of Pericles', in Samons (2007), 46–69.

—, and Kurt Raaflaub (eds), *Democracy, Empire, and the Arts in Fifth-Century Athens* (Cambridge, Mass.: Harvard University Press, 1998).

Boegehold, Alan (ed.), *The Lawcourts at Athens: Site, Buildings, Equipment, Procedure, and Testimonia* (Princeton: The American School of Classical Studies at Athens, 1995; = *The Athenian Agora*, vol. 28).

Bonfante, Larissa, and Leo Raditsa, 'Socrates' Defense and His Audience', *Bulletin of the American Society of Papyrologists* 15 (1978), 17–23.

Bonner, Robert, 'The Legal Setting of Plato's *Apology*', *Classical Philology* 3 (1908), 169–77 (repr. in Brooks (2007), 147–55).

Bosworth, A. Brian, 'The Humanitarian Aspect of the Melian Dialogue', *Journal of Hellenic Studies* 113 (1993), 30–44.

Bowie, Angus, 'Tragic Filters for History: Euripides' *Supplices* and Sophocles' *Philoctetes*', in Christopher Pelling (ed.), *Greek Tragedy and the Historian* (Oxford: Oxford University Press, 1997), 39–62.

Bowra, Maurice, 'Euripides' Epinician for Alcibiades', *Historia* 9 (1960), 68–79 (repr. in Maurice Bowra, *On Greek Margins* (London: Oxford University Press, 1970), 134–48).

Bremmer, Jan, 'Literacy and the Origins and Limitations of Greek Atheism', in Jan den Boeft and Ton Kessels (eds), *Actus. Studies in Honour of H. L. W. Nelson* (Utrecht: Instituut voor Klassieke Talen, 1982), 43–55.

—, 'Scapegoat Rituals in Ancient Greece', *Harvard Studies in Classical Philology* 87 (1983), 299–320 (repr. in Richard Buxton (ed.), *Oxford Readings in Greek Religion* (Oxford: Oxford University Press, 2000), 271–93).

*–, 'Atheism in Antiquity', in Michael Martin (ed.), *The Cambridge Companion to Atheism* (Cambridge: Cambridge University Press, 2007), 11–26.

*Brickhouse, Thomas, and Smith, Nicholas, *Socrates on Trial* (Oxford: Oxford University Press, 1989).

—, *Plato's Socrates* (New York: Oxford University Press, 1994).

—, *Plato and the Trial of Socrates* (London: Routledge, 2004).

*— (eds), *The Trial and Execution of Socrates: Sources and Controversies* (New York: Oxford University Press, 2002).

Broadie, Sarah, 'Rational Theology', in Long (1999), 205–24.

Brock, Roger, 'Athenian Oligarchs: The Numbers Game', *Journal of Hellenic Studies* 109 (1989), 160–4.

Brooks, Richard (ed.), *Plato and Modern Law* (Aldershot: Ashgate, 2007).

*Bruit Zaidman, Louise, and Pauline Schmitt Pantel, *Religion in the Ancient Greek City*, trans. by Paul Cartledge (Cambridge: Cambridge University Press, 1992; later reprints have enlarged bibliographies).

Brunt, Peter, 'Thucydides and Alcibiades', *Revue des études grecques* 65 (1952), 59–96 (repr. in Peter Brunt, *Studies in Greek History and Thought* (Oxford: Oxford University Press, 1993), 17–46).

Buck, Robert, 'The Character of Theramenes', *Ancient History Bulletin* 9 (1995), 14–24.

—, *Thrasybulus and the Athenian Democracy: The Life of an Athenian Statesman* (Wiesbaden: Steiner, 1998; = *Historia* Einzelschrift 120).

*Bugh, Glenn, *The Horsemen of Athens* (Princeton: Princeton University Press, 1988).

Bultrighini, Umberto (ed.), *Democrazia e antidemocrazia nel mondo greco* (Alessandria: Edizioni dell'Orso, 2005).

Burnyeat, Myles, 'The Impiety of Socrates', in Aminadav Dykman and Wlad Godzich (eds), *Platon et les poètes: Hommage à George Steiner* (Geneva: University of Geneva, 1996), 13–36; revised version repr. in *Ancient Philosophy* 17 (1997), 1–12 (repr. in Brickhouse and Smith (2002), 133–45; repr. in Kamtekar (2005), 150–62).

Bussanich, John, 'Socrates the Mystic', in John Cleary (ed.), *Traditions of Platonism: Essays Presented to John Dillon* (Aldershot: Ashgate, 1999), 29–51.

—, 'Socrates and Religious Experience', in Ahbel-Rappe and Kamtekar (2006), 200–13.

Cairns, Douglas, and Ronald Knox (eds), *Law, Rhetoric, and Comedy in Classical Athens: Essays in Honour of Douglas M. MacDowell* (Swansea: Classical Press of Wales, 2004).

Calhoun, George, *Athenian Clubs in Politics and Litigation* (Austin, Tex.: Bulletins of the University of Texas 262, 1913).

Carawan, Edwin, 'The Athenian Amnesty and the "Scrutiny of the Laws" ', *Journal of Hellenic Studies* 122 (2002), 1–23.

—, 'Andocides' Defence and MacDowell's Solution', in Cairns and Knox (2004), 103–12.

—, 'Amnesty and Accountings for the Thirty', *Classical Quarterly* n.s. 56 (2006), 57–76.
*Carey, Christopher, 'Legal Space in Classical Athens', *Greece and Rome* n.s. 41 (1994), 172–86.
—, 'The Shape of Athenian Laws', *Classical Quarterly* n.s. 48 (1998), 93–109.
Carter, L. B., *The Quiet Athenian* (Oxford: Oxford University Press, 1986).
Cartledge, Paul, 'Alcibiades of Athens: A Patriot for Whom?', *History Today*, Oct. 1987, 15–21.
*—, 'The Socratics' Sparta and Rousseau's', in Anton Powell and Stephen Hodkinson (eds), *Sparta: New Perspectives* (Swansea: The Classical Press of Wales, 1999), 311–37.
*—, 'Greek Political Thought: The Historical Context', in Rowe and Schofield (2000), 11–22.
Christ, Matthew, *The Litigious Athenian* (Baltimore: Johns Hopkins University Press, 1998).
—, *The Bad Citizen in Classical Athens* (Cambridge: Cambridge University Press, 2006).
Chroust, Anton-Hermann, *Socrates, Man and Myth. The Two Socratic Apologies of Xenophon* (London: Routledge & Kegan Paul, 1957).
*Cohen, David, *Law, Sexuality, and Society: The Enforcement of Morals in Classical Athens* (Cambridge: Cambridge University Press, 1991).
—, *Law, Violence and Community in Classical Athens* (Cambridge: Cambridge University Press, 1995).
*Colaiaco, James, *Socrates Against Athens: Philosophy on Trial* (London: Routledge, 2001).
Connor, W. Robert, 'Two Notes on Diopeithes the Seer', *Classical Philology* 58 (1963), 115–18.
*—, *The New Politicians of Fifth-century Athens* (Princeton: Princeton University Press, 1971; repr. Indianapolis: Hackett, 1992).
—, 'The Other 399: Religion and the Trial of Socrates', in Michael Flower and Mark Toher (eds), *Georgica: Greek Studies in Honour of George Cawkwell* (London: Institute of Classical Studies, 1991; = *Bulletin of the Institute of Classical Studies* suppl. vol. 58), 49–56.
Csapo, Eric, 'The Politics of the New Music', in Murray and Wilson (2004), 207–48.
D'Angour, Armand, 'The New Music – So What's New?', in Goldhill and Osborne (2006), 264–83.
Davidson, James, 'Dover, Foucault and Greek Homosexuality: Penetration and the Truth of Sex', *Past and Present* 170 (2001), 3–51.
—, 'Revolutions in Human Time: Age-class in Athens and the Greekness of Greek Revolutions', in Goldhill and Osborne (2006), 29–67.
Davies, John, *Athenian Propertied Families 600–300 BC* (London: Oxford University Press, 1971 [second edition in preparation]).
*—, *Wealth and the Power of Wealth in Classical Athens* (Salem, NH: Ayer, 1984).
Davies, Malcolm, 'Sisyphus and the Invention of Religion ("Critias" TrGF 1 (43)

F19 = B 25 DK)', *Bulletin of the Institute of Classical Studies* 36 (1989), 16–32.

Destrée, Pierre, and Nicholas Smith (eds), *Socrates' Divine Sign: Religion, Practice, and Value in Socratic Philosophy* (Kelowna: Academic Printing & Publishing, 2005; = *Apeiron* 38.2).

Develin, Robert, *Athenian Officials, 684–321 BC* (Cambridge: Cambridge University Press, 1989).

*Dillon, John, *Salt and Olives: Morality and Custom in Ancient Greece* (Edinburgh: Edinburgh University Press, 2004).

Domingo Gygax, Marc, 'Plutarch on Alcibiades' Return to Athens', *Mnemosyne* series 4, 59 (2006), 481–500.

Donlan, Walter, 'The Role of *Eugeneia* in the Aristocratic Self-image During the Fifth Century B.C.', in Eugene Borza and Robert Carrubba (eds), *Classics and the Classical Tradition: Essays Presented to Robert E. Dengler* (University Park, Pa.: Pennsylvania State University Press, 1973), 63–78.

—, *The Aristocratic Ideal in Ancient Greece* (Lawrence, Kan.: Coronado, 1980; repr. in *The Aristocratic Ideal and Selected Essays* (Wauconda, Ill.: Bolchazy-Carducci, 1999).

Dover, Kenneth, 'Socrates in the *Clouds*', in Vlastos (1971), 50–77.

*—, *Greek Popular Morality in the Time of Plato and Aristotle* (Oxford: Blackwell, 1974; updated edn, Cambridge, Mass.: Harvard University Press, 1989).

—, 'The Freedom of the Intellectual in Greek Society', *Talanta* 7 (1976), 24–54 (repr. with addendum in Kenneth Dover, *The Greeks and Their Legacy* (Oxford: Oxford University Press, 1988), 135–58).

—, *Greek Homosexuality* (London: Duckworth, 1978).

Edmunds, Lowell, 'Aristophanes' Socrates', *Proceedings of the Boston Area Colloquium in Ancient Philosophy* 1 (1985), 209–30.

Edwards, Michael, 'Antiphon the Revolutionary', in Cairns and Knox (2004), 75–86.

Ellis, Walter, *Alcibiades* (London: Routledge, 1989).

Euben, J. Peter, 'Philosophy and Politics in Plato's *Crito*', *Political Theory* 6 (1978), 149–72.

—, *Corrupting Youth: Political Education, Democratic Culture, and Political Theory* (Princeton: Princeton University Press, 1992).

Farenga, Vincent, *Citizen and Self in Ancient Greece: Individuals Performing Justice and the Law* (New York: Cambridge University Press, 2006).

*Farrar, Cynthia, *The Origins of Democratic Thinking: The Invention of Politics in Classical Athens* (Cambridge: Cambridge University Press, 1988).

—, 'Ancient Greek Political Theory as a Response to Democracy', in John Dunn (ed.), *Democracy, The Unfinished Journey: 508 B.C. to A.D. 1993* (Oxford: Oxford University Press, 1992), 17–39.

—, 'Gyges' Ring: Reflections on the Boundaries of Democratic Citizenship', in Sakellariou (1996), 109–36.

Ferguson, John, 'On the Date of Socrates' Conversion', *Eranos* 62 (1964), 70–3.

Finley, Moses, 'The Freedom of the Citizen in the Greek World', *Talanta* 7 (1976), 1–23 (repr. in Moses Finley, *Economy and Society*, ed. by Brent Shaw and Richard Saller (New York: Viking, 1982), 77–94).

—, 'Socrates and Athens', in Moses Finley, *Aspects of Antiquity: Discoveries and Controversies* (2nd edn, Harmondsworth: Penguin, 1977), 60–73.

Flensted-Jensen, Pernille, et al. (eds), *Polis and Politics: Studies in Ancient Greek History Presented to Mogens Herman Hansen* (Copenhagen: Museum Tusculanum Press, 2000).

*Forde, Steven, *The Ambition to Rule: Alcibiades and the Politics of Imperialism in Thucydides* (Ithaca, NY: Cornell University Press, 1989).

Forrest, W. George, 'An Athenian Generation Gap', *Yale Classical Studies* 24 (1975), 37–52.

Fuks, Alexander, *The Ancestral Constitution: Four Studies in Athenian Party Politics at the End of the Fifth Century B.C.* (London: Routledge & Kegan Paul, 1953; repr. Westport, Conn.: Greenwood, 1971).

—, 'Notes on the Rule of the Ten at Athens', *Mnemosyne* series 4, 6 (1953), 198–207 (repr. in Alexander Fuks, *Social Conflict in Ancient Greece* (Jerusalem/Leiden: Magnes/Brill, 1984), 289–98).

—, 'Kritias, Pseudo-Herodes, and Thessaly', *Eos* 48.2 (1956), 47–50 (repr. in Alexander Fuks, *Social Conflict in Ancient Greece* (Jerusalem/Leiden: Magnes/Brill, 1984), 299–302).

Fuqua, Charles, 'Possible Implications of the Ostracism of Hyperbolus', *Transactions and Proceedings of the American Philological Association* 96 (1965), 165–79.

Furley, William, *Andokides and the Herms. A Study of Crisis in Fifth-century Religion* (London: Institute of Classical Studies, 1996; = *Bulletin of the Institute of Classical Studies* suppl. vol. 65).

*Gagarin, Michael, and David Cohen (eds), *The Cambridge Companion to Ancient Greek Law* (Cambridge: Cambridge University Press, 2005).

*Garland, Robert, *Introducing New Gods: The Politics of Athenian Religion* (London: Duckworth, 1992).

—, 'Strategies of Religious Intimidation and Coercion in Classical Athens', *Boreas* 24 (1996), 91–9.

Garner, Richard, *Law and Society in Classical Athens* (London: Croom Helm, 1987).

Garnsey, Peter, 'Religious Toleration in Classical Antiquity', in William Sheils (ed.), *Persecution and Toleration* (Oxford: Blackwell, 1984), 1–27.

Gera, Deborah Levine, 'Xenophon's Socrateses', in Trapp (2007), 33–50.

*Gill, Christopher, *Greek Thought* (Oxford: Oxford University Press, 1995; = *Greece and Rome*, New Surveys in the Classics 25 [second edition in preparation]).

Golden, Mark, *Sport and Society in Ancient Greece* (Cambridge: Cambridge University Press, 1998).

Goldhill, Simon, and Robin Osborne (eds), *Rethinking Revolutions through Ancient Greece* (Cambridge: Cambridge University Press, 2006).

Gómez-Lobo, Alfonso, *The Foundations of Socratic Ethics* (Indianapolis: Hackett, 1994).

Gomme, Arnold, et al., *An Historical Commentary on Thucydides* (5 vols, London/Oxford: Oxford University Press, 1945–81).

*Green, Peter, *Armada from Athens: The Failure of the Sicilian Expedition, 415–413 B.C.* (London: Hodder and Stoughton, 1970 [second edition in preparation]).

—, 'Socrates, Strepsiades and the Abuse of Intellectualism', *Greek, Roman, and Byzantine Studies* 20 (1979), 15–25.

—, 'Rebooking the Flute Girls: A Fresh Look at the Chronological Evidence for the Fall of Athens and the ὀκτάμηνος ἀρχή of the Thirty', *Ancient History Bulletin* 5 (1991), 1–16 (repr. in Peter Green, *From Ikaria to the Stars: Classical Mythification, Ancient and Modern* (Austin: University of Texas Press, 2004), 144–59).

*Gribble, David, *Alcibiades and Athens: A Study in Literary Presentation* (Oxford: Oxford University Press, 1999).

*Guthrie, W. K. C., *A History of Greek Philosophy*, vol. 3: *The Sophists and Socrates* (Cambridge: Cambridge University Press, 1969; also in two parts: *The Sophists* (1971), *Socrates* (1971)).

Halliwell, Stephen, 'Comic Satire and Freedom of Speech in Classical Athens', *Journal of Hellenic Studies* 111 (1991), 48–70.

Hansen, Mogens, 'The Political Powers of the People's Court in Fourth-century Athens', in Murray and Price (1990), 215–43.

*—, *The Athenian Democracy in the Age of Demosthenes*, trans. by J. A. Crook (Oxford: Blackwell, 1991; new edn, Bristol: Bristol Classical Press, 1999).

—, 'The Ancient Athenian and the Modern Liberal View of Liberty as a Democratic Ideal', in Ober and Hedrick (1996), 91–104.

—, 'The Trial of Sokrates – from the Athenian Point of View', in Sakellariou (1996), 137–70 (also in *Historisk-filosofiskes Meddelelser* 71 (Copenhagen: Royal Danish Academy of Sciences and Letters, 1995)).

Harris, Edward, 'Was All Criticism of Athenian Democracy Necessarily Anti-democratic?', in Bultrighini (2005), 11–23.

—, and Lene Rubinstein (eds), *The Law and the Courts in Ancient Greece* (London: Routledge, 2004).

Henderson, Jeffrey, 'Attic Old Comedy, Frank Speech, and Democracy', in Boedeker and Raaflaub (1998), 255–73.

Henrichs, Albert, 'The Atheism of Prodicus', *Cronache Ercolanesi* 6 (1976), 15–21.

Herman, Gabriel, *Ritualised Friendship and the Greek City* (Cambridge: Cambridge University Press, 1987).

*—, *Morality and Behaviour in Democratic Athens: A Social History* (Cambridge: Cambridge University Press, 2006).

Holt, Wythe, 'Socrates on Democracy', *Legal Studies Forum* 14 (1990), 291–317.

Hornblower, Simon, *A Commentary on Thucydides* (3 vols, Oxford: Oxford University Press, 1991/1996 [third volume in preparation]).

*—, *The Greek World 479–323 BC* (3rd edn, London: Routledge, 2002).

Hubbard, Thomas, 'Popular Perceptions of Elite Homosexuality in Classical Athens', *Arion* n.s. 6 (1998), 48–68.

Humphreys, Sally, 'Economy and Society in Classical Athens', *Annali* 39 (1970), 1–26 (repr. in Sally Humphreys, *Anthropology and the Greeks* (London: Routledge & Kegan Paul, 1978), 136–58).

—, 'Public and Private Interests in Classical Athens', *Classical Journal* 73 (1977–8), 97–104 (repr. in Rhodes (2004), 225–36).

Hunter, Virginia, *Policing Athens: Social Control in the Attic Lawsuits, 420–320 BC* (Princeton: Princeton University Press, 1994).

—, 'The Prison of Athens: A Comparative Perspective', *Phoenix* 51 (1997), 296–326.

Irwin, Terence, 'Socrates and Athenian Democracy', *Philosophy and Public Affairs* 18 (1989), 184–205 (revised version repr. as 'Was Socrates Against Democracy?' in Kamtekar (2005), 127–49).

Janko, Richard, 'The Derveni Papyrus (Diagoras of Melos, *Apopyrgizontes Logoi?*): A New Translation', *Classical Philology* 96 (2001), 1–32.

—, 'God, Science and Socrates', *Bulletin of the Institute of Classical Studies* 46 (2002–3), 1–18.

—, 'Socrates the Freethinker', in Ahbel-Rappe and Kamtekar (2006), 48–62.

Jones, A. H. M., 'The Athenian Democracy and Its Critics', *Cambridge Historical Journal* 11 (1953), 1–26 (repr. in A. H. M. Jones, *Athenian Democracy* (Oxford: Basil Blackwell, 1957), 41–72).

Joyal, Mark, 'Socrates' Divine Sign', in Mark Joyal, *The Platonic* Theages (Stuttgart: Steiner, 2000), 65–103.

Kahn, Charles, 'Pre-Platonic Ethics', in Stephen Everson (ed.), *Companions to Ancient Thought*, vol. 4: *Ethics* (Cambridge: Cambridge University Press, 1998), 27–48.

*Kamtekar, Rachana (ed.), *Plato's Euthyphro, Apology, and Crito: Critical Essays* (Lanham, Md.: Rowman and Littlefield, 2005).

—, 'The Politics of Plato's Socrates', in Ahbel-Rappe and Kamtekar (2006), 214–27.

Kateb, George, 'Socratic Integrity', in Ian Shapiro and Robert Adams (eds), *Integrity and Conscience* (New York: New York University Press, 1998), 77–112.

Kebric, Robert, 'Implications of Alcibiades' Relationship with Endius', *Mnemosyne* series 4, 29 (1976), 72–8.

Kerferd, George, *The Sophistic Movement* (Cambridge: Cambridge University Press, 1981).

Klosko, George, *The Development of Plato's Political Theory* (2nd edn, Oxford: Oxford University Press, 2006).

Kraut, Richard, *Socrates and the State* (Princeton: Princeton University Press, 1984).

—, 'Socrates, Politics, and Religion', in Smith and Woodruff (2000), 13–23.

*Krentz, Peter, *The Thirty at Athens* (Ithaca, NY: Cornell University Press, 1982).

Lanni, Adriaan, *Law and Justice in the Courts of Classical Athens* (Cambridge: Cambridge University Press, 2006).

Lefkowitz, Mary, 'Commentary on Vlastos', *Proceedings of the Boston Area Colloquium in Ancient Philosophy* 5 (1989), 239–46.

Lewis, David, 'After the Profanation of the Mysteries', in Ernst Badian (ed.), *Ancient Society and Institutions: Studies Presented to Victor Ehrenberg* (Oxford: Blackwell, 1966), 177–91.

—, 'Sparta as Victor', in David Lewis et al. (eds), *The Cambridge Ancient History*, vol. 6: *The Fourth Century BC* (2nd edn, Cambridge: Cambridge University Press, 1994), 24–44.

*—, et al. (eds), *The Cambridge Ancient History*, vol. 5: *The Fifth Century BC* (2nd edn, Cambridge: Cambridge University Press, 1992).

Lewis, Sian (ed.), *Ancient Tyranny* (Edinburgh: Edinburgh University Press, 2006).

Lintott, Andrew, *Violence, Civil Strife and Revolution in the Classical City* (London: Croom Helm, 1982).

Littman, Robert, 'The Loves of Alcibiades', *Transactions and Proceedings of the American Philological Association* 101 (1970), 263–76.

Loening, Thomas, *The Reconciliation Agreement of 403/402 BC in Athens: Its Content and Application* (Wiesbaden: Steiner, 1987; = *Hermes* Einzelschrift 53).

Long, Anthony (ed.), *The Cambridge Companion to Early Greek Philosophy* (Cambridge: Cambridge University Press, 1999).

—, 'How Does Socrates' Divine Sign Communicate with Him?', in Ahbel-Rappe and Kamtekar (2006), 63–74.

Low, Polly, *Interstate Relations in Classical Greece: Morality and Politics* (Cambridge: Cambridge University Press, 2007).

Luban, David, 'Some Greek Trials: Order and Justice in Homer, Hesiod, Aeschylus and Plato', *Tennessee Law Review* 54 (1987), 279–325.

MacDowell, Douglas, *Andokides: On the Mysteries* (Oxford: Oxford University Press, 1962).

*—, *The Law in Classical Athens* (London: Thames and Hudson, 1978).

Mansfeld, Jaap, 'The Chronology of Anaxagoras' Athenian Period and the Date of His Trial', *Mnemosyne* series 4, 32 (1979), 39–69 and 33 (1980), 17–95 (partial repr. in Jaap Mansfeld, *Studies in the Historiography of Greek Philosophy* (Assen: Van Gorcum, 1990), 264–306).

Marr, J. L., 'Andocides' Part in the Mysteries and the Hermae Affairs', *Classical Quarterly* n.s. 21 (1971), 326–38.

*Marrou, Henri-Irénée, *A History of Education in Antiquity*, trans. by George Lamb (New York: Sheed and Ward, 1956).

McPherran, Mark, *The Religion of Socrates* (University Park, Pa.: Pennsylvania State University Press, 1996).

Meiggs, Russell, *The Athenian Empire* (London: Oxford University Press, 1972).

Meijer, P. A., 'Philosophers, Intellectuals and Religion in Hellas', in Henk Versnel (ed.), *Faith, Hope and Worship: Aspects of Religious Mentality in the Ancient World* (Leiden: Brill, 1981), 217–63.

*Mikalson, Jon, *Athenian Popular Religion* (Chapel Hill: University of North Carolina Press, 1983).

—, 'Religion and the Plague in Athens, 431–423 B.C.', in *Studies Presented to Sterling Dow on His Eightieth Birthday* (*Greek, Roman, and Byzantine Monographs* 10 (1984)), 217–25.

—, *Ancient Greek Religion* (Oxford: Blackwell, 2005).

Mitchell, Lynette, 'Tyrannical Oligarchs at Athens', in S. Lewis (2006), 178–87.

Mitscherling, Jeff, 'Socrates and the Comic Poets', *Apeiron* 36 (2003), 67–72.

Momigliano, Arnaldo, 'Freedom of Speech and Religious Tolerance in the Ancient World', in Sally Humphreys, *Anthropology and the Greeks* (London: Routledge & Kegan Paul, 1978), 179–93.

Montgomery, John (ed.), *The State Versus Socrates* (Boston: Beacon Press, 1954).

Moreno, Alfonso, *Feeding the Democracy: The Athenian Grain Supply in the Fifth and Fourth Centuries BC* (Oxford: Oxford University Press, 2007).

Morgan, Michael, 'Socratic Piety as Plato Saw It', ch. 1 in Michael Morgan, *Platonic Piety* (New Haven: Yale University Press, 1990), 7–31.

Morrison, Donald, 'On the Alleged Historical Reliability of Plato's *Apology*', *Archiv für Geschichte der Philosophie* 82 (2000), 235–65 (repr. in Kamtekar (2005), 97–126).

—, 'Some Central Elements of Socratic Political Theory', *Polis* 18 (2001), 27–40.

*Muir, John, 'Religion and the New Education: The Challenge of the Sophists', in Pat Easterling and John Muir (eds.), *Greek Religion and Society* (Cambridge: Cambridge University Press, 1985), 191–218.

*Mulgan, Richard, 'Liberty in Ancient Greece', in Zbigniew Pelczynski and John Gray (eds), *Conceptions of Liberty in Political Philosophy* (New York: St Martin's Press, 1984), 7–26.

—, 'Aristotle's Analysis of Democracy and Oligarchy', in David Keyt and Fred Miller (eds), *A Companion to Aristotle's Politics* (Oxford: Blackwell, 1991), 307–22.

*Munn, Mark, *The School of History: Athens in the Age of Socrates* (Berkeley, Ca.: University of California Press, 2000).

—, *The Mother of the Gods, Athens, and the Tyranny of Asia* (Berkeley, Ca.: University of California Press, 2006).

Murray, Oswyn, 'The Affair of the Mysteries: Democracy and the Drinking Group', in Oswyn Murray (ed.), *Sympotica: A Symposium on the Symposion* (Oxford: Oxford University Press, 1990), 149–61.

—, and Simon Price (eds), *The Greek City from Homer to Alexander* (Oxford: Oxford University Press, 1990).

Murray, Penelope, and Peter Wilson (eds), *Music and the Muses: The Culture of Mousike in the Classical Athenian City* (Oxford: Oxford University Press, 2004).

Nagy, Blaise, 'Alcibiades' Second "Profanation" ', *Historia* 43 (1994), 275–85.

*Nails, Debra, *The People of Plato: A Prosopography of Plato and Other Socratics* (Indianapolis: Hackett, 2002).

—, 'The Trial and Death of Socrates', in Ahbel-Rappe and Kamtekar (2006), 5–20.

Nill, Michael, *Morality and Self-interest in Protagoras, Antiphon and Democritus* (Leiden: Brill, 1985).

Nussbaum, Martha, 'Aristophanes and Socrates on Learning Practical Wisdom', *Yale Classical Studies* 26 (1990), 43–97 (repr. in Prior (1996), vol. 1, 74–118).

*Ober, Josiah, *Mass and Elite in Democratic Athens: Rhetoric, Ideology, and the Power of the People* (Princeton: Princeton University Press, 1989).

—, *The Athenian Revolution: Essays on Ancient Greek Democracy and Political Theory* (Princeton: Princeton University Press, 1996).

*—, *Political Dissent in Democratic Athens: Intellectual Critics of Popular Rule* (Princeton: Princeton University Press, 1998).

—, 'Political Conflict, Political Debate, and Political Thought', in Robin Osborne (ed.), *Classical Greece, 500–323 BC* (Oxford: Oxford University Press, 2000), 111–38.

—, *Athenian Legacies: Essays on the Politics of Going On Together* (Princeton: Princeton University Press, 2005).

—, and Charles Hedrick (eds), *Dēmokratia: A Conversation on Democracies, Ancient and Modern* (Princeton: Princeton University Press, 1996).

—, and Barry Strauss, 'Drama, Political Rhetoric, and the Discourse of Athenian Democracy', in John Winkler and Froma Zeitlin (eds), *Nothing to Do with Dionysos? Athenian Drama in Its Social Context* (Princeton, NJ: Princeton University Press, 1990), 237–70.

O'Connor, David, 'Socrates and Political Ambition', *Proceedings of the Boston Area Colloquium in Ancient Philosophy* 14 (1998), 31–51.

Olsen, Frances, 'Socrates on Legal Obligation: Legitimation Theory and Civil Disobedience', *Georgia Law Review* 18 (1984), 929–66 (repr. in R. George Wright (ed.), *Legal and Political Obligation: Classic and Contemporary Texts and Commentary* (Lanham, MD: University Press of America, 1992), 69–99).

Osborne, Robin, 'The Erection and Mutilation of the Hermai', *Proceedings of the Cambridge Philological Society* n.s. 31 (1985), 47–73.

—, 'Law in Action in Classical Athens', *Journal of Hellenic Studies* 105 (1985), 40–58.

—, and Simon Hornblower (eds), *Ritual, Finance, Politics: Athenian Democratic Accounts Presented to David Lewis* (Oxford: Oxford University Press, 1994).

*Ostwald, Martin, *From Popular Sovereignty to the Sovereignty of Law: Law, Society, and Politics in Fifth-century Athens* (Berkeley, Ca.: University of California Press, 1986).

—, *Oligarchia: The Development of a Constitutional Form in Ancient Greece* (Stuttgart: Steiner, 2000; = *Historia* Einzelschrift 144).

O'Sullivan, Lara, 'Athenian Impiety Trials in the Late Fourth Century B.C.', *Classical Quarterly* n.s. 47 (1997), 136–52.

Palmer, Michael, 'Alcibiades and the Question of Tyranny in Thucydides', *Canadian Journal of Political Science* 15 (1982), 103–24.

Parker, Robert, *Miasma: Pollution and Purification in Early Greek Religion* (Oxford: Oxford University Press, 1983).

*—, *Athenian Religion: A History* (Oxford: Oxford University Press, 1996).

—, *Polytheism and Society at Athens* (Oxford: Oxford University Press, 2005).

Penner, Terry, 'Socrates', in Rowe and Schofield (2000), 164–89.

Pesely, George, 'Socrates' Attempt to Save Theramenes', *Ancient History Bulletin* 2 (1988), 31–3.

Peterson, Sandra, 'An Authentically Socratic Conclusion in Plato's *Phaedo*: Socrates' Debt to Asclepius', in Naomi Reshotko (ed.), *Desire, Identity and Existence: Essays in Honour of T. M. Penner* (Kelowna, BC: Academic Printing & Publishing, 2003), 33–52.

*Poulakos, John, *Sophistical Rhetoric in Classical Greece* (Columbia, SC: University of South Carolina Press, 1995).

Powell, C. Anton, 'Religion and the Sicilian Expedition', *Historia* 28 (1979), 15–31.

Prandi, Luisa, 'Textual Arguments for the Date of the *In Alcibiadem* in the *Corpus* of Andokides', in Cairns and Knox (2004), 65–73.

Price, Simon, *Religions of the Greeks* (Cambridge: Cambridge University Press, 1999).

*Prior, William (ed.), *Socrates: Critical Assessments*, 4 vols (London: Routledge, 1996).

—, 'The Historicity of Plato's *Apology*', *Polis* 18 (2001), 41–57.

—, 'The Portrait of Socrates in Plato's *Symposium*', *Oxford Studies in Ancient Philosophy* 31 (2006), 137–66.

*Raaflaub, Kurt, 'Democracy, Oligarchy, and the Concept of the "Free Citizen" in Late Fifth-century Athens', *Political Theory* 11 (1983), 517–44.

—, 'Contemporary Perceptions of Democracy in Fifth-century Athens', *Classica et Mediaevalia* 40 (1989), 33–70 (also in W. Robert Connor et al., *Aspects of Athenian Democracy* (Copenhagen: Museum Tusculanum Press, 1990), 33–70).

—, 'Equalities and Inequalities in the Athenian Democracy', in Ober and Hedrick (1996), 139–74.

—, 'Stick and Glue: The Function of Tyranny in Fifth-century Athenian Democracy', in Kathryn Morgan (ed.), *Popular Tyranny: Sovereignty and Its Discontents in Ancient Greece* (Austin: University of Texas Press, 2003), 59–93.

—, 'The Alleged Ostracism of Damon', in Geoffrey Bakewell and James Sickinger (eds), *Gestures: Essays in Ancient History, Literature and Philosophy Presented to Alan L. Boegehold* (Oxford: Oxbow, 2003), 317–31.

Rankin, Herbert, *Sophists, Socratics and Cynics* (London: Croom Helm, 1983).

Raubitschek, Antony, 'The Case Against Alcibiades (Andocides IV)', *Transactions and Proceedings of the American Philological Association* 79 (1948), 191–210 (repr. in Antony Raubitschek, *The School of Hellas: Essays on Greek History, Archaeology, and Literature*, ed. by Dirk Obbink and Paul Vander Waerdt (Oxford: Oxford University Press, 1991), 116–31).

Reeve, C. D. C., *Socrates in the* Apology: *An Essay on Plato's* Apology of
    Socrates (Indianapolis: Hackett, 1989).
Rhodes, Peter, 'The Five Thousand in the Athenian Revolutions of 411 BC',
    Journal of Hellenic Studies 92 (1972), 115–27.
—, 'Athenian Democracy after 403 BC', *Classical Journal* 75 (1979–80),
    305–23.
—, ' "What Alcibiades Did, or What Happened to Him" ' (Inaugural Lecture
    pamphlet, University of Durham, 1985).
—, 'Political Activity in Classical Athens', *Journal of Hellenic Studies* 106
    (1986), 132–44 (repr. in Rhodes (ed.) (2004), 185–206).
—, 'The Athenian Code of Laws, 410–399 BC', *Journal of Hellenic Studies* 111
    (1991), 87–100.
—, *A Commentary on the Aristotelian* Athenaion Politeia (2nd edn, Oxford:
    Oxford University Press, 1992).
*—, *The Athenian Empire* (2nd edn, Oxford: Oxford University Press, 1993;
    = *Greece and Rome* New Surveys in the Classics 17).
—, 'The Ostracism of Hyperbolus', in Osborne and Hornblower (1994),
    85–98.
—, 'Who Ran Democratic Athens?', in Flensted-Jensen et al. (2000), 465–77.
*— (ed.), *Athenian Democracy* (Edinburgh: Edinburgh University Press, 2004).
—, 'Democracy and Its Opponents in Fourth-century Athens', in Bultrighini
    (2005), 275–89.
Roberts, Jennifer Tolbert, 'Aristocratic Democracy: The Perseverance of
    Timocratic Principles in Athenian Government', *Athenaeum* n.s. 64 (1986),
    355–69.
*—, *Athens on Trial: The Antidemocratic Tradition in Western Thought*
    (Princeton: Princeton University Press, 1994).
de Romilly, Jacqueline, *The Great Sophists in Periclean Athens*, trans. by Janet
    Lloyd (Oxford: Oxford University Press, 1992).
Rowe, Christopher, 'Democracy and Sokratic-Platonic Philosophy', in Boedeker
    and Raaflaub (1998), 241–53.
*—, and Malcolm Schofield (eds), *The Cambridge History of Greek and Roman
    Political Thought* (Cambridge: Cambridge University Press, 2000).
de Ste Croix, Geoffrey, 'The Constitution of the 5000', *Historia* 5 (1956), 1–23.
Sakellariou, Michel (ed.), *Démocratie athénienne et culture* (Athens: Academy of
    Athens, 1996).
Samons, Loren, *What's Wrong with Democracy? From Athenian Practice to
    American Worship* (Berkeley: University of California Press, 2004).
— (ed.), *The Cambridge Companion to the Age of Pericles* (Cambridge:
    Cambridge University Press, 2007).
Schiappa, Edward, *Protagoras and Logos: A Study in Greek Philosophy and
    Rhetoric* (Columbia, SC: University of South Carolina Press, 1991).
*Schofield, Malcolm, 'I. F. Stone and Gregory Vlastos on Socrates and
    Democracy', in Charlotte Witt and Mohan Matthen (eds), *Ancient
    Philosophy and Modern Ideology* (Kelowna, BC: Academic Printing &
    Publishing, 2000; = *Apeiron* special issue), 281–301.

Seager, Robin, 'Alcibiades and the Charge of Aiming at Tyranny', *Historia* 16 (1967), 6–18.

—, 'Elitism and Democracy in Classical Athens', in Frederic Jaher (ed.), *The Rich, the Well Born and the Powerful* (Urbana: University of Illinois Press, 1973), 7–26.

Sealey, Raphael, 'The Revolution of 411 B.C.', in Raphael Sealey, *Essays in Greek Politics* (New York: Manyland, 1970), 111–32.

—, 'Democratic Theory and Practice', in Samons (2007), 238–57.

*Sluiter, Ineke, and Ralph Rosen (eds), *Free Speech in Classical Antiquity* (Leiden: Brill, 2004).

Smith, Nicholas, and Paul Woodruff (eds), *Reason and Religion in Socratic Philosophy* (New York: Oxford University Press, 2000).

Sourvinou-Inwood, Christiane, 'What is *Polis* Religion?', in Murray and Price (1990), 295–322 (repr. in Richard Buxton (ed.), *Oxford Readings in Greek Religion* (Oxford: Oxford University Press, 2000), 13–37).

Spence, Iain, *The Cavalry of Classical Greece: A Social and Military History with Particular Reference to Athens* (Oxford: Oxford University Press, 1993).

Steinberger, Peter, 'Was Socrates Guilty as Charged? *Apology* 24c–28a', *Ancient Philosophy* 17 (1997), 13–29.

Stem, Rex, 'The Thirty at Athens in the Summer of 404', *Phoenix* 57 (2003), 18–34.

Stokes, Michael, 'Socrates' Mission', in Barry Gower and Michael Stokes (eds), *Socratic Questions* (London: Routledge, 1992), 26–81.

Stone, I. F., *The Trial of Socrates* (New York: Little, Brown, 1988).

Strauss, Barry, *Athens after the Peloponnesian War: Class, Faction and Policy 403–386 BC* (London: Croom Helm, 1986).

*—, *Fathers and Sons in Athens: Ideology and Society in the Era of the Peloponnesian War* (Princeton: Princeton University Press, 1993).

*—, and Josiah Ober, 'The Alcibiades Syndrome', in Barry Strauss and Josiah Ober, *The Anatomy of Error: Ancient Military Disasters and Their Lessons for Modern Strategists* (New York: St Martin's Press, 1990), 44–73.

Sutton, Dana, 'Critias and Atheism', *Classical Quarterly* n.s. 31 (1981), 33–8.

Tarrant, Harold, 'Alcibiades in Aristophanes' *Clouds* I and II', *Ancient History: Resources for Teachers* 19 (1989), 13–20.

Taylor, Alfred, *Varia Socratica* (Oxford: James Parker, 1911).

*Taylor, Christopher, *Socrates: A Very Short Introduction* (Oxford: Oxford University Press, 1998).

—, 'Socrates the Sophist', in Lindsay Judson and Vassilis Karasmanis (eds), *Remembering Socrates: Philosophical Essays* (Oxford: Oxford University Press, 2006), 157–68.

Taylor, Martha, 'Implicating the *Demos*: A Reading of Thucydides on the Rise of the Four Hundred', *Journal of Hellenic Studies* 122 (2002), 91–108.

Thomas, Rosalind, 'Law and the Lawgiver in Athenian Democracy', in Osborne and Hornblower (1994), 119–33.

Todd, Stephen, 'Factions in Early-Fourth-Century Athens?', *Polis* 7 (1987), 32–49.

—, '*Lady Chatterley's Lover* and the Attic Orators: The Social Composition of the Athenian Jury', *Journal of Hellenic Studies* 110 (1990), 146–73 (repr., with retrospect, in Edwin Carawan (ed.), *Oxford Readings in the Attic Orators* (Oxford: Oxford University Press, 2007), 312–58).

*—, *The Shape of Athenian Law* (Oxford: Oxford University Press, 1993).

—, 'Revisiting the Herms and the Mysteries', in Cairns and Knox (2004), 87–102.

*Trapp, Michael (ed.), *Socrates from Antiquity to the Enlightenment* (Aldershot: Ashgate, 2007).

Vander Waerdt, Paul, 'Socratic Justice and Self-sufficiency: The Story of the Delphic Oracle in Xenophon's *Apology of Socrates*', *Oxford Studies in Ancient Philosophy* 11 (1993), 1–48.

—, 'Socrates in the *Clouds*', in Paul Vander Waerdt (ed.), *The Socratic Movement* (Ithaca, NY: Cornell University Press, 1994), 48–86.

Vickers, Michael, 'Alcibiades on Stage: *Philoctetes* and *Cyclops*', *Historia* 36 (1987), 171–97.

—, 'Alcibiades on Stage: *Thesmophoriazousae* and *Helen*', *Historia* 38 (1989), 41–65.

—, 'Alcibiades in Cloudedoverland', in Ralph Rosen and Joseph Farrell (eds), *Nomodeiktes: Studies in Honor of Martin Ostwald* (Ann Arbor, Mich.: University of Michigan Press, 1993), 603–18.

—, *Pericles on Stage: Political Comedy in Aristophanes' Early Plays* (Austin: University of Texas Press, 1997).

—, 'Alcibiades and Aspasia: Notes on the *Hippolytus*', *Dialogues d'histoire ancienne* 26 (2000), 7–17.

Villa, Dana, *Socratic Citizenship* (Princeton: Princeton University Press, 2001).

Vlastos, Gregory (ed.), *The Philosophy of Socrates: A Collection of Critical Essays* (Garden City, NY: Doubleday, 1971).

—, 'The Historical Socrates and Athenian Democracy', *Political Theory* 11 (1983), 495–515 (repr. in Robert Sharples (ed.), *Modern Thinkers and Ancient Thinkers* (London: UCL Press, 1993), 66–89; repr. in Vlastos (1994), 87–108; repr. in Prior (1996), vol. 2, 25–44; repr. in Brooks (2007), 123–44).

—, 'Platis's *Socrates' Accusers*', *American Journal of Philology* 104 (1983), 201–6 (repr. in Gregory Vlastos, *Studies in Greek Philosophy*, vol. 2: *Socrates, Plato, and Their Tradition* (Princeton: Princeton University Press, 1995), 19–24).

—, 'Socratic Piety', *Proceedings of the Boston Area Colloquium in Ancient Philosophy* 5 (1989), 213–38 (updated version (= ch. 6 of Gregory Vlastos (1991)) repr. in Prior (1996), vol. 2, 144–66; repr. in Smith and Woodruff (2000), 55–73; repr. in Kamtekar (2005), 49–71).

—, *Socrates: Ironist and Moral Philosopher* (Cambridge: Cambridge University Press, 1991).

—, *Socratic Studies*, ed. by Myles Burnyeat (Cambridge: Cambridge University Press, 1994).

Wade-Gery, H. Theodore, 'Kritias and Herodes', *Classical Quarterly* 39 (1945), 19–33 (repr. in H. Theodore Wade-Gery, *Essays in Greek History* (Oxford: Blackwell, 1958), 271–92).

Wallace, Robert, 'Charmides, Agariste and Damon: Andokides 1.16', *Classical Quarterly* 42 (1992), 328–35.

—, 'The Athenian Laws against Slander', in Gerhard Thür (ed.), *Symposion 1993, Vorträge zur Griechischen und Hellenistischen Rechtsgeschichte* (Cologne: Böhlau, 1994), 109–24.

*—, 'Private Lives and Public Enemies: Freedom of Thought in Classical Athens', in Alan Boegehold and Adele Scafuro (eds), *Athenian Identity and Civic Ideology* (Baltimore: Johns Hopkins University Press, 1994), 27–55.

—, 'Law, Freedom, and the Concept of Citizens' Rights in Democratic Athens', in Ober and Hedrick (1996), 105–19.

—, 'The Sophists in Athens', in Boedeker and Raaflaub (1998), 203–22.

—, 'Damon of Oa: A Music Theorist Ostracized?', in Murray and Wilson (2004), 249–67.

—, 'Law and Rhetoric: Community Justice in Athenian Courts', in Konrad Kinzl (ed.), *A Companion to the Classical World* (Oxford: Blackwell, 2006), 416–31.

*—, 'Plato's Sophists, Intellectual History after 450, and Sokrates', in Samons (2007), 215–37.

Wallach, John, 'Socratic Citizenship', *History of Political Thought* 9 (1988), 393–413 (repr. in Prior (1996), vol. 2, 69–91).

—, *The Platonic Political Art: A Study of Critical Reason and Democracy* (University Park, Pa.: Pennsylvania State University Press, 2001).

Webster, Thomas, *Athenian Culture and Society* (London: Batsford, 1973).

Westlake, H. D., 'Alcibiades, Agis, and Spartan Policy', *Journal of Hellenic Studies* 58 (1938), 31–40.

—, *Individuals in Thucydides* (Cambridge: Cambridge University Press, 1968).

Whitehead, David, 'Sparta and the Thirty Tyrants', *Ancient Society* 13–14 (1982–3), 105–30.

—, 'Competitive Outlay and Community Profit: Philotimia in Democratic Athens', *Classica et Mediaevalia* 34 (1983), 55–74.

—, 'Cardinal Virtues: The Language of Public Approbation in Democratic Athens', *Classica et Mediaevalia* 44 (1993), 37–75.

—, 'Athenian Laws and Lawsuits in the Late Fifth Century BC', *Museum Helveticum* 58 (2002), 3–28.

Wildberg, Christian, 'The Rise and Fall of the Socratic Notion of Piety', *Proceedings of the Boston Area Colloquium in Ancient Philosophy* 18 (2002), 1–28.

Wilson, Emily, *The Death of Socrates: Hero, Villain, Chatterbox, Saint* (London: Profile Books, 2007).

Wohl, Victoria, *Love Among the Ruins: The Erotics of Democracy in Classical Athens* (Princeton: Princeton University Press, 2002).

*Wolpert, Andrew, *Remembering Defeat: Civil War and Civic Memory in Ancient Athens* (Baltimore: Johns Hopkins University Press, 2002).

—, 'The Violence of the Thirty Tyrants', in S. Lewis (2006), 213–23.

Wood, Ellen Meiksins, 'Demos versus "We, the People": Freedom and Democracy Ancient and Modern', in Ober and Hedrick (1996), 121–37.

*—, 'Socrates and Democracy: A Reply to Gregory Vlastos', *Political Theory* 14 (1986), 55–82 (repr. in Prior (1996), vol. 2, 45–68).

—, and Neal Wood, *Class Ideology and Ancient Political Theory* (Oxford: Blackwell, 1978).

Woodbury, Leonard, 'The Date and Atheism of Diagoras of Melos', *Phoenix* 19 (1965), 178–211.

—, 'Socrates and Archelaus', *Phoenix* 25 (1971), 299–309.

—, 'Socrates and the Daughter of Aristides', *Phoenix* 27 (1973), 7–25.

Woodhead, A. G., 'Peisander', *American Journal of Philology* 75 (1954), 132–46.

Woodruff, Paul, 'Rhetoric and Relativism: Protagoras and Gorgias', in Long (1999), 290–310.

—, 'Natural Justice?', in Victor Caston and Daniel Graham (eds), *Presocratic Philosophy: Essays in Honour of Alexander Mourelatos* (Aldershot: Ashgate, 2002), 195–204.

—, 'Socrates and Political Courage', *Ancient Philosophy* 27 (2007), 289–302.

Wylie, Graham, 'What Really Happened at Aegospotami?', *L'Antiquité classique* 55 (1986), 125–41.

Yates, Velvet, '*Anterastai*: Competition in Eros and Politics in Classical Athens', *Arethusa* 38 (2005), 33–47.

Yunis, Harvey, *A New Creed: Fundamental Religious Beliefs in the Athenian Polis and Euripidean Drama* (Göttingen: Vandenhoeck and Ruprecht, 1988; = Hypomnemata 91).

—, *Taming Democracy: Models of Political Rhetoric in Classical Athens* (Ithaca, NY: Cornell University Press, 1996).

—, 'The Constraints of Democracy and the Rise of the Art of Rhetoric', in Boedeker and Raaflaub (1998), 223–40.

Index